# The Applied Psychologist

Second Edition

# The Applied Psychologist

Second Edition

*Edited by*
*James Hartley* and *Alan Branthwaite*

**Open University Press**
Buckingham · Philadelphia

Open University Press
Celtic Court
22 Ballmoor
Buckingham
MK18 1XW

e-mail: enquiries@openup.co.uk
world wide web: http://www.openup.co.uk

and
325 Chestnut Street
Philadelphia, PA 19106, USA

First published 1989

First published in this second edition 2000

A catalogue record of this book is available from the British Library

ISBN   0 335 20285 3 (hb)   0 335 20284 5 (pb)

*Library of Congress Cataloging-in-Publication Data*
The applied psychologist / edited by James Hartley and Alan
    Branthwaite. – 2nd ed.
        p.     cm.
    Includes bibliographical references and index.
    ISBN 0–335–20285–3 (hardcover). – ISBN 0–335–20284–5 (pbk.)
    1. Psychology–Vocational guidance.   2. Psychology, Applied–
Vocational guidance.   I. Hartley, James. Ph. D.   II. Branthwaite,
Alan. Ph. D.
BF76.A63   1999
158–dc21                                                      99–25143
                                                                  CIP

Typeset by Graphicraft Limited, Hong Kong
Printed in Great Britain by Redwood Books, Trowbridge

# Contents

# List of figures, tables and boxes

## Figures

## Tables

## Boxes

# Notes on contributors

**James Hartley** is Research Professor in the Department of Psychology at the University of Keele. He is an expert on the psychology of text design, and on teaching and learning in higher education. His books include *Designing Instructional Text* (3rd edn) (1994) and *Learning and Studying* (1998).

**Alan Branthwaite** is Qualitative Research and Development Director at Millward Brown, an international market research company, and part of the WPP group of communication and research companies. He is the winner of three successive Atticus awards given annually by WPP to 'honour original published thinking in marketing services' and is a regular contributor to international conferences. He was formerly a Lecturer in Social Psychology at the University of Keele.

**Alastair Ager** is Professor of Applied Psychology and Director of the Centre for International Health Studies at Queen Margaret College, Edinburgh, working in the areas of organizational development, psychosocial intervention, disability and cross-cultural health psychology. He is editor of *Refugees: Perspectives on the Experience of Forced Migration* (1999).

**Clare Allen** is Director of Organizational Development in South Birmingham Mental Health National Health Service (NHS) Trust. Her professional background is in clinical and organizational psychology. Her recent work has included establishing a 'well-being service' for NHS staff – providing workplace counselling together with stress prevention measures.

**Simon Baron-Cohen** is Lecturer in Psychopathology in the Departments of Experimental Psychology and Psychiatry at the University of Cambridge. He is also Fellow in Experimental Psychology at Trinity College, Cambridge and co-director of the Autism Research Centre, Cambridge. He is the author of *Mindblindness: An Essay on Autism and Theory of Mind* (1995).

**Michael Boulton** is Senior Lecturer in Psychology at the University of Keele. He has conducted research on the causes and consequences of childhood bullying since the late 1980s and has published extensively on these topics. He also contributes regularly to training courses designed to help teachers and childcare professionals improve children's relationships with their peers.

**J. Fredrik Brown** is a clinical psychologist specializing with children and people with learning difficulties. When writing his chapter for this book he worked with Professor Cullen at the North Staffordshire Combined Healthcare NHS Trust. He now works with the Phoenix Trust in Bristol.

**Jennifer Brown** is Senior Lecturer and Director of the MSc in Forensic Psychology at the University of Surrey. Her main research interests are occupational stress and the role of women officers in the police service. Previously she was the research manager for Hampshire Constabulary where she worked on organizational and operational aspects of policing. She is co-author (with Elizabeth Campbell) of *Stress and Policing* (1994).

**Chris Cullen** is a consultant clinical psychologist with North Staffordshire Combined Healthcare NHS Trust and Professor in the Psychology of Learning Disabilities at the University of Keele. His clinical work is in the area of learning disabilities and his research interests are in staff training, challenging behaviour, sexual abuse and autism.

**Helen Graham** is Lecturer in Psychology at the University of Keele with extensive experience in counselling training. Her publications include *Complementary Therapies in Context* (1999) and *A Picture of Health* (1995).

**John Hegarty** is Lecturer in Psychology and Director of the MA in Community Care (Learning Disability) at the University of Keele. He is co-facilitator of the Cancer Support Group at North Staffordshire Royal Infirmary which he helped to found in 1981. He co-edited (with Richard DeCann) *Psychology in Radiography* (vols 1 and 2) (1986, 1988).

**John McLeod** is Professor of Counselling at the School of Social and Health Sciences of Abertay, Dundee. Originally trained in person centred counselling, he has published several books and papers on counselling including *An Introduction to Counselling* (2nd edn) (Open University Press, 1998) and *Narrative and Psychotherapy* (1997).

**Michelle Meadows** is Lecturer in Psychology at the University of Staffordshire. She works with the Manchester Driver Behaviour Research Group whose aim is to improve road safety by furthering understanding of the psychology of driving. She is currently involved in a number of projects funded by the Department of Environment, Transport and the Regions.

**Aidan Moran** is Professor of Psychology and Director of the Psychology Research Laboratory at University College, Dublin. He is Official Psychologist to the Irish Olympic Squad and author of *The Psychology of Concentration in Sports Performers* (1996) and *Managing Your Own Learning at University* (1997).

**Stephen Stradling** is Reader in Psychology at the Transport Research Unit at Napier University, Edinburgh. He was formerly Senior Lecturer and a member of the Manchester Driver Behaviour Research Group in the Department of Psychology at Manchester University. He has published widely on counselling and stress, and his books (with others) include *Developing Cognitive-Behavioural Counselling* (1995) and *Brief Group Counselling* (1998).

# Preface

The plan for the first edition of this book was conceived on the last day of January 1986, when we were driving down to London for a meeting to discuss research with British Telecom. On that journey we discussed our views on applied psychology. We had both been struck by the wide range of applications that psychology had, and how psychology could reach into all manner of practical, personal, social and occupational problems. Indeed the number of problems where a psychological input might be useful seemed boundless. However, at the back of both our minds was a long held dissatisfaction with textbooks in this field which typically discuss occupational, clinical, educational and other areas of applied psychology separately. We knew from experience that solving problems does not always depend upon the particular domain in which the problems lie. Different occupational, clinical or educational problems might be approached in the same way. Thus we concluded that it did not matter much to applied psychology whether the problem was a management one, a health one or an educational one. What mattered was the approach that psychologists took to solving problems across different domains.

We developed this argument on our journey, and in this second edition we illustrate it in more detail. Here we identify seven general overlapping roles that applied psychologists might have and, together with our co-authors, we provide two illustrative chapters for each role. This means that there is no specific chapter that describes any one particular kind of applied psychologist, such as an occupational or a clinical psychologist. What there is, however, is an attempt to show that psychologists have multiple skills that can be applied in a wide variety of settings.

In compiling *The Applied Psychologist* we and our co-authors have been helped by many people, individually and collectively, and we would like to acknowledge here their assistance. The main changes between the first and the second edition of the text stem from the widening scope of applied psychology, and the increase in the number of national and international experts in the field who have been able to help us. These changes reflect the development of applied psychology since 1989 and promise well for its future.

We enjoyed putting this text together. We hope you enjoy reading it.

*James Hartley and Alan Branthwaite*

# The roles and skills of applied psychologists

## *James Hartley and Alan Branthwaite*

**What do psychologists do . . . ? How do they work . . . ?
How useful is their training . . . ?**

People in their professional lives play a variety of roles and use a variety of skills to carry out their work effectively. Applied psychologists are people who, in their jobs, try to use their skills to help other people – teachers, parents and children; doctors, nurses and patients; managers, union representatives and workers; and the general public. The majority of applied psychologists work in four main areas: clinical psychology, educational psychology, occupational psychology and government service (e.g. as prison psychologists). In any of these areas applied psychologists may offer advice to others on the basis of knowledge, theory, specifically collected data or experience. Each of these sources of advice has its own advantages and limitations: data from especially commissioned studies may be specific but may lack controls and replication; experience is often able to take complex factors into account, but it may be subjective. In practice most advice is based on all four sources.

A conventional approach in texts on applied psychology is to take each of these four areas in turn, perhaps to add some more – such as forensic and sports psychology – and to discuss in separate chapters the work involved in each (e.g. see Spurgeon *et al.* 1994; Coolican 1996; Sternberg 1997). In reality, however, the work which psychologists actually do in these various areas has more similarities than differences. It is the subject matter of their jobs that differs, rather than the roles, skills and ways of working.

So another approach is to consider the ways an applied psychologist uses specialized roles and skills appropriately in different situations – rather like the way in which someone fitting a new kitchen takes on the role of plumber, electrician, joiner, plasterer, painter and decorator as appropriate. It is this latter approach that we take in this book. We see applied psychologists as skilled technicians who operate in a number of different roles, and these roles are present in each of the areas of activity mentioned above.

In this text we have identified seven overlapping roles played by applied psychologists. This list is not exhaustive, but we consider these roles to be the most important and the most widely used. In their work, applied psychologists exercise these roles in varying degrees and at varying times; sometimes, indeed, the different roles may conflict. However, each section of this book is concerned with explaining and exploring one particular role in detail in order to give it prominence.

What then are these roles? How far can we characterize them? We have given them rather pretentious titles in order to encapsulate their qualities. Let us consider each in turn and look at some of the issues relating to each one.

## A: The psychologist as counsellor

A counsellor is a person who gives counsel – or advice – usually to individuals but sometimes to organizations (see Chapters 1 and 2). The psychologist as counsellor uses a number of skills to help people to talk openly, to express their feelings and ideas, to draw out responses and reactions, to help them explore their problems more deeply and more thoroughly, and to see their concerns from different perspectives.

The role of the counsellor is prominent in treating illnesses and in helping people to cope better in their lives (McLeod 1998). Psychologists use counselling in treating agoraphobia or school phobia, marriage crises, victims of hijackings, etc. But the roles and techniques of the counsellor are also used in many other areas. In personnel selection, market research interviews and wage bargaining, psychologists use counselling skills to help those involved express themselves and formulate their views and opinions.

The skills used by trained counsellors are discussed in Chapters 1 and 2. Broadly speaking there are two approaches in use. One uses a more directive style, in which the counsellor takes more initiative and is more authoritative in the interaction. An alternative is a less directive approach that takes a lower profile and lets the patient or the client take the initiative. In practice most psychologists use both strategies depending on the needs of the particular case and the progress that has been made. The two approaches involve different styles of questioning (suggestive, firm or realistic versus open, encouraging, explorative or tentative). Experience is important in knowing which style might be more appropriate and productive at a given point.

## B: The psychologist as colleague

Psychologists often work as members of a team with other professionals – such as doctors, engineers and computer programmers – and psychology makes only one contribution to the whole team effort. However, as colleagues in such multidisciplinary teams, psychologists provide a particular perspective and approach over and above their knowledge, expertise and specialized techniques.

The perspective of a psychologist working as a colleague is to draw attention to the human factors that may be pertinent to the system or the solution of a problem. Other professionals in the team, for instance, will focus on the electronics, the physical engineering, the medical, biological or pharmacological aspects of the system, which are equally relevant and important, but each of which is only a part of the total working system. By their training psychologists consider problems from the point of view of the end-user – or recipient – and are more conscious of the perspective of the individual in the system, like the pilot of an aircraft, the operator in a nuclear power plant or the reader of a patient information leaflet. A long time ago, Howarth (1975) pointed out that many errors (in architectural planning and in designing control panels, to give but two examples) could have been avoided if psychologists had been involved at the design stage. Indeed, Howarth suggested that one of the chief functions of psychologists was to prevent other experts from 'going it alone'. So (as shown in Chapters 3 and 4) the psychologist as colleague in health care and policing will draw attention to potential problems arising out of subjective interpretations and experiences, individual differences and biases, and interactions between human characteristics and the demands of the situation.

## C: The psychologist as expert

As an expert a psychologist may be called in as a consultant to advise on some topic, such as the design of an advertisement or methods of improving sports performance (as discussed in Chapters 5 and 6). In carrying out the role of 'expert', psychologists draw upon specialized knowledge, concepts, theories and their practical experience. This helps them to review the situation, to analyse and interpret findings, and perhaps to carry out some experiments of their own. In the USA presidential commissions have called upon such expertise by asking psychologists to present reports on topics such as the effects of pornography on people and on the consequences of viewing violence on television. In the UK psychologists, similarly, have been asked to help with reports on topics such as 'recovered memory' (where previously forgotten memories, say of childhood trauma, are 'recovered' during therapy), child sexual abuse, post-traumatic stress disorder, educational testing in schools and even examining PhD theses.

As independent experts, psychologists also bring different insights into some of the problems and difficulties that may be experienced in social systems such as factories, schools, libraries, hospitals, prisons and transport.

The people who create and manage such systems tend to see them from their own point of view, and come to accept them as they stand. Outside observers, however, may see things in a different way. Bull (1982), for example, observed the briefing of police officers at the beginning of their shifts, and noticed that they were being given far more information than they could easily assimilate. For Bull (a psychologist) this obvious factor partly explained the police officers' failure to remember all of the information they were given. But memory overload was not an aspect that the senior police officers (non-psychologists) in charge of the briefings had considered. They appeared to view memory as being like a tape recorder, and they regarded a police officer's inability to remember as a sign of lack of motivation. (Other aspects of policing which have benefited from the expertise of psychologists are described in Chapter 4.)

## D: The psychologist as toolmaker

Psychologists develop tools, measures and techniques for use in analysing and resolving problems. These tools have a wide range of applications and are used for different ends. The most obvious examples are the personality, intelligence and ability tests used by personnel managers, educationalists and health workers to improve selection (see Furnham 1992; Anastasi 1993; Shackleton 1994).

However, there are other techniques and procedures that are employed in different fields to aid learning, improve performance and resolve problems. Operant conditioning and behaviour modification programmes (see Chapter 12) are used in homes for learning-disabled people, in prisons, in treating phobias and social deviancy and in training guide dogs for visually-disabled people and sniffer dogs for police and customs work. Similar techniques are used for teaching social skills, and in assertiveness training to overcome shyness and/or improve the quality of life among lonely or mentally ill people (Argyle 1988). Chapter 14 also includes another example – showing how this approach can be used in planning humanitarian assistance.

Tools are developed and used to measure behaviour accurately in order to investigate issues that are of widespread social concern, or of relevance to public policy and planning. But this is not necessarily an easy task. Chapter 8, for instance, shows how difficult it can be to devise precise tools to answer some of the basic questions about differences between men and women.

In developing such tools and techniques it is often assumed that psychologists create tools that they can readily give away for non-psychologists to use (Miller 1980). But difficulties can arise when non-psychologists start using psychologists' tools without being fully aware of how they were developed, how they should be used and what precautions are needed in interpreting the results. Measures of text difficulty provide a case in point (see Chapter 7) but probably a better instance comes from fields like intelligence testing (Howe 1997).

Some psychologists have argued that it is more useful for psychologists to *share* their psychological tools with experts from other disciplines, and thus they advocate our Role B – the psychologist as colleague. However, there are other complex situations when Role C – the psychologist as expert – may be more appropriate.

## E: The psychologist as detached investigator

Psychologists are trained as students to collect and analyse data, to draw conclusions and to write reports. Psychology as a discipline emphasizes the need for objectivity and controlled experimentation, and encourages psychologists to be conscious of the dangers of subjectivity and bias. Many applied psychologists conduct evaluation studies in a scientific manner in order to collect data and assess the evidence for and against a particular point of view. Thus, for example, there are studies on the effects of noise on productivity, of different teaching styles, and of different methods of psychotherapy and counselling (e.g. see Haselgrave 1995; Kember 1997; Strupp 1993 respectively). Chapters 9 and 10 illustrate the usefulness of this approach in relation to assessing the amount of stress experienced by fire-fighters which affects their work, and in forming public policy about home-work, but they also draw attention to the difficulties which are involved in being neutral and impartial.

It has sometimes been argued that the detached approach of the scientific method is inappropriate for studying topics in psychology because, first, it is impossible to study people in a scientific way when perception and judgement is coloured by experiences and wishes, second, it is impossible to control many of the relevant interacting variables that affect behaviour, and third, the results of one study are always specific to one particular set of conditions – and thus one cannot generalize widely from them. (Interested readers might enjoy the exchanges about this issue between Morgan (1998), Sherrard (1998) and Cooper and Stevenson (1998) in *The Psychologist* 11(10).)

Attempts to overcome these difficulties usually require psychologists to use more flexible but less precise methods and analyses which are more subjective but also more insightful (as in the role of expert). The data from such investigations, like those from more precise experiments, are still open to scrutiny and are thus more objective than are simple value judgements. Psychologists argue that the biases of outside observers are likely to be less partial than are those of people who hold a vested interest.

## F: The psychologist as theoretician

Theories consist of several principles (or a collection of general interrelated laws) that are put forward as an explanation of a set of facts and empirical findings. In collecting evidence to intervene in a problem, or give advice, theories can suggest the underlying mechanisms or processes that might be involved, where to look for causes, and how to design specific inquiries to support or reject a particular point of view. Theories help applied psychologists to explain and predict on a wide scale and in circumstances which may not necessarily have been studied before. Of course, there are always dangers in not knowing the precise range of application of a theory or its limits of application, but these can be discovered by further testing and checking. Often theories derived from studies in one situation can be the starting point for explorations of a new problem (see Chapters 11, 12 and 14) and experiences in applied fields can help to build up and qualify existing theories (Broadbent 1971; Coolican 1996).

Theories provide the link between laboratory studies and the 'real' world. Theories are the means by which results from studies under artificial circumstances can be applied to practical problems. Although laboratory studies are artificially restricted and controlled, it is possible, by varying the parameters and conditions across a series of studies, to identify causal relationships between variables. Thus, for example, multiple laboratory and field studies of inter-group relationships enable us to predict conditions that will foster harmonious working relationships between groups in the real world (Argyle 1989; Duck 1998). Chapters 11, 12 and 14 illustrate the ways in which very different theories can be useful to the applied psychologist in understanding 'real' problems, and how general theories can be built up out of experience in attempting to solve specific problems.

## G: The psychologist as change agent

Psychology has the scope and the potential for helping people, institutions and organizations in a wide range of circumstances. Psychologists believe that their work will change people and society for the better (whatever they perceive this to be). Most of these changes which empower individuals are relatively uncontroversial. Social skills training, for example, is used to help delinquents, unemployed people, mentally ill people and members of the public to cope with the everyday encounters and situations that they find stressful (Argyle 1988). However, other kinds of social engineering may be deemed more controversial. For instance, the researchers involved in the *Girls into Science* project in the 1980s deliberately set out to design instructional materials and experiences that would encourage more girls to take up science in British secondary schools and beyond (Kelly 1987). The chapters in this section reflect this continuum: trying to reduce bullying in schools (Chapter 13) is seen as relatively uncontroversial and desirable. However, psychological interventions in the field of humanitarian aid (Chapter 14) raise many issues about the rights of people and relationships between one culture and another.

Psychologists may work independently and try to change things but (as noted above) they often have to work for other people. In this case they may be cast into a number of different roles by their employers or by the clients who commission their work. Psychologists may be required to be inventors or problem solvers; they may be expected to be mediators or arbiters between competing factions; they may be required to support and to confirm a prejudged opinion (and not to 'rock the boat'); or they may be made scapegoats – carrying the blame if things go wrong. (All of these roles have been observed in business and industrial contexts, and no doubt occur in other contexts too.)

In addition, work conducted by psychologists in one area of investigation may be taken up by non-psychologists in ways that may not have been foreseen. Thus, for example, psychologists' work on sensory deprivation, obedience and reactions to imprisonment formed the basis for innovations in interrogation techniques (Watson 1980; Gudjonsson 1992). Thus psychologists acting as agents for change need to be conscious of their reasons and motivations for conducting their research and of the potential for exploitation of the results by others.

The chapters that follow in this book have each been written by psychologists who are working primarily in one of these seven roles. The authors of each chapter were asked:

1 to sketch briefly the main issues involved in the topic of their title
2 to write their chapter to illustrate one of our suggested seven roles that their work entails.

The resulting text shows that applied psychologists are people who employ many different roles and skills. Although each chapter focuses on one specific role, each one also shows that applied psychologists do not restrict themselves to single roles. The psychologist as counsellor might well be a detached analyst on occasions, and vice versa. In this book the different roles have been emphasized in order to show that applied psychologists use a variety of different skills in their everyday work and that, while the nature of this work may differ, these multiple roles – in different degrees – are common to them all.

---

*Discussion questions*

1 What difficulties might you expect in convincing some professional people who are not psychologists that psychologists might make a contribution to their area of expertise?

2 Can you think of examples where it might be appropriate for psychologists to share their skills rather than to provide tools for non-psychologists to use?

3 Should psychologists be agents for change? What difficulties do you see in this role for psychologists? Does this role conflict with being a detached analyst?

4 Working in small groups, see if you can put in rank order of importance the seven roles for applied psychologists outlined in this chapter.

## Further reading

Coolican, H. (1996) *Applied Psychology*. London: Hodder and Stoughton. A readable, more typical, introductory text on applied psychology, with chapters on sport, health, environmental and forensic psychology in addition to the major topics of clinical, educational and occupational psychology.

Fagan, T. K. and VandenBos, G. (eds) (1993) *Exploring Applied Psychology: Origins and Critical Analyses*. Washington, DC: American Psychological Association. This text contains five 'Master Lectures' delivered at the American Psychological Association's 1992 Annual Conference, tracing the history and development of educational, occupational and counselling psychology.

Spurgeon, P., Davies, R. and Chapman, A. (eds) (1994) *Elements of Applied Psychology*. Reading, UK: Harwood. A more substantial general textbook than Coolican's, with individual chapters on specialist topics written by separate experts.

Sternberg, R. J. (ed.) (1997) *Career Paths in Psychology: Where Your Degree Can Take You*. Washington, DC: American Psychological Association. An American text that illustrates the occupations available for psychology graduates in the applied field by using case history accounts from established professionals.

Warr, P. B. (ed.) (1996) *Psychology at Work*, 4th edn. Harmondsworth: Penguin. This is a revised edition of a classic text on occupational psychology, which is difficult going in parts. Comparisons between the first, second, third and fourth editions illustrate clearly how occupational psychology has developed since 1971.

## References

Anastasi, A. (1993) A century of psychological testing: origins, problems and progress, in T. K. Fagan and G. VandenBos (eds) *Exploring Applied Psychology: Origins and Critical Analyses*. Washington, DC: American Psychological Association.

Argyle, M. (1988) *Bodily Communication*, 2nd edn. London: Methuen.

Argyle, M. (1989) *The Social Psychology of Work*, 2nd edn. Harmondsworth: Penguin.

Broadbent, D. E. (1971) Relationships between theory and application in psychology, in P. B. Warr (ed.) *Psychology at Work*, 1st edn. Harmondsworth: Penguin.

Bull, R. (1982) Can experimental psychology be applied psychology?, in S. Canter and D. Canter (eds) *Psychology in Practice*. Chichester: Wiley.

Coolican, H. (1996) *Applied Psychology*. London: Hodder and Stoughton.

Cooper, N. and Stevenson, C. (1998) 'New science' and psychology. *The Psychologist*, 11(10): 484–5.

Duck, S. W. (1998) *Human Relationships*, 3rd edn. London: Sage.

Furnham, A. (1992) *Personality at Work*. London: Routledge.

Gudjonsson, G. H. (1992) *The Psychology of Interrogation, Confessions and Testimony*. Chichester: Wiley.

Haselgrave, C. M. (1995) Auditory environment and noise assessment, in J. R. Wilson and E. N. Corlett (eds) *Evaluation of Human Work*, 2nd edn. London: Taylor and Francis.

Howarth, I. (1975) The uses of psychology, in W. E. C. Gilham (ed.) *Psychology Today*. London: Hodder Teach Yourself Books.

Howe, M. J. A. (1997) *IQ in Question: The Truth about Intelligence*. London: Sage.

Kelly, A. (ed.) (1987) *Science for Girls*. Milton Keynes: Open University Press.

Kember, D. (1997) A reconceptualisation of the research into university academics' conceptions of teaching. *Learning and Instruction*, 7(3): 255–75.

McLeod, J. (1998) *An Introduction to Counselling*, 2nd edn. Buckingham: Open University Press.

Miller, G. A. (1980) Giving away psychology in the 80s. *Psychology Today*, 13: 38–50.

Morgan, M. (1998) Qualitative research: science or pseudo-science? *The Psychologist*, 11(10): 481–3, 488.

Shackleton, V. (1994) Recruitment and selection, in P. Spurgeon, R. Davies and A. Chapman (eds) *Elements of Applied Psychology*. Reading, UK: Harwood.

Sherrard, C. (1998) Social dimensions of research. *The Psychologist*, 11(10): 486–7.

Spurgeon, P., Davies, R. and Chapman, A. (eds) (1994) *Elements of Applied Psychology*. Reading, UK: Harwood.

Sternberg, R. J. (ed.) (1997) *Career Paths in Psychology: Where Your Degree Can Take You*. Washington, DC: American Psychological Association.

Strupp, H. H. (1993) Psychotherapy research: evolution and current trends, in T. K. Fagan and G. VandenBos (eds) *Exploring Applied Psychology: Origins and Critical Analyses*. Washington, DC: American Psychological Association.

Watson, P. (1980) *War on the Mind*. Harmondsworth: Penguin.

## Section *A*

# The psychologist as counsellor

# Chapter 1

## What is counselling?
## A personal view

## Helen Graham

Hardly a day passes without us hearing that someone, somewhere, has been offered counselling following some event or experience. It may be after an accident, a natural disaster, abuse, bereavement, divorce, drug addiction, a diagnosis of AIDS, a debilitating or terminal illness, a genetic disorder, the birth of a handicapped child, fertility treatment, redundancy, being released from imprisonment or a hostage situation, or winning the national lottery. Indeed, when there are major disasters, whole teams of counsellors are mobilized to give counselling. Few of us question this. Yet we need to question it very seriously. We have to ask what is being given here and why; how is it received; whether it is wanted, appropriate or effective; and what are its consequences and implications.

## Counselling: a lay approach

If we take the initial question, what is counselling, we run into the first of several problems because the answer is not as straightforward as we might suppose. My dictionary defines counselling as 'giving advice or guidance on conduct'. The problem lies not with this definition, but with the way in which this advice is given and its consequent effects. One lay interpretation is that counselling means telling someone what to do, or what not to do. But this approach is authoritarian and directive. It implies that the person giving the advice or counsel has access to information or knowledge that the other person does not have, and that they are wiser in some way. In this sense, therefore, this person is superior to, or of different status from, the other. By telling a person what to do, or not to do, the authoritative person is directing him or her in some way. Implicitly therefore, they are more powerful.

---

> ***Box 1.1*  A case history**
>
> Jackie has fallen behind with her work and has not submitted an important assignment which contributes to her final course result. The scenario is this. Having found herself short of cash after the vacation when she'd been travelling in Europe, Jackie took on a job in a bar at a nightclub, several evenings a week during the term. At first everything was fine. Her working hours were OK, she was earning money, able to attend lectures and do her work. She enjoyed the job and made friends in the club, so after a few weeks she would stay on after work finished and have a few drinks and a laugh. She began staying later and later so that it was an effort to get up for lectures the next day. She missed some lectures and fell asleep in others. She also found that she was spending most of her earnings on drink and so she began to get anxious. She was becoming more and more hard up and not getting her work done. She knew she was falling behind so, being anxious, she found that chatting and drinking at the club meant she could put it out of her mind for a while. The net result was that she hadn't completed her assignment. Her student friends are understandably concerned about her; she is obviously stressed and anxious and not coping at all well. She has become depressed, and is drinking and smoking heavily. She spends most of her time in college worrying about the situation and seeking the advice of friends.

However, it is easy to appreciate the shortcomings of this kind of counselling. Imagine the common occurrence in student life depicted in Box 1.1. What advice would you give Jackie?

One of Jackie's friends says: 'Well if I were you I'd just get my head down and get on with the assignment.'
'But I can't do that,' says Jackie. 'I'm too stressed and/or depressed to concentrate on anything.'

Another friend says: 'Well if I were you I'd go and see your tutor and explain. I'm sure you'll be treated sympathetically.'
'But you know my tutor,' says Jackie. 'We don't get on and he takes a really tough line on late work and I've missed some of his lectures and tutorials. I can't possibly do that.'

Another friend says: 'Well if I were you I'd just stick anything down on paper. You'll get credit for handing something in.'
'No, I can't do that,' says Jackie. 'I really want a good course mark and that would ruin my chances.'

Someone else says: 'If I were you I'd copy someone else's work. No one will ever know.'
'I can't do that either,' says Jackie. 'If I were to be found out I'd get

zero, and I'd be no better off. Even if I wasn't found out I couldn't live with myself as a cheat.'

So what has been achieved here? After agonizing for an hour or two, Jackie may feel a bit better for having expressed her angst but, as soon as she leaves her friends, she is likely to feel a lot worse – because nothing has altered.

Her friends – all instant lay counsellors – probably all feel quite good. The encounter has passed the time rather well. Their opinions have been sought; they have been experts; they have given the best advice. They have said what they would do. It has been a bit of an ego trip for them being able to offer their advice, but the truth is that in the same position as their friend they probably would have done none of the things that they advised her to do, and for exactly the same reasons. But it doesn't matter – advice is cheap – and it's not their problem anyway. They've done their bit as friends, so they can't be blamed. If Jackie doesn't do as she's told that is her problem.

Most of us have a tendency to engage in this kind of activity, whether invited to or not. Typically, therefore, lay counselling goes something like this:

- 'If I were you I'd invest in a personal pension scheme' (financial counselling)
- 'If I were you I'd study law' (careers counselling)
- 'If I were you I'd leave him immediately' (marriage guidance counselling)
- 'If I were you I'd give up sex altogether' (AIDS counselling)

We tend to assume we are all 'counsellors' inasmuch as we listen to other people's problems and offer advice, and that to a greater or lesser degree listening is 'natural', an innate, inborn activity. However, this assumption tends to confuse listening with our desire to be heard, that is, for others to listen to us. It also fails to distinguish between *hearing*, the perception of sound, which is for most people a natural and inborn activity, and *listening*, the selective process of attending to sound, which is a complex and acquired skill which requires learning and practice (see pp. 24–6).

When lay counsellors volunteer their services they are commonly assumed to have some kind of wisdom or knowledge that they can pass on to others that will be of help to them. This assumption does a great deal for the volunteers; it is always good for the ego to be regarded as an expert. It is also good for relevant authorities because it seems that something is being done; action is being taken, so they cannot be criticized for not having tried to help the victims. And, of course, it is good for the rest of us because it absolves us from any responsibility for having to do anything ourselves. On hearing that a team of counsellors has been arranged we may think 'Well that's all right then' and promptly forget about it and the person or persons on the receiving end of such wise counsel.

But is it good for the recipient? The person receiving this kind of counselling, however well intended, may not want it, and for support to be truly helpful it must be regarded as such by the recipient (Cook and Oltjenbruns 1998). If there has been an accident, disaster, death, even a divorce, people may be too stunned to take in anything at all. They may feel bitter, resentful, angry. They may want to be alone and not hassled. They may want space to deal with their feelings. They may object to someone sympathizing or 'empathizing', saying 'I know it hurts now but in time you'll get over it', or 'Try and see the positive side of it', or 'One day you'll look back and laugh at this', or 'If I were you I'd go home and get some sleep' or 'Have a nice cup of tea'. Interventions of this kind are undesirable (Rando 1984).

## Loss and bereavement

Relatively little attention has been given to the positive outcomes of grief, but a growing literature suggests that personal growth can occur as a result as well as feelings of loss. Thus interventions of the 'look on the bright side' sort are inappropriate. It is likely that personal and social growth triggered by a loss 'can only be identified by those who are at some point in the resolution process and *not* in the acute phase of grief' (Cook and Oltjenbruns 1998: 122).

Following any kind of loss, whether loss of a loved one or loss of face, several stages of bereavement are identifiable (Kubler-Ross 1969; Bowlby 1980). There is a stage of denial in which the person cannot believe what has occurred. He or she wants to wake up and discover it was all an unpleasant dream. A guilty phase often follows, characterized by feelings of self-blame and recrimination: 'If I had been there this wouldn't have happened' or 'If I'd acted differently this could have been avoided'. There may also be anger, usually directed at others, and attribution of blame; it is now *their* fault that this happened: if the doctor had made the correct diagnosis, if the driver of the car had not been drunk, if God were just, and so on. This may be followed by grief, sadness or depression. Finally there is reconciliation and acceptance of the loss.

These stages vary in duration from person to person and with the circumstances. They are not necessarily sequential and the emotions may be ordered differently. Hence these stages do not adequately reflect the uniqueness of grief (Bugen 1979), but they can be discerned in most instances of loss. Consider the reaction to the death of Diana, Princess of Wales in August 1997. Initially this was of mass disbelief. It took days for the fact of her death to penetrate public consciousness. Following this universal sense of shock, there was a phase during which people reasoned that she would still be alive 'if only' she had been wearing a seatbelt, remained in Sardinia, had not been divorced, had been in different company, and had a police escort. Then there was the anger towards the paparazzi; Prince Charles and the royal family, for their treatment of her; and Mr Al Fayed, for employing an unsuitable driver. Then there was a shared sense of overwhelming sadness and grief, as reflected in the millions of tributes paid to her. Finally there was acceptance that none of this changed the situation; Diana was dead and life went on without her.

Although individuals differ in the rate at which they progress through these stages, and the order in which they do so, it is considered that for healthy adjustment to occur they must proceed through all of them (Kubler-Ross 1969; Bowlby 1980). However, if a person becomes arrested at any stage – stuck there – then they are likely to experience profound problems, or what has been termed 'complicated grief' (Rando 1993). They can be arrested at the stage of denial, or guilt, or anger, or depression – sometimes indefinitely. A parent in denial may keep a child's bedroom exactly as it was when he or she died and refuse to accept that the child will not be coming back to occupy it. Fans who believe that Elvis is still alive are also 'stuck' in denial. In extreme cases, individuals may keep the body of a dead person in bed for years rather than acknowledge the death. This response has been termed the *mummification* of the deceased person (Aiken 1985). Some people cannot come to terms with their guilt – real or imagined – for the loss of a loved one, whether through death, separation or divorce. Others cannot let go of their anger, often because they do not realize they are angry, such as the woman who told me that if her son were alive today, she would kill him for the pain he had caused her by his death while pursuing a dangerous hobby she disapproved of. *Chronic mourning* (Bowlby 1980) may occur when the manifestations of grief are unusually intense and protracted; prolonged depression is not uncommon. Self-destructive behaviour, violence directed towards others, inability to talk about or remember the deceased, and loss of contact with reality may also occur when grief is unresolved (Demi and Myles 1987).

These people all need help at the points where they become stuck and this is unlikely to be evident at the outset. These effects tend to be delayed. Indeed, in some cases, it appears that some people are not given help because they were previously given counselling at the time of the trauma (Dicks 1997). However, most post-traumatic stress victims need counselling many years after the event, as the experience of Vietnam veterans shows graphically (Dicks 1997). Most people who have experienced serious trauma need long-term support rather than quick fix solutions, and positive resolution is correlated with the long-term availability of social support (Parkes and Weiss 1983). Unfortunately, such extended support is often lacking, and many people do not recognize the need to offer support beyond the immediacy of the loss (Sprang *et al.* 1993).

## The shortcomings of quick fix counselling

Some so-called 'bereavement counselling' is provided shortly after the death of a loved one and, in the experience of many people that I have spoken to, it amounts to little more than helping them to put on a brave face. One person whose husband committed suicide told me that bereavement counselling enabled her to erect quickly a defensive wall around herself which helped her to cope with the painful aftermath of his death. Years later she has neither mourned for him nor dealt with the many feelings his death gave rise to, including profound anger. She knows only too well that her pain and other feelings were never examined, much less worked through, and that they will erupt at some time in the future.

Bowlby (1980) observed that if grief is inhibited, and individuals refuse to allow themselves to feel the emotional pain of their loss, the grief manifests itself through a variety of physical symptoms, such as headache and other psychosomatic conditions, rather than the normal signs of loss. Grief may be expressed directly but much later than the loss. When grief is delayed in this way, a subsequent loss may trigger a greatly magnified grief reaction that is really tied to the earlier loss. An example (cited by Cook and Oltjenbruns 1998) is that of a woman who never mourned the death of her mother five years earlier but became emotionally and physically immobilized when her pet cat aged 3 months was run over and killed. She admitted that she had loved her mother so much that she had refused to think of her death so that she would not be consumed by sorrow. The sudden death of her cat brought these thoughts and feelings to the surface. 'If the bereaved are encouraged to identify and express their emotions, they are more likely to become reconciled to their loss instead of inhibiting their grief or prematurely aborting it' (Cook and Oltjenbruns 1998: 123). It is therefore helpful to communicate to bereaved people that it is normal, necessary and permissible to grieve (Rando 1984), rather than to encourage cover up of emotions.

The latter can be likened to a situation where a wound has been treated by the speedy application of a sticking plaster. Superficially the wound may seem to heal after a few days or so, but if dirt, bacteria or other contaminants have been sealed in by the plaster rather than expressed they will fester away and may erupt much later as an abscess, boil or septicaemia. Emotional wounds are much the same. The potentially damaging emotions that accompany them have to be expressed rather than hastily covered up and repressed if they are not to give rise to serious problems at a later stage.

The potentially harmful consequences of quick fix counselling were highlighted by Yvonne McEwan in 1997. Speaking at the European Practitioners Trauma Conference in September 1997, McEwan put the cat among the pigeons by describing the burgeoning counselling industry as unstructured, unregulated, ethically bankrupt and highly destructive. She pointed out that, since a fire at Bradford City football stadium in May 1985, the disaster scene has become a growth industry and has created a victim culture, in which the rights of victims are being sacrificed. McEwan observed that those who help with stress and bereavement in the wake of tragedies can be insensitive. Victims may have to endure overzealous and ignorant counsellors. In Dunblane, Scotland, for example, where 16 children and their teacher were shot dead in their primary school in March 1996, McEwan claimed that there were more counsellors than victims.

It is McEwan's view that most people who witness terrible accidents or see loved ones killed do not need counsellors; they recover by relying on their own inner resources and the support of family and friends. The idea that they need counselling is a western invention. As she points out, there is no mandatory debriefing by counsellors after environmental disasters and famines such as those in Africa: people simply get on with their lives. McEwan (1998) suggested that following a trauma, individuals should do likewise. They should think twice about counselling, look at their past coping strategies and how friends and family helped them. They should also consider their goals and aspirations for the future, asking themselves 'Where do I go from here?' rather than 'Why me?'

McEwan despairs at our blind faith in the need for trauma counselling, claiming that research has shown it to be 'at best useless, and at worst harmful' (personal communication, March 1998). Her claims are not totally unfounded. Bisson *et al.* (1997) showed that serious burns victims who received immediate counselling suffered greater post-traumatic stress when followed up than those who did not receive counselling, and other studies have shown that psychological debriefing has no obvious effects (e.g. Brom *et al.* 1993; Hobbs *et al.* 1996; Lee *et al.* 1996).

While I agree that, normally, people do not need counselling in such situations, I think there is a broader issue here. With the decline of organized religions during the twentieth century, people in distress turn to doctors rather than priests, vicars or rabbi. Doctors have not been trained to deal with emotional pain and the help they give to people suffering in this way is usually in the form of a pharmacological quick fix – such as antidepressants to the bereaved and tranquillizers to the distraught – in the same way as they give painkillers to reduce physical pain. It is a case of the old saying: 'If you only have a spanner you tend to treat everything as if it were a nut'. These remedies do not address the problem, they simply reduce the individual's capacity for response, and by so doing they imply that emotional responses are in some way undesirable, unnatural and to be avoided at all costs, whereas they are in fact healthy coping behaviours.

## Professional counselling: the example of Carl Rogers

Given all of the above, it is often very difficult for people to realize that the main features of lay counselling are totally incompatible with the theory and practice of counselling as advanced by the distinguished American psychologist, Carl Rogers, in the 1950s and 1960s (Rogers 1951, 1967, 1971, 1980). Rogers is widely regarded as the founding father of what is often referred to as 'the counselling movement' and has been perhaps the most significant contributor to theory, practice and research in this field.

Rogers' ideas about counselling are so diametrically opposed to commonly held ideas of counselling both then and now that it seems perverse that he chose to adopt the term counselling at all. Certainly it would have avoided a great deal of confusion if he had used another term altogether. Rogers took the view that no one can make decisions for another person, act for them or solve their problems because these are matters of personal responsibility and choice. The notion 'If I were you' is simply untenable, because one is not. Accordingly, any kind of change or action must proceed from the individual concerned.

Rogers' major field of psychological study was perception, and specifically the area of phenomenology – the study of the way people perceive the phenomena of their existence. In other words, he was primarily concerned with how people see themselves and their world. He took the view that if individuals can be helped to see themselves and the situation they find themselves in, they will be able to perceive the options available to them and make choices. This amounts to acquiring greater freedom from perceiving greater degrees of freedom for action and taking greater responsibility for one's life. Implicitly it is empowering because it enables people to make changes and take control for themselves. The counsellor's role is merely to facilitate their clients' exploration of themselves, their situation and the choices available to them. The counsellor does not interpret, evaluate or judge.

Jackie, the fictional student described in Box 1.1, cannot see that she can act in any way; all options seem closed to her; she sees herself as having no choice and thus no control over her situation. A 'Rogerian' counsellor would help Jackie to explore and understand her feelings about her situation and those underpinning her decisions not to act in certain ways. The counsellor would help her to see that by not acting she is nevertheless making a choice which has a number of consequences, and that she is responsible for them. Ultimately the situation *is* in her control, whether she acknowledges this or not. By considering all the alternatives available to her and her personal needs in the situation, she can responsibly choose the most appropriate course of action for her.

## Core conditions of counselling

Rogers viewed the potential for change and self-development as residing primarily within the person, but he recognized that another person could be a facilitator or catalyst for change, providing they could establish a relationship characterized by three qualities, which he referred to as core conditions for growth. Rogers said,

> I can state the overall hypothesis in one sentence, as follows: If I can provide a certain kind of relationship, the other person will discover within himself the capacity to use that relationship for growth; and change and personal development will occur.
>
> (Rogers 1967: 33)

The core conditions of that relationship are, first, *genuineness* or authenticity. The person offering the relationship (the counsellor) must be aware of his or her feelings and, so far as is appropriate, be able to express these rather than present any facade or phony face or front to the other person.

The second core condition is *unconditional positive regard* for the person, that is, the counsellor must be non-judgemental; able to value, respect and care for another person irrespective of their condition, behaviour, attitudes and feelings. The counsellor must be able to distinguish the sinner from the sin; to approve of the individual without necessarily approving of their thoughts, beliefs or actions.

Third, the counsellor must strive to achieve *empathy;* to understand the feelings and meanings which the other person is experiencing.

Hence, counsellors assume no role, no facade, no false front, no authority: they are real or genuine; open, accepting and non-directive. The implications of Rogers' core conditions are that the relationship between the counsellor and the other person is equal and democratic. Authority and responsibility for change and action reside in the individual, not the counsellor. Rogers claimed that simply being genuine, open and caring is sufficient to establish the conditions in which other people feel free to be themselves and express that self.

What we have here is a statement of a phenomenological method. The counsellor must be able to be real and honest in the situation, to respect and value the individuality of the other person, and be able to 'bracket him or herself' or put the self out of the equation so as to make the other person the object of their attention or study in order to understand the way that individuals experience and make sense of themselves and their world. Ultimately therefore counselling is a pursuit of meaning, of genuine understanding. It embodies the ideal of true friendship – which is why in the USA counselling and therapy have both been described as the purchase of friendship (Schofield 1964). Ironically it is because friendship so rarely offers these ideal qualities that people are obliged to try and buy it from professionals.

From these principles developed by Rogers it can be argued that the profession has developed a quasi-scientific language to give it kudos. Certainly complex terminology is a feature of much so-called counselling, and this gives rise to much confusion and misunderstanding among both counsellors and their clients.

Empathy, for example, is one of the most widely misunderstood terms in common usage. It is often interpreted as the ability to stand in someone else's shoes and have the same experience as them. Only a moment's reflection will show that this is nonsense. We cannot be in another's shoes. We can never experience their experience. The notion is absurd and meaningless, and was not intended by Rogers. By empathy Rogers meant listening attentively – with full attention. The words 'therapy' and 'therapist' derive from the Greek word *therapeia* meaning attendance. Therapy is, literally, attending, so a therapist is someone who attends. A counsellor, in the Rogerian sense, is a therapist. Indeed, Rogers did not distinguish between counselling and psychotherapy inasmuch as they are both concerned with attending to others. What does this actually mean?

The word attention derives from the Latin verb *attendere* meaning to reach out. Attention is reaching out to another. If you are to reach out to another with any prospect of making contact with them you have to ensure that there is nothing in the way. Normally when we attend to others there is a good deal in the way – our ego, ourself and all the baggage that this implies. Our ego tends to take our attention. We may be concerned about how we appear to others; whether we make a good impression; whether they like us; whether they think we know what we are doing. We may be worried that we might be inadequate or fail; that we are not really able to help. We may be quite uninterested in others. They may take up time we want to spend on ourselves. We may be more interested in our own affairs, or the weather, or racing from Catterick, or a million and one other things that relate to us and not them, and while that is the case we cannot give them our full attention. It is like being called to the phone in the middle of a favourite TV programme which you really want to see, to hear a friend droning on about her problems. Do you really care at that moment? Can you fully attend, knowing that the *X Files* or *EastEnders* is proceeding without you? It is hard to give someone your full attention when you have had a sizzling row with your partner that morning, or a letter saying the house is about to be repossessed, or an appointment to go for a hospital check up, or a meeting with your bank manager. Yet if we are to give another person our full attention that is precisely what we must be able to do. We must be able, temporarily at least, to suspend our ego, to enter into an ego-less state. This is why in some literature you will find the counselling attitude described as a Zen state, a meditative state or an altered state of consciousness. It is altered from our usual state of preoccupation with ourself and our world (Lesh 1984).

## Barriers to attending

Our ego is a major preoccupation for us all. We are very attached to it. We want to strengthen it, rather than diminish it or lose it. One of the main ways we build and strengthen our ego is through the roles we adopt and the power and authority invested in them. These give us status, standing, an identity, respect and so on. We invest a great deal of importance in them. Some roles are more prestigious and powerful than others and are therefore sought by many. Some people (e.g. Jourard 1971) suggest that the role of counsellor or therapist is sought by some people precisely because it does wonders for the ego. People are thus attached to the role and act in that role in ways they see as consistent with it. So, for example, a male psychologist or psychotherapist might grow a beard in the time-honoured manner of Freud – and this is how 'shrinks' are usually depicted in the media. The problem is that the role – the persona – can come between people and act as a barrier to any real contact.

Thus the 'helping' role of the counsellor can in itself be a major barrier. The attitude of non-doing at the core of Rogerian counselling, in which the counsellor neither takes over a person's problems nor tries to solve them, is quite alien to the western world, with its obsessive concern for performance and achievement. It is especially difficult for men who are particularly conditioned to the idea of 'doing'. Jourard (1971) observed that passivity often constitutes a threat to masculine identity, so male counsellors are frequently attracted to 'manly' active therapeutic techniques which make them feel that they are doing something to or for clients that will help them. This 'technical behaviour' may impress clients, but Jourard (1971) suggests, in striving to manipulate both themselves and their clients rather than responding openly and spontaneously, counsellors may provoke vigorous defences in their clients. So, at best, 'technique' proves unproductive, and at worst constitutes an act of alienation or hostility. This is no less true of attempts to 'do' things to put others at ease, such as offering cigarettes or coffee, affecting certain mannerisms or postures, which are a feature of many would-be counselling approaches. Jourard observed that many people assume a 'professional' manner as soon as they are in the presence of clients or patients. These acts invariably put people on their guard, because they are aware that they are devices to manipulate them or the situation to the other person's advantage. Thus, despite appearances to the contrary, such counsellors are attending to themselves rather than others.

Jourard claimed that the helping role could prove not only unhelpful but downright dangerous, and even deadly in some instances. He observed nurses in hospitals and found that some of them were so concerned to give the impression of being good nurses by putting patients at their ease, that they did not listen to what patients were trying to tell them. Instead they would keep insisting, as they tucked in the sheets and pumped up the pillows, that they should not worry and that they were in the best of hands. As a result in some cases, despite all the apparent attention given to patients, the nurses failed to attend to what they were trying to communicate. Thus they did not discover that patients had allergies to penicillin or other drugs, which when subsequently administered, proved almost or actually fatal (Jourard 1971).

Empathy is often confused with sympathy, and many people perceive counselling as 'lending a sympathetic ear'. However, sympathy means feeling sorry for someone or pitying them. Implicitly this puts the sympathizer in a superior position to the pitiful person, who may feel patronized and alienated. A sympathetic ear may therefore be a barrier to effective listening.

## The principle of reflection

To the extent that counsellors can put aside or suspend their egos and withdraw themselves from an encounter with another person, albeit temporarily, the other person is effectively talking to themself, much as they might if speaking into a mirror. In so doing they may confront features of themselves, possibly for the first time, and be able to use this new awareness for personal growth and change.

This concept of mirroring, or *reflection*, is central to Rogerian theory, in which the counsellor is conceived as mirror like, reflecting back the content and manner of a person's attempts at communication as faithfully as possible without the distortions that arise from egotistical involvements; that is, from the counsellor's hunches, theories, speculations, experiences, ideas on life, and so on. Rogers claimed that when confronted with such sustained reflection, people attend more closely to themselves and begin to see themselves more clearly. Their awareness progresses from the general to the specific, from superficial to deep, from thoughts to feelings, and from the abstract to the concrete.

## The effectiveness of Rogerian counselling

Certainly there is evidence to suggest that when the core conditions specified by Rogers are met, counselling is highly effective (Rogers 1980; Cramer 1992; but see Bozarth 1997). However, for me questions about whether or not counselling works or is effective are largely irrelevant. The more important question is how many counsellors and would-be counsellors actually understand what is required of them in a client centred Rogerian approach and how many of them can achieve it. In my experience very few meet the first criterion. They view counselling as a set of skills or techniques, a doing rather than a quality of being. And, for the most part – again in my experience – this is how counselling is taught. Even those who realize what counselling is really about cannot necessarily achieve the ego-less state necessary for full and genuine attending to another for very long – which has all kinds of practical implications for counselling as a full-time profession.

Unsurprisingly, most of the considerable research literature on the effectiveness of counselling highlights the importance of the individual therapist; indicating that it is not the approach, methods, style or anything else that seems to bring about positive results but the personal qualities of the coun-sellors themselves (e.g. see Bozarth 1997).

## Counselling outcomes

As to outcomes, it is obviously difficult to assess self-growth, development, actualization, self-empowerment and so on. Most of the literature seems to agree that the major shift that occurs during counselling is heightened self-esteem (see Cramer 1992). This is partly because, being valued uncondition-ally by someone else, the person comes to feel more self-value and worth and to listen to him or herself. By so doing the person implicitly acknowledges his or her own authority: that he or she is someone worth listening to.

It follows from this that a major gain from good counselling or therapy is increased self-awareness or self-knowledge. People who know themselves better tend to feel more secure and confident, and in turn to listen to their own authority with more respect. This is of the greatest importance. I believe that one of the most pertinent observations made about therapy was by the former psychologist Richard Alpert, who became the guru Ram Dass. He observed that you can go only as high as your therapist (Dass 1978). In other words you can be facilitated in your growth and development only to the extent that the therapist is facilitating their own self-growth and develop-ment. Such a person will be seeking to empower other people just as they are also striving towards self-empowerment. They will realize that ultimately the only authority you should follow is your own authority and it should be at all times encouraging you to stand on your own feet as your own expert and person.

## The psychologist as counsellor: listening to others

In this chapter I have tried to show that professional counselling is rather more complex than many people suppose, and that it is not something that should be undertaken lightly. The main contribution that psychologists as counsellors can make, in my view, is to emphasize the role and the power of listening seriously to others. As psychologists we can contribute to this in a number of ways. We can provide an understanding of the cognitive aspects of counselling and listening. For example, Barker's (1971) listening model pro-vides a framework for the analysis and discussion of all aspects of the listen-ing process. Furthermore, as listening (as opposed to hearing) is an acquired skill, we can help with training and instruction. Finally, we can help with indicating the likely barriers to communication in a listening situation.

In my own training workshops we have focused on developing an aware-ness of these personal barriers to effective listening. For example, in one exercise, participants are invited to listen to truthful statements generated by others in response to a given topic, for example, personal aggression. So, for example, one person might start with the statement, 'I get really angry when people who see themselves in some kind of position of authority try to patronize me.' Another might begin, ' I find that I am frequently very aggress-ive towards certain kinds of women.'

Most listeners experience difficulty in recalling this initial statement, irrespective of its length and complexity. This finding usually highlights, sometimes forcefully, the extent to which we tend not to hear others, and the strategies that we have adopted which promote this kind of 'deafness'. However, with practice, problems of hearing and recall are usually quickly remedied. What proves difficult for virtually every 'listener' is for them to suspend those aspects of themselves that inevitably obtrude between them and another. Typically this occurs in a number of ways, such as the tendency to give advice, provide solutions, dismiss a concern as trivial and fill silences which the person is using to explore their thoughts and feelings.

Other barriers to effective listening might include certain mannerisms, attitudes or anxiety. For example, some 'listeners' constantly interject with phrases such as 'I see' (when it is clear that they do not), and others may say 'Yes, dear', with all the patronizing overtones that this implies.

Generally people find these features relatively easy to identify, although harder to overcome. Frequently they find these insights threatening to their view of themselves, and requiring a close examination of their self-concept. Many find that this in itself is of help in their own personal growth and devel-opment, but others retreat further behind the defence of their professional role. However, the workshop situation is essentially experiential and it provides participants with the opportunity to explore these strategies with others, and to compare the outcomes with those advocated in counselling theory.

For most people, this experience is initially salutary, highlighting not only impediments to effective listening but also their own concerns, conflicts, preoccupations and problems. They quickly realize that self-awareness is para-mount in counselling, and that they themselves have a good deal to learn in this respect. Therefore, rather than seeing the counselling relationship as a one-way authoritarian process, the recipient of which is the client, they come to see it as a relationship of quality and mutuality, a sharing, through which both parties may grow and develop. They appreciate that to become effective listeners they first have to free themselves.

That this has not been grasped previously by many people is reflected in the results of a survey I conducted during 1987 on three groups of profes-sional and voluntary counsellors. Of those attending the workshops 70 per cent indicated that they had not previously given any consideration to the skills involved in effective listening. Nevertheless 66 per cent had considered themselves as good listeners. Perhaps not surprisingly, therefore, 92 per cent found that their view of their own listening skill had altered during the course of the workshops; 90 per cent found listening to others demanding, and 88 per cent reported that they found listening skills difficult to master in practice. Given all this, it is perhaps not too surprising to find the following anguished and anonymous plea among the annals of the journal *The Profes-sional in Practice – Skill Development*:

*Listen*

When I ask you to listen to me
  and you start giving advice
  you have not done what I asked.

When I ask you to listen to me
  and you begin to tell me why I shouldn't feel that way,
  you are trampling on *my feelings*.

When I ask you to listen to me
  and you feel you have to do something to solve my problem
  you have failed me, strange as it may seem.

Listen. All I asked was that you listen,
  not talk or do – just hear me.
Advice is cheap: 10 cents will get you both Dear Abby and
  Billy Graham in the same newspaper.
And I can do for myself: I'm not helpless,
  Maybe discouraged and faltering, but not helpless.

When you do something for me *that* I can and *need* to do
  *for myself,* you contribute to my fear and weakness.

But when you accept as a simple fact that I do feel what I feel,
  no matter how irrational, then I can quit trying to convince
  you and get about the business of understanding what's
  behind this irrational feeling.
  And when that's clear, the answers are obvious and I
  don't need advice.

Irrational feelings make sense when we understand what's
  behind them.

Perhaps that's why prayer works, sometimes, for some people,
  because God is mute, and he doesn't give advice or
  try to fix things. 'They' just listen and let you
  work it out for yourself.

So please listen and just hear me. And, if you want to
  talk, wait a minute for your turn: and I'll listen to you.

---

*Discussion question and exercises*

1 What are the possible limitations of accepting clients at 'face value'?

2 Listen to someone for two minutes giving them your full attention; then two minutes of half attention; then two minutes of no attention. What effect does this have on the speaker? What kinds of material typically occupy you when you are not attending fully to the other person?

3 Listen to someone for two to three minutes while engaging in one of the following: writing on a notepad; looking intermittently at your watch; filling a pipe or rolling a cigarette; doodling; looking out of the window; repeatedly saying 'hmm', 'yes' or 'right'. Note the effects on the speaker and, afterwards, discuss his or her responses with the speaker.

# Further reading

Binik, Y. M., Cantor, J., Ochs, E. and Meana, M. (1997) From the couch to the keyboard: psychotherapy in cyberspace, in S. Kiesler (ed.) *Culture of the Internet*. Mahwah, NJ: Erlbaum. Not as mad as it sounds, this chapter offers an interesting perspective on the future of counselling.

Feltham, C. (ed.) (1997) *Which Psychotherapy? Leading Exponents Explain their Differences.* London: Sage. This text describes a variety of different counselling procedures, and thus complements the section on Rogerian counselling in this chapter.

Mearns, D. and Thorne, B. (1988) *Person-Centred Counselling in Action.* London: Sage. This widely read text gives a fuller exposition of client centred counselling than space allowed here.

# References

Aiken, L. R. (1985) *Death, Dying and Bereavement.* Rockleigh, NJ: Allyn and Bacon.

Barker, L. B. (1971) *Listening Behavior.* Englewood Cliffs, NJ: Prentice Hall.

Bisson, J. I., Jenkins, P. L., Alexander, J. and Bannister, C. (1997) Randomised controlled trial of psychological debriefing for victims of acute burn trauma. *British Journal of Psychiatry*, 171: 78–91.

Bowlby, J. (1980) *Attachment and Loss, vol. 3, Loss, Sadness and Depression.* New York: Basic Books.

Bozarth, J. D. (1997) The person-centered approach, in C. Feltham (ed.) *Which Psychotherapy?* London: Sage.

Brom, D., Kleber, R. J. and Hofman, M. C. (1993) Victims of traffic accidents: incidence and prevention of post-traumatic stress disorder. *Journal of Clinical Psychology*, 49(2): 131–40.

Bugen, L. A. (1979) *Death and Dying: Theory, Research, Practice.* Dubuque, IA: William C. Brown.

Cook, A. S. and Oltjenbruns, K. A. (1998) *Dying and Grieving: Lifespan and Family Perspectives,* 2nd edn. Fort Worth: Harcourt Brace.

Cramer, D. (1992) *Personality and Psychotherapy.* Buckingham: Open University Press.

Dass, R. (1978) *Journey of Awakening: A Meditator's Guidebook.* London: Bantam.

Demi, A. S. and Miles, M. S. (1987) Parameters of normal grief: a Delphi study. *Death Studies*, 11(6): 397–412.

Dicks, S. (1997) From Vietnam to Hell, in D. N. Sattler and V. Shabatay (eds) *Psychology in Context: Voices and Perspectives.* Boston, MA: Houghton Mifflin.

Hobbs, M., Mayou, M., Harrison, B. and Worlock, P. (1996) A randomised controlled trial of psychological debriefing for victims of road traffic accidents. *British Medical Journal*, 313: 1438–9.

Jourard, S. M. (1971) *The Transparent Self.* New York: Van Nostrand.

Kubler-Ross, E. (1969) *On Death and Dying.* New York: Macmillan.

Lee, C., Slade, P. and Lygo, V. (1996) The influence of psychological debriefing on emotional adaptation in females following early miscarriage. *British Journal of Medical Psychology*, 69: 47–58.

Lesh, T. V. (1984) Zen meditation and the development of empathy in counselors, in D. H. Shapiro and R. N. Walsh (eds) *Meditation: Classical and Contemporary Perspectives.* New York: Aldine.

McEwan, Y. (1997) Has trauma care become a travesty? *European Practitioners Trauma Conference*, London, September.

McEwan, Y. (1998) Television interview. *Trust Me I'm a Doctor.* BBC2 broadcast 24 March.

Parkes, C. H. and Weiss, R. S. (1983) *Recovery from Bereavement*. New York: Basic Books.

Rando, T. (1984) *Grief, Dying and Death: Clinical Interventions for Caregivers*. Champaign, IL: Research Press.

Rando, T. (1993) *Treatment of Complicated Mourning*. Champaign, IL: Research Press.

Rogers, C. R. (1951) *Client-Centred Therapy*. London: Constable.

Rogers, C. R. (1967) *On Becoming a Person: A Therapist's View of Psychotherapy*. London: Constable.

Rogers, C. R. (1971) *On Encounter Groups*. Harmondsworth: Penguin.

Rogers, C. R. (1980) *A Way of Being*. Boston, MA: Houghton Mifflin.

Schofield, W. (1964) *Psychotherapy: The Purchase of Friendship*. Englewood Cliffs, NJ: Prentice Hall.

Sprang, M. V., McNeil, J. S. and Wright, R. (1993) Grief among surviving family members of homicide victims: a causal approach. *Omega*, 26(2): 145–60.

# Chapter 2

# Counselling at work

## James Hartley and Clare Allen

We are familiar with counselling being given in a wide variety of circumstances, as Helen Graham discussed in Chapter 1. Here we consider the application of counselling in one particular setting – the workplace. You may have come across the idea of 'workplace' or 'staff' counselling and wondered how is this distinct from any other counselling, and why it is provided at work? Does it make a difference?

In this chapter we shall discuss the following issues:

- What are the main objectives of counselling at work?
- What do workplace counsellors do?
- What causes stress, and how can workplace counsellors help?

In addition, we shall look at these questions:

- How does psychology help in providing counselling at work?
- Does workplace counselling actually make a difference?
- What is the future for workplace counselling?

## What is workplace counselling?

Perhaps the keys to the definition of workplace counselling are occupational and economic ones. Workplace counselling is counselling that is paid for by an organization for its employees. Thus there are at least three components: the organization, the employee(s) and the counsellor(s). These three components, however, can vary in their relationships to one another. For example, both the employee and the counsellor can work for and be paid by the same organization, or the organization can subcontract the counselling to a separate agency, or the organization can pay for an employee to hire an

---

**Box 2.1   Some different roles for counsellors in workplace counselling**

*Example 1*

Carole is employed by the British Council as its full-time staff counsellor. Her main task is to offer confidential counselling for all UK-based staff and those working overseas who have been appointed in London – approximately 1800 employees. Family members may also use the service. Clients refer themselves by telephoning directly to Carole for an appointment. She is free to agree with clients the number of sessions required, how she will work with them and whether an outside referral would be appropriate.

*Example 2*

Nigel is a counsellor in private practice who is employed by a large company to work with its employees on a sessional basis. Employees approach their personnel officer, who gives the go ahead for them to approach Nigel for counselling. Nigel is restricted to eight sessions with each client and has to negotiate with the personnel officer if there is a suggestion that this time be extended. Usually, with the agreement of both client and Nigel, a further eight sessions can be utilized. After this, clients need to pay for their own counselling.

*Example 3*

Margaret works in a student counselling service in higher education, which she and her colleague were instrumental in setting up. She is employed by the institution to see students and, where appropriate, staff for counselling. The line manager is the pro-rector responsible for student services. The counselling team have their own counselling suite, and by and large are free to run the service as they choose. They assess all students who come to the service, work with a number of them themselves and refer others to counsellors on placement with the service (who are frequently counsellors in training).

*Source*: extracts adapted, with permission, from Carroll (1996) and Sage Publications Ltd

---

independent counsellor. Box 2.1 illustrates these differences; Carroll (1996) extends this discussion further.

## Why provide counselling at work?

Employees are people employed to do a job so, it could be argued, personal problems are their own business and their own responsibility. Part of the explanation for an increase in the provision of workplace counselling since the mid-1970s derives from changes in our views of work and workers. In the past, mechanistic views of organizations were dominant. The efficient working of the system was emphasized, ineffective parts needed to be fixed, and individual employees were often thought of as replaceable small cogs in the large machine. But as the environment of organizations has become less certain and technologies less routine, new research has shown that treating employees well increases motivation and productivity (Cooper and Cartwright 1994). Consequently there has been more emphasis on cultures that value employees – and this includes providing advice and counselling. One recent initiative in the UK demonstrating this change in emphasis is 'Investors in People'. Organizations are currently accredited as 'Investors in People' when they can demonstrate that employee training and development contributes to the individual's and the organization's overall objectives (*Investors in People* 1998).

Another important strand in the development of counselling in the workplace has been the development of Employee Assistance Programmes (EAPs), originally in the USA but now also in the UK (see Berridge *et al.* 1997). Initially, in the USA in the 1960s, EAPs were work-based programmes designed largely to reduce the effects of alcoholism at work but, later, they extended their coverage to a wider range of social issues. Berridge *et al.* (1997: 13) define an EAP as 'a systematic, organized and continued provision of counselling, advice and assistance, provided or funded by the employer, designed to help employees and (in most cases) their families with problems arising from work-related and external sources'. In the late 1980s there were in the region of 10,000 EAPs in the USA; by the end of 1994, there were around 1 million UK employees, and in many instances their families, covered by EAPs (Carroll 1996).

So, conceptions of work and what makes for effective organizations have changed. It now makes sense to invest in support and development for employees, and in increasing their motivation. It also makes good financial sense. Elkin and Rosch (1990) estimated that unhealthy, stressful working in US industry led to a loss of 550 million working days per year, and that more than half of this sickness absence was stress related. For the UK we have the following statistics (Carroll 1996):

• One in five of the working population suffers some form of mental illness each year (approximately 6 million people).
• Some 90 million working days are lost each year as a result of mental illness.
• When asked about the 'true' reason for absence from work, over half of the employees felt that emotional/personal problems were to blame.
• Between 30 and 40 per cent of all sickness from work involves some form of mental illness or emotional stress.
• Approximately 20 per cent of any workforce is affected by personal problems that have an impact on their performance.

In addition there are now legal imperatives to address stress at work and employers have a 'duty of care' to protect their employees' health (and safety) at work – both physical and mental. Since the 1990s some companies have been successfully sued by their employees for failing in this duty. In the UK, government policy also encourages employers to improve health at work, as in the government Green Paper, *Our Healthier Nation* (Department of Health 1998). Workplace counselling, then, is promoted by humanitarian, economic and legal issues.

## What is the main focus of counselling at work?

Counselling at work is driven by – at least – two interacting concerns. These may complement each other or conflict, which can put the counsellor in a difficult position. These two concerns are those of the individual, and those of the organization for whom the individual works.

The question arises of what is being targeted for change? Is it the concerns of the individual – e.g. issues of mood, stress, behaviour, work-related competencies and skills? Or is it the concerns of the employer – e.g. issues of absence or turnover rates, performance targets and quality? Or is it some combination of both – e.g. issues concerning interpersonal skills at work? Furthermore, are the concerns of the counsellor ones of prevention (through training) or treatment (involving counselling)?

Fundamentally, the issue is whether work-based counselling should be restricted to difficulties that arise in the workplace, or whether it should have a broader application to include any issues that give rise to distress. At work, people try to do their jobs, exercising their skills and the knowledge they have acquired through training and experience. At home they are also the same people who have family and friends, social and personal experiences. Obviously people do not behave in the same way in these different places, and in these different roles, but the two do influence each other. If people have just completed a rewarding task at work that has given them a sense of achievement and of being valued for what they do, they may well return home feeling buoyant and particularly well disposed towards their family. You may have noticed how hard work, if fulfilling, can increase energy rather than deplete it. In contrast, financial problems at home, or significant upheavals, such as moving house, can be preoccupying even when we go to work, leaving us less energy and attention to do our job well. Counselling support may enable people to cope with this extra pressure, while continuing to do their jobs – clearly a benefit to their employers.

So the issues that lead employees to consult a workplace counsellor are as likely to be personal as they are to be work related (Highley-Marchington and Cooper 1997), and often there is an overlap. Even purely work-related difficulties – which may have their origin in external, objective work situations – can affect individuals differently. Perceptions and interpretations vary. Think about the following example:

> One individual may experience the way her manager talks to her as patronizing. Perhaps, because there are echoes with an experience of authoritarian parents, when she felt belittled and angry, the present relationship rekindles these feelings with the same intensity, interfering with her ability to do her job and to enjoy it. She feels powerless to address her manager in the way that a young dependent

child can feel in relation to her parents. Another individual, in a similar role, more self-confident, may also experience the manager's patronizing style and be angered by it. However, she is able to explain assertively to the manager that this is his problem. The manager may then be able to modify his behaviour (we hope).

The point here is that the second individual believes more strongly in her capacity to address the problem and to change it because of who she is as an individual. The first individual, with no improvement in the situation, is more likely to experience pressure and distress. This can in turn lead to illness, whether physical or psychological, being off work and even leaving this particular employment. So, the impact of something or someone at work can vary, depending upon individuals' perceptions and their responses. Furthermore, damaging consequences for the workers are also damaging for the organization that employs them. An organization will want to minimize the costs of recruiting new staff and training them, or paying for sick leave and replacement staff.

## What do workplace counsellors do?

Workplace counsellors work with both personal and workplace issues with managers and staff, as shown in Figure 2.1. In this section of the chapter we shall give one example from each of the four cells to indicate the nature of what can be done.

|               | Personal problems | Workplace problems |
|---------------|:-----------------:|:------------------:|
| Manager       | 1                 | 2                  |
| Staff member  | 3                 | 4                  |

*Figure 2.1*   The focus of workplace counselling

### 1   A manager's personal problem

At this point we need to remember that (as Graham described in Chapter 1) much of counselling is a non-judgemental, active listening process. The aim is to help someone understand the situation and his or her place in it, and thereby choose a way forward. Managers are just as likely as staff members to have personal problems at home that might affect their performance at work. For example:

Mary, a production supervisor, has just experienced the death of her father, and is trying to cope with the difficulties her mother is facing with the onset of Alzheimer's disease. Mary is facing bereavement and loss on the one hand, and trying to ensure an appropriate quality of life for her mother on the other. She is also struggling to balance her commitment to her career and her commitment to her mother.

Here the counsellor helps Mary to explore these dilemmas and to come to some resolution. The counsellor provides support in helping Mary work through her bereavement, and introduces her to a voluntary carers' network or support group that will be able to provide help for her mother.

## 2   A manager's workplace problem

The second example also illustrates this non-judgemental approach.

> A manager seeks counselling advice. One of the staff in a building society branch, who provides counter service to customers, has been off sick for three months. She had been depressed following a miscarriage but she has now recovered and she has told her manager that she is ready to return to work. However, in her letter to the manager she is critical of his style, saying that she found his response to her earlier plight unsympathetic. The manager also finds that this woman's colleagues have expressed concern about her performance.

Here the manager needs to make his expectations clear, but in a supportive way. The counsellor can empathize with the manager's experience of being criticized, which he had felt was unjustified. The manager can also be helped to clarify his task and to rehearse how to help this staff member back to work, sensitively, using some of his own reactions to help him to anticipate how she might be likely to feel.

## 3   A staff member's personal problem

The example given earlier (p. 32) of a staff member's difficulty with the patronizing behaviour of her manager illustrates this area of work. Counselling support in this situation may help the first individual to understand better her own feelings, and to develop sufficient self-confidence to raise the issue with her manager – perhaps rehearsing possible outcomes with the counsellor's support.

## 4   A staff member's workplace problem

> In a group, members of a team working with learning-disabled adults complain of mental exhaustion and 'burnout'. Some are talking of 'jacking it in'.

Here the counsellor needs to explore a variety of issues. It may be that some members of the team feel that they are inadequately rewarded, in terms of pay, recognition or career advancement. These issues need to be recognized and addressed. The counsellor may negotiate with the group to be allowed to feed these issues back to the senior management. Members of the group might be encouraged to focus on examples of individual achievements. Morale, generally, may be improved through peer support, and by making the meeting a regular occurrence, possibly attended by senior managers.

Table 2.1 provides a summary of possible activities of counsellors at different levels of intervention.

***Table 2.1***   Activities of counsellors at different levels of intervention

| Level of intervention | Activity |
| --- | --- |
| Individual | Advice<br>Consultation<br>Counselling |
| Group | Training in awareness of stress and self-management skills<br>Assessing risks to psychological health<br>Facilitating staff groups<br>Process consultancy (i.e. facilitating understanding) |
| Organization | Management development<br>Feedback on trends<br>Advice on policies<br>Developing new systems and resources |

## Causes of stress in the workplace

Undoubtedly one of the main causes of difficulty for employees is handling stress. The term 'stress' is used to cover a multitude of problems and symptoms but, for the sake of clarity, we can initially distinguish between two different sources of stress. These are

- environmental factors, such as noise, crowding and pace of work.
- subjective psychological factors, such as feelings of strain and overwork.

As noted earlier, individual differences between people affect their perceptions and judgements about both of these factors. In the workplace, of course, these two sources of stress combine. Box 2.2 lists some contributors to stress in the workplace.

The question arises of how much, if at all, these stressors contribute to illness. (This issue is explored further in Chapter 3.) Some researchers in the field of stress have distinguished between what they call 'major life-events' and 'daily hassles'. 'Major life-events' occur relatively rarely but have significant effects (such as the death of a parent) (see Box 2.3). 'Daily hassles' occur relatively frequently but do not have so much significance (such as temporarily losing a phone number) (see Box 2.4).

*Box 2.2*  **Stress in the workplace: some contributing factors**

| | |
|---|---|
| *Physical environment* | Light |
| | Noise |
| | Temperature |
| | Vibration and motion |
| | Ventilation |
| | Ergonomic factors |
| |    (e.g. design of workspace/machinery) |
| | |
| *Job characteristics* | Pace of work (self-paced or externally driven) |
| | Repetition |
| | Shift work |
| | Task attributes |
| | |
| *Organizational structure* | Centralized / decentralized |
| | Position in hierarchy |
| | Internal control versus imposed demands |
| | |
| *Organizational culture* | 'How things are done' |
| | Competitiveness / insecurity |
| | |
| *Roles* | Role ambiguity |
| | Role overload / underload |
| | |
| *Relationships* | Supervisors / managers |
| | Colleagues |
| | Team |
| | Clients / customers |
| | |
| *Personnel practices* | Starting work |
| | Training |
| | Feedback |
| | Rewards / punishments |
| | Career development |
| | Career transitions |
| | Job future |

**Box 2.3** An early example of a well known scale measuring the stress of major life-events

| Rank | Life-event | Mean value |
|---|---|---|
| 1 | Death of spouse | 100 |
| 2 | Divorce | 73 |
| 3 | Marital separation | 65 |
| 4 | Jail term | 63 |
| 5 | Death of close family member | 63 |
| 6 | Personal injury or illness | 53 |
| 7 | Marriage | 50 |
| 8 | Fired at work | 47 |
| 9 | Marital reconciliation | 45 |
| 10 | Retirement | 45 |
| 11 | Change in health of family member | 44 |
| 12 | Pregnancy | 40 |
| 13 | Sex difficulties | 39 |
| 14 | Gain of new family member | 39 |
| 15 | Business readjustment | 39 |
| 16 | Change in financial state | 38 |
| 17 | Death of close friend | 37 |
| 18 | Change to different line of work | 36 |
| 19 | Change in number of arguments with spouse | 35 |
| 20 | Mortgage over $10,000 (approx. £5000 in 1967) | 31 |
| 21 | Foreclosure of mortgage or loan | 30 |
| 22 | Change in responsibilities at work | 29 |
| 23 | Son or daughter leaving home | 29 |
| 24 | Trouble with in-laws | 29 |
| 25 | Outstanding personal achievement | 28 |
| 26 | Wife begins or stops work | 26 |
| 27 | Begin or end school | 26 |
| 28 | Change in living conditions | 25 |
| 29 | Revision of personal habits | 24 |
| 30 | Trouble with boss | 23 |
| 31 | Change in work hours or conditions | 20 |
| 32 | Change in residence | 20 |
| 33 | Change in schools | 20 |
| 34 | Change in recreation | 19 |
| 35 | Change in church activities | 19 |
| 36 | Change in social activities | 18 |
| 37 | Mortgage or loan of less than $10,000 | 17 |
| 38 | Change in sleeping habits | 16 |
| 39 | Change in number of family get-togethers | 15 |
| 40 | Change in eating habits | 15 |
| 41 | Vacation | 13 |
| 42 | Christmas | 12 |
| 43 | Minor violations of the law | 11 |

(To measure your personal stress score tick off events that have occurred to you over a given period of time – say 12 months – and add up the scores given on the right.)

*Source*: reprinted from Holmes and Rahe (1967), with permission of Elsevier Science

> ***Box 2.4***  **The ten most frequently expressed hassles of middle-aged adults**
>
> 1 Concerns about weight
> 2 Health of a family member
> 3 Rising prices of common goods
> 4 Home maintenance
> 5 Too many things to do
> 6 Misplacing or losing things
> 7 Outside home maintenance
> 8 Property, investment or taxes
> 9 Crime
> 10 Physical appearance
>
> *Source*: reprinted from Kanner *et al.* (1981) with permission of Plenum Publishing

Clearly scales such as these are fraught with difficulties (Banyard 1996):

- Major life-events are quite rare and many people will score near to zero.
- Some of the items in the scales are vague or ambiguous.
- There are large individual differences in our ability to cope with stressful events.
- There are large cultural and subcultural differences in our experience of events.
- The value of events changes with time and changing social customs.
- Some of the items will have greater value for some groups in society rather than others.

In connection with this final point we may note that more specific life-events scales have now been published. Renner and Mackin (1998), for instance, have described a life-events scale for US university psychology students.

Some researchers question whether major life-events or minor daily hassles actually do contribute to illness and, if they do, which contribute most to our feelings of stress and illness. In one study designed to assess this, students completed measures of major life-events and daily hassles at three points in time during their transition from school to university, as well as measures of health and well-being (Wagner *et al.* 1988). These times were one month before leaving school, two weeks into university, and two and a half months later. The aim of the study was to see if major life-events (such as transition to college) had a greater impact on health than did the more minor daily hassles. Interestingly, the results showed that the two sorts of stressors were interrelated. More specifically the major life-events led to an increase in stress which, in turn, led to an increase in the perceived stress of daily hassles which, in turn, led to an increase in psychological symptoms. So, this research suggests, the two sorts of stress combine in an additive way.

## How do workplace counsellors help with stress?

Psychotherapeutic interventions to combat stress may be in the form of treatment (counselling) for stress, or training courses designed to prevent its occurrence. Counsellors offering such courses tailor their contents to meet the needs of the participants. A staff group may ask a counsellor to help them identify the sources of pressure in their own work area and introduce improvements within their control. For example, counter staff who deal with complaints are often exposed to the negative feelings and sometimes the aggressive behaviour of customers. Others may require help in coping with stressful events that arise in their work so that they can function efficiently. For example, nurses in an intensive care baby unit use highly technological skills, yet there is still a high mortality rate, with ensuing distress. In these situations support by a counsellor could include helping staff to acknowledge emotions at work and exploring with them ways of coping. This could take the form of regular meetings with the objective of expressing, discussing and understanding the pressures, and providing emotional support by recognizing the shared nature of workers' experiences. (See Chapter 9 for a discussion of counselling fire-fighters after stressful events.)

More general stress management training courses may be offered to any members of an organization in order to prevent stress from occurring. Undoubtedly some attendees at such courses will be suffering from stress, but, for the majority, the aim will be to learn how to limit stress and to cope better with it. For example:

> A graphic designer attending a three-day stress management programme learnt to recognize that his typical response to stress was to overwork, gradually losing his ability to prioritize. He practised breathing techniques to reduce his physical arousal and to help calm his anxiety. Cognitive components in the course helped him to explore some of the unchecked assumptions that he held, such as believing that his team leader would see him as a failure, reducing the performance of the whole team. He rehearsed approaching his team leader to seek feedback and to discuss priorities in his workload. He was able to apply what he learned, monitor the effect of fluctuating work pressures, and to take constructive action before becoming unduly stressed.

Hardy and Barkham (1999) describe how staff management training courses are typically offered to groups of staff in anything ranging from 1-hour sessions to 20-week courses. The programmes vary, but they generally contain an educational element about the causes of stress; training in relaxation; self-evaluation and goal setting; and skills training in related areas such as assertion, time management and problem solving. The courses thus help people to recognize previously unrecognized sources of difficulty, and to learn how to deal with them.

***Table 2.2***  Areas and topics in psychology

| Area | Topic |
|------|-------|
| Organizational psychology | Motivation<br>Human factors<br>Organizational structures<br>Organizational change<br>Selection procedures<br>Goal setting<br>Leadership<br>Effects of physical environment<br>Human factors |
| Developmental and educational psychology | Early childhood experiences<br>Identity issues<br>Coping styles<br>Self-efficacy<br>Cognitive development<br>Rewards and punishments<br>Physical disabilities<br>Learning disabilities<br>Bullying<br>Child abuse<br>Ethnic and gender issues |
| Clinical and abnormal psychology | Family history of mental health problems<br>Mild mental health disorders<br>Severe mental health disorders<br>Anxiety and depression<br>Aggression |
| Health psychology | Stress (including post-traumatic stress)<br>Bereavement and loss<br>Coping styles<br>Culture and health<br>Personality styles (e.g. type A person)<br>Stress management<br>Time management<br>Health promotion |
| Research skills | Designing questionnaires and surveys<br>Interpreting evidence<br>Writing reports<br>Giving presentations<br>Designing leaflets |

## How does psychology help in providing counselling at work?

Workplace counsellors draw on a surprisingly wide knowledge base, much of which is derived from psychology. Table 2.2 highlights some of these topics and indicates which areas of psychology depend on them.

# Does workplace counselling make a difference?

This question can be addressed in a number of ways, depending upon the kind of question you have in mind. Does counselling make people feel better? Are people better able to cope with stress after counselling? Are there gains for the organization from counselling (such as reduced absenteeism or increased productivity)? Do employees feel better disposed to employers who offer counselling? And so on.

Of course, the methods available to evaluate counselling differ widely and there are questions about their validity and reliability (see Berridge *et al.* 1997). Apart from training courses, most counselling interventions are made on a one to one basis. Individuals may report improvements but it is not easy to generalize from samples of one. As the following example illustrates, the outcomes depend upon the individual client and counsellor involved, on the client's particular problems, the counsellor's reactions, and on how both the client and the counsellor perceive the situation. The client may feel better, but might this have happened anyway, or with some different form of treatment, and did the counselling achieve as much as it could?

> Peter reported problems with sleeping and violent nightmares to his doctor. Much to his surprise, his doctor told him he was suffering from stress. So he sought out counselling to supplement the doctor's medication. The counsellor arranged for once weekly sessions at a fee specified as 'what Peter thought it appropriate to pay'. It transpired that Peter considered himself a 'workaholic' as an office manager, and that he maintained a lover, unbeknown to his wife and children. He spent much of his time juggling with these constraints. Non-directive counselling over a period of two years allowed him to sort out his work and marital problems. The basic gain for Peter was the fact that the counselling sessions forced him to answer questions about himself and his behaviour which he normally avoided, and to come to terms more with his feelings. Peter considered that the counselling was a success, and recommended it for others, but he still thinks that more could have been achieved had he allowed himself to go further with his counsellor.

It is perhaps not surprising to find that workplace counselling does not always have the marked effects that one might hope (see Highley-Marchington and Cooper 1997; Hardy and Barkham 1999). Nonetheless, there have been some successes, and here we shall describe three studies, each one designed to answer a different question about the effectiveness of counselling.

## An evaluation study of counselling focusing on improvements for the individual

Barkham *et al.* (1999) describe a study carried out in Sheffield with clients suffering from problems at work and who were depressed; 116 people (67 men and 49 women) were allocated randomly into either a cognitive behavioural or a psychodynamic interpersonal intervention. Both treatments were run by the same (three) counsellors, and each treatment had only three sessions – the first two were one week apart and the third was three months later. (The idea here was that the client and counsellor could work hard on the client's problems in the first two sessions and then that the gains made here could be built upon by the client in the intervening period before the third session.)

The clients completed before and after measures of depression (the Beck Inventory), a symptom checklist and an inventory of personal problems. The results indicated that there were no significant differences between the effectiveness of the two types of counselling initially: both treatments led to substantial improvements in levels of depression, work behaviours and attitudes. However, it appeared that the clients had responded better to the cognitive behavioural treatment when the measures were taken again after one year.

Barkham *et al.* (1999) concluded that this brief approach to counselling individuals in the workplace was highly successful, and they suggested that it could be applied in a variety of settings (e.g. primary care, medical settings and Employee Assistance Programmes).

## An evaluation study focusing on improvements for the organization

Allinson *et al.* (1989) describe how stress counselling was introduced into the Occupational Health Service of the British Post Office in 1986, starting with two in-house counsellors. From the start the service was available on an open access basis, and its use spread rapidly throughout the entire organization, including cleaners, postmen and women, postal officers and executives, technical engineers and senior staff. The ratio of men to women using the service was 73 to 27 per cent, which matched that in the Post Office as a whole, so there was no indication that men were less ready to avail themselves of the service. The average number of interviews at the start was three, with 75 per cent of the cases requiring four or fewer interviews. The effect of the service was a substantial reduction in absenteeism and in the duration of absences that did occur. There were also many fewer disciplinary cases.

## An evaluation study of stress management programmes

Kagan *et al.* (1995) compared the effectiveness of different stress management training programmes in controlling physiological reactions, coping with people and increasing self-awareness. Progressive muscle relaxation was used in the first programme to help course members control their physiological reactions. Assertiveness training, crisis intervention skills, listening skills and negotiating skills were used in the second programme to help participants develop their skills of coping with people. Training in problem solving and insight therapy was used in the third programme to increase interpersonal awareness. Participants (over 300 employees of a US emergency medical service) were assigned to one or more of these programmes, and the outcomes were assessed with before and after standardized self-report measures and an unobtrusive job performance measure. All three programmes led to improvements in the management of stress in the short term (1 week) and this was sustained for 9 to 16 months. The self-awareness programme was particularly effective in the long term.

## What is the future for workplace counselling?

In this final section we shall speculate about the future for work-based counselling. We see work-based counselling as an expanding profession for at least four (overlapping) reasons.

1 There is much greater acceptance now – by both employers and employees – that problems at home and in the workplace can profoundly affect job performance, and that it is no longer 'macho' to ignore this.
2 There is much less stigma today in seeking help. The concept of 'stress' and its effects have percolated widely through the national conscious.
3 There is increasingly useful research on these issues, and we are now in a better position to be able to understand the complex relationships between psychological distress and its effects at work. This research will undoubtedly continue.
4 People nowadays feel entitled to expect better conditions at work, and thus they are likely to react more positively to organizations that demonstrate commitment to their workers. Indeed, it is becoming harder for employers not to be seen as committed when people are seeking employment.

Work-based counselling will thus expand because employers are having to value human beings, in all their complexity, as an essential resource. Long may they continue to do so.

---

*Discussion questions*

1 What is the priority focus for workplace counsellors? Should their work aim to prevent potential causes of stress or be directed at those needing help and relief from distress? Should they direct their efforts to work with individuals, groups or the whole organization?

2 Whose responsibility is it to reduce the effects of stress at work? Employees? Employers? Work-based counsellors?

3 What ethical dilemmas arise in workplace counselling? For example, should workplace counsellors prioritize the needs of the organization or the needs of the client? (See also the discussion on 'insider'/ 'outsider' roles for psychologists on pp. 71–2.)

## Further reading

Berridge, J., Cooper, C. L. and Highley-Marchington, C. (1997) *Employee Assistance Programmes and Workplace Counselling.* Chichester: Wiley. A collection of chapters on aspects of work-based counselling, including practical examples and research evaluations.

Carroll, M. (1996) *Workplace Counselling.* London: Sage. A lively, readable book that covers in more detail the issues raised in this chapter, and more.

Carroll, M. and Walton, M. (eds) (1997) *Handbook of Counselling in Organizations.* London: Sage. A more challenging book that is of particular interest for those who are thinking of becoming workplace counsellors.

## References

Allinson, T., Cooper, C. L. and Reynolds, P. (1989) Stress counselling in the workplace: the Post Office experience. *The Psychologist,* 2(9): 384–8.

Banyard, P. (1996) *Applying Psychology to Health.* London: Hodder and Stoughton.

Barkham, M., Shapiro, D. A., Hardy, G. E. and Rees, A. (1999) Psychotherapy in two-plus-one sessions: outcomes of a randomized controlled trial of cognitive-behavioral and psychodynamic-interpersonal therapy for subsyndromal depression. *Journal of Consulting and Clinical Psychology,* 67: 201–11.

Berridge, J., Cooper, C. L. and Highley-Marchington, C. (1997) *Employee Assistance Programmes and Workplace Counselling.* Chichester: Wiley.

Carroll, M. (1996) *Workplace Counselling.* London: Sage.

Cooper, C. L. and Cartwright, S. (1994) Healthy mind: healthy organization – a proactive approach to occupational stress. *Human Relations,* 47: 455–71.

Cooper, C. L., Sadri, G., Allinson, T. and Reynolds, P. (1990) Stress counselling in the Post Office. *Counselling Psychology Quarterly,* 3(1): 3–11.

Department of Health (1998) *Our Healthier Nation.* London: HMSO.

Elkin, A. J. and Rosch, P. J. (1990) Promoting mental health at the workplace. *Occupational Medicine: State of the Art Review,* 5(4): 734–54.

Hardy, G. E. and Barkham, M. (1999) Psychotherapeutic interventions for work stress, in R. Payne and J. Firth-Cozens (eds) *Stress in Health Care Professionals,* 2nd edn. Chichester: Wiley.

Highley-Marchington, C. and Cooper, C. L. (1997) An evaluation of employee assistance and workplace counselling programmes in the UK, in M. Carroll and M. Walton (eds) *Handbook of Counselling in Organizations.* London: Sage.

Holmes, T. H. and Rahe, R. H. (1967) The social readjustment rating scale. *Journal of Psychosomatic Research,* 11: 213–18.

Investors in People (1998) Investors in people: how to get started, *I. I. P. 64b.* London: Investors in People, UK.

Kagan, N. I., Kagan, H. and Watson, M. G. (1995) Stress reduction in the workplace: the effectiveness of psychoeducational programs. *Journal of Counseling Psychology,* 42: 71–8.

Kanner, A. D., Coynes, J. C., Schaefer, C. and Lazarus, R. S. (1981) Comparison of two modes of stress measurement: daily hassles and uplifts versus major life events. *Journal of Behavioural Medicine,* 4: 1–39.

Renner, M. J. and Mackin, R. S. (1998) A life stress instrument for classroom use. *Teaching of Psychology,* 25(1): 46–8.

Wagner, B., Compas, B. E. and Howell, D. C. (1988) Daily and major life events: a test of an integrative model of psychosocial stress. *American Journal of Community Psychology,* 16(2): 189–205.

*Section* **B**

# The psychologist as colleague

# Chapter 3

# Psychologists, doctors and cancer patients

## John Hegarty

I am up to my chin in marking, university administration, planning conferences, supervising student projects and the other (multiple!) preoccupations of a university teacher. The telephone rings: 'Dr Hegarty! It's Pat
– social worker at the Douglas Macmillan Home. Would you be able to
visit one of our patients? She is interested in psychological approaches to
cancer.' I agree to go. Later I telephone the nurse at the home (a cancer care
hospice) responsible for day care to arrange a convenient time. I visit the
patient at the home and discuss her attitudes, feelings and actions about
cancer.

But why am I, as a psychologist, visiting such a medical centre and working with patients? Why should it be important for a cancer patient's mental
events to be relevant to what is primarily a physical problem – the occurrence of abnormal, cancerous cells in the body? And why, with all the might
of modern scientific medicine and the high technology of cancer diagnosis
and treatment, is it still thought to be important for someone like me, a
psychologist, to talk, encourage and support patients? These questions will
be answered in this chapter as I describe the work of psychologists as colleagues with medical staff and patients in treating cancer.

## What is cancer?

Cancer is a generic term for over 200 medical conditions. Some say, indeed,
that there are as many different cancers as there are patients, since there
are large individual differences even within the same type of cancer. What
cancers have in common is a disorder of the mechanism which normally
regulates cell division such that a mass of cells will start to grow unchecked,

causing a swelling (tumour) of new tissue (neoplasm). Common sites for such abnormal growths are the lung, colon and breast. Some tumours are benign or non-malignant because they confine themselves to one site of the body but, in others, cells break away (metastasize) and grow in other parts of the body. When disease is disseminated in this way it is hard to treat and potentially life threatening.

'Cancer' is a taboo word, and it is only in the last few years that the fashion of not mentioning the word to patients has changed. For many people 'cancer' is still a feared word, suggesting inevitable death, pain and a long, creeping illness. In reality, heart disease is the bigger killer in developed countries, causing about 50 per cent of all deaths compared to cancer's 20 per cent. Many people have growths successfully treated with no recurrence. For other people the disease remains stable for many years. Modern drugs and techniques have markedly reduced pain and discomfort and increased the quality of life. Slowly, cancer's bad reputation is being shaken off, and people are increasingly able to talk about it openly and view it more objectively.

Nonetheless, with few exceptions, the effectiveness of treatment for the most common cancers has stayed the same for many decades despite a terrific volume of medical research and the introduction of new methods. Treatment still remains much as it was in the 1940s: surgical removal of tumours, the killing of cancer cells by radiation (radiotherapy) and the poisoning or starvation of cancer cells by drugs (chemotherapy).

## Psychological approaches to cancer

Because conventional medical treatment has failed to produce distinctive advances in cure rates (and because medical treatment can have unwanted side-effects which make the treatment unpleasant) a movement has grown up, predominantly since 1980, to promote alternative approaches to the conventional ones. These new approaches look to diet, meditation, spiritual healing and various psychological therapies to promote the body's own natural defences against cancer. Cancer help centres (such as the Bristol Cancer Help Centre in the UK), self-help groups and national associations have been formed to promote knowledge and to spread information about alternative methods (or 'complementary approaches', as many people prefer to call them, emphasizing that patients can use them in parallel with conventional medical treatment). Although there is little scientific evidence that these approaches reduce the disease, they have been increasingly accepted as an adjunct to conventional treatment. Some people, including those within the medical profession, have hailed the combination of conventional and complementary approaches as the 'new approach to cancer'.

Psychological aspects of patients and families are central to the 'new approach to cancer'. In this chapter I shall consider the main elements of these psychological aspects of cancer and thus outline the professional heritage that the psychologist brings to the medical team treating people with cancer and supporting their relatives. I shall discuss two main areas of work:

- psychological aspects of the causes of cancer and its prognosis
- psychotherapy, counselling and support for people with cancer.

# Psychological aspects of the causes of cancer and its prognosis

During the eighteenth and nineteenth centuries physicians noted cases in which emotional distress was a precursor of cancer. Building on these early observations a number of studies have considered the relationship between personality, emotional distress and cancer. This now extensive literature can be divided into four kinds of approach:

- The cancer-prone personality
- Stress and cancer
- Individual coping strategies for stress
- Psycho-neuro-immunology.

## The cancer-prone personality

Psychoanalytic researchers (especially LeShan 1966) believed that they had discovered a typical life history pattern in people with cancer. This was characterized by the loss of an important emotional relationship prior to the onset of symptoms and the presence of other, unresolved emotional conflicts. These writers believed that the patient's particular personality was unable to cope with the loss, resulting in despair, depression, hopelessness and helplessness.

Other researchers have tried, through prospective and retrospective studies, to find firm support for such suggestions about the possibility of a cancer-prone personality. This area of research is fraught with methodological difficulties, and no clear picture has emerged. Nevertheless, Temoshok and Heller (1984) in a major review of these studies concluded that there are indeed personality factors associated with the occurrence of cancer. The most salient of these are a difficulty in expressing emotions, or even feeling them; such traits as niceness, industriousness, perfectionism, sociability and defensiveness; and a tendency to react with hopelessness and helplessness to stress.

If we accept their conclusion, it does seem that personality factors are implicated. But how could they possibly affect what is happening at the bodily level of cells? For many people the link between personality and cancer lies in concepts of stress.

## Stress and cancer

Since stressful events have physiological as well as psychological effects on people it is reasonable to look to stress as a cause of disease. Stress increases the likelihood of cancer occurring in animals under experimental conditions, and a variety of studies have claimed a link between stress and a variety of human diseases, including cancer (see Rosch 1984 for review).

There have, however, been notable negative findings from well controlled, large-scale studies such as the one by Jones (1986), which was based on an analysis of population census data in the UK.

Partly, these results have occurred because 'stress' is an elusive concept, difficult to define and to measure. But also it appears that how people deal with stress is more important than how they deal with the nature of stressful events themselves. So a body of research has grown up on individuals' strategies for coping with stress.

## Individual coping strategies for stress

Interesting and potentially clinically valuable work has been done with a view to finding out whether some ways of coping with stress are better than others. Early ideas were characterized by psychoanalytic views of 'ego defence mechanisms' which were seen as ways in which the self was protected from emotional pain. 'Denial' is one example of such a mechanism, seen by psychoanalysts as an unwillingness (often unconscious) to admit the 'truth' of a distressing state of affairs. As humanistic and behavioural approaches within psychology have tended to supersede psychoanalytic ones in recent years, the notion of a 'coping strategy' has come to replace that of 'defence mechanism'. Coping strategies are seen to be partly conscious (deliberate) and partly unconscious (unthinking or habitual) ways in which individuals reduce unacceptable levels of stress. Importantly, it is believed by many that such strategies can be taught or strengthened during stress management training.

These ideas can be seen applied to understanding psychological aspects of cancer in the important work of Greer and his colleagues at the Faith Courtauld Unit, King's College Hospital, London. In now classic research, Greer et al. (1979) interviewed women who had had a recent diagnosis of breast cancer and asked them about how they viewed the diagnosis. On the basis of their replies the researchers characterized the responses of women to their threatening and potentially stressful diagnosis in one of four ways. These were whether their attitude was characterized by:

- 'fighting spirit' (for example, 'This is not going to get me')
- 'denial' ('I'm being treated for a lump, but it is not serious', despite being told clearly the diagnosis)
- 'stoic acceptance' ('I feel all illness is God's will, and if this is what He intends for me, so be it')
- 'giving up' ('Well, there's no hope with cancer is there!').

The women were then followed up for a period of five years. The numbers of women still alive at that time showed that 'fighting spirit' and 'denial' reactions were associated with a significantly higher life expectancy than 'stoic acceptance' or 'giving up'. A follow-up at 15 years (Greer et al. 1990) confirmed the correlation of improved prognosis with these reactions.

Such research (and there is an ever-growing body of work which supports it) appears to give scientific support to the advice often given by well-meaning professionals and laypeople 'to think positive' in the face of a diagnosis of cancer. It suggests the value of having psychological resources which will allow individuals to adapt to, rather than succumb to, a severe threat to their well-being. It might even be possible to teach such strategies to people who neither have nor use them.

### Psycho-neuro-immunology

As you read this you may wonder how someone's attitudes could possibly affect physiological processes in their body. Such doubt is a stumbling block for anyone wishing to believe in a psychological approach to cancer – particularly for doctors who are trained to see the body as a complex machine working without much need of the supervisory role of mind. Indeed, one consultant once said to me categorically and emphatically, 'Look, cancer is an autonomous process and cannot be affected by the mind.' This is a modern example of the old debate about whether mind and body are one or separate.

Fortunately, there is now a middle ground for mind–body monists and dualists to meet upon. Scientific research has given us insights into the complex realm of psychophysiology – the interface that exists between body and mind and in which the emotions figure large. One need only think of the bodily changes that occur when we are excited or aroused by an idea – or how powerful depression can be when we are bereaved – to realize that bodily responses occur very rapidly after an idea with emotional significance.

In addition to this lay understanding, psychologists can offer examples of relevant research on topics such as perceptual defence, subliminal perception and placebo effects which demonstrate the very close and subtle linkages between mind and body. Of particular relevance to cancer is work which considers the role of mental events in the workings of the immune system (psycho-neuro-immunology). This is relevant because of the widely held view that cancer is a disorder of the immune system in which mechanisms that normally identify and destroy potentially cancerous cells cease to function. Research is increasingly showing that stress reduces the immune system's ability to fight disease – so that it is possible that severe stress occurring in a person prone to cancer could so depress the immune system that cancer cells could gain a foothold and grow into a tumour. (An introduction to the field of psycho-neuro-immunology is given by Ader *et al.* 1991.)

## Psychotherapy, counselling and support for people with cancer

The previous section of this chapter, on psychological aspects of the causes of cancer and its prognosis in individual cases, suggested that there was indeed a link between the occurrence of cancer, life-events which cause stress and one's personality as it affects one's attitude to such stress. The link between these may lie in how the emotions affect those aspects of the immune system which keep cancerous cells in check within the body. I suggested that the links between mind and immune system might be used constructively in therapy – by producing positive emotions which could stimulate immune response. I now want to look in more detail at what lines of inquiry are being taken to investigate whether psychological therapy could come to be as important in treatment as surgery, radiotherapy and chemotherapy, playing its part not in isolation but as an adjuvant therapy to medical methods.

## Adjuvant psychological therapy

The outcome studies reviewed by Temoshok and Heller (1984) and the work of Greer *et al.* (1979, 1990) suggest that those people more likely to get cancer are also those more likely to have less favourable outcomes. In other words, if you want to live longer upon knowing that you have cancer it would seem best if you have the personality which allows you either to live life as if nothing very bad has happened or to find resources to fight for your life. Spiritual healers have long noted the occurrence of marked regressions of cancer following healing interventions, and there are many medically documented accounts of growth plateaux or regressions of tumours – showing that such occurrences are at least physically possible (even if the mechanisms underlying such restraint or regression are unclear). Despite this picture, little systematic research has been done to see if help can be given to people which would improve their prognosis. Pioneering examples of a psychological element in treatment are the work of the Simontons in the USA and Meares in Australia.

Simonton *et al.* (1980) emphasize that theirs is a 'self-help' approach and that it is not designed to replace conventional treatment but to supplement it. Patients are taught progressive relaxation and encouraged to spend time daily in practising this technique. During the periods of relaxation, patients are asked to imagine their cancer and their body's immune system fighting cancerous cells. In addition, patients are asked to find a counsellor to support them and work on any negative feelings they may have. Additional parts of this self-help programme, which is described in more detail in a later section, include regular exercise, setting and achieving personal goals and tapping spiritual help within themselves.

The prognosis and quality of life for 159 patients with a diagnosis of medically incurable malignancy who followed the programme were studied and compared with national norms (Simonton *et al.* 1980). The average expected survival for the group was 12 months. At the time of the study, 63 patients were alive, having had an average survival of 24.4 months. Patients who died during the study had survived on average 20.3 months. Simonton *et al.* concluded that their approach significantly lengthened survival time by a factor of 1.5 to 2.0. In addition, patients maintained higher than usual levels of everyday activity, signifying an improvement in their quality of life.

Meares' approach aimed to regress the patient to a primitive state of being characterized by stillness and peace and in which healing could take place. He reported no controlled studies but cited a number of case histories which showed unexpected regression of cancer (Meares 1979).

I personally believe that these approaches are a significant contribution to cancer treatment and care. Medical opinion about them is divided. On the one hand, doctors will agree that the attitude of the patient is vitally important; they will agree too that it is important to do everything possible to support people who have cancer. On the other hand, they tend not to agree that it is right to offer patients a specific package and imply that it will cure them, or even influence the course of the disease. They see that as engendering 'false hope', as likely to make patients feel guilty if they fail to cure themselves, or likely to put excessive pressure on them at a time when they need help rather than extra work.

The way forward, undoubtedly, lies in carrying out more studies in which a structured psychological element is included in routine cancer treatment. In view of the likely benefits (that survival time can be doubled by adding in a psychological package such as that suggested by Simonton *et al.*) it is surprising that so few have been done. It is methodologically difficult to carry out such studies, which require the random allocation of patients to experimental and control groups and where the doctors and nurses administering the treatment are blind to which groups the patients are in. This is possibly one explanation for the paucity of trials. But some attempts have been made to carry out controlled studies, notably by an American psychiatrist, Dr David Spiegel, and Dr Fawzy Fawzy, heading a team at the University of California at Los Angeles. These projects are examples of a psychological approach in a medical setting and both have attempted to see whether adding such an approach produces improved outcomes for patients' prognosis.

Spiegel *et al.* (1989) reported a 10-year follow-up of 89 women with breast cancer, some of whom had taken part in a support group designed to boost their self-confidence, help them to express emotions and to teach them self-hypnosis. Women who had taken part in the support group lived, on average, about twice as long as women who had not.

Fawzy and his colleagues offered six weekly 90-minute sessions of group therapy to patients with early malignant melanoma in which they were instructed in a range of coping strategies. Assessment of the patients and those in a control group showed that the intervention successfully reduced psychological distress in the short term. Moreover, these interventions appeared to produce changes in immune function: 5–6 years after the intervention there was a statistically significant improvement in survival for patients in the therapy group. Fawzy (1994) provides a helpful, short overview of this research, whilst Fawzy *et al.* (1995) give an excellent critical review of the field.

## Psychosocial support

Despite these provocative studies, the idea that a psychological approach may affect the course of the disease itself is still extremely controversial, although it is commonly accepted that patients with cancer and their relatives need support and encouragement. Although few centres, at least in the UK, have a psychologist as part of their clinical team, psychological perspectives are being increasingly introduced as centres aim to build a more systematic support and counselling service for patients and relatives. This is true both within the National Health Service settings and in the voluntary or private sector clinics offering alternative approaches to treatment. There is a wide range of psychological approaches. Current examples commonly include hypnosis, guided visual imagery, anxiety management techniques including progressive relaxation, cognitive therapy for depression, psychoanalytic therapy aimed at personality change and humanistic therapies aimed at promoting personal development and responsibility. Broadly, these approaches may be described as 'psychological healing', this phrase usefully forming a convenient conceptual bridge between psychological literature and practice and the valuable work of other disciplines in providing emotional support and encouragement to patients and relatives. In fact, while there are outward differences in the kinds of techniques used within the various therapeutic approaches, it should not be forgotten that all techniques share common features. Any therapeutic approach typically involves:

- a relationship of support
- an emphasis on change for the better
- specific techniques for the individual to draw on for help, often oriented towards the notion of 'self-help'.

A relationship which has these features, whether it has the label of 'therapy' or 'counselling' or not – and wherever it occurs – is psychotherapeutic.

Do such therapeutic relationships have beneficial results? Well, since we all need them at times of crisis, and as they are a feature of every human society, they are, presumably, indispensable and hence effective. However, studies have looked at whether observable benefits do occur as a result of structured intervention. Notable amongst these is the study of Gordon *et al.* (1980), who systematically assessed the value of counselling for 157 cancer patients in the USA, comparing them with another 151 whose problems were assessed but who received no structured counselling. The results showed that the counselling was effective in that patients in the intervention group more rapidly became less anxious, hostile and depressed than the control group, experienced a more realistic outlook on life, returned to work more quickly and used their time more actively.

## Psychologists working with doctors

I have now sketched the scope of psychological involvement with cancer patients. Summarizing this, it seems that a link between mind, emotion and cancer has been demonstrated sufficiently strongly to argue for a psychological element in treatment, as an adjunct to conventional medical treatment (or to alternative approaches for patients opting for these). In addition, patients and relatives need support during treatment and illness in which psychological methods and perspectives add to what occurs in a caring human relationship. I now want to argue for the importance of psychologists working alongside doctors and other members of the medical team as equal colleagues and illustrate some of the issues involved. Let me give four examples.

### Example 1

The work of Simonton, Matthews-Simonton and Creighton (1980) has already been mentioned. Carl Simonton, an oncologist in the USA, was puzzled by the individual variation in his patients' responses to treatment and he saw a connection between their attitude and their response. Patients with a 'will to live' seemed to fare better than those who had given up, and it also seemed to him that mental attitude was a good prognostic indicator of response to treatment. He and his wife Stephanie Matthews-Simonton, a psychologist, then worked together to develop an approach which could be offered to patients in addition to conventional treatment. The package they evolved is a self-help approach since it relies on patients taking responsibility for helping themselves to get well again. Their approach incorporates patients carrying out daily relaxation exercises, visualizing their body fighting the cancer, setting goals and achieving them, exercising, approaching rather than avoiding fearful and stressful ideas, building a support network, being self-assertive, contacting an inner spiritual strength and having the support of a counsellor. This approach has been controversial but it represents the most highly developed example of teamwork between doctors and psychologists. Importantly, they not only developed an approach in which doctors and psychologists worked together but also incorporated a psychological approach into conventional medical treatment.

## Example 2

Bindemann, a clinical psychologist working at the Department of Clinical Oncology, Glasgow, has routinely offered training in relaxation methods for patients receiving chemotherapy, particularly those showing symptoms of chronic psychological distress. This relaxation training takes place individually with patients who are hospitalized or who are attending hospital as outpatients. The benefits of relaxation for patients appear to be an improvement in the quality of life, improvement in night sleep, easier nursing care, reduced requirement for psychotropic and analgesic drugs and reduced side-effects of anti-cancer drugs (Bindemann *et al.* 1986).

## Example 3

Dr Leslie Walker, a psychologist, is Director of the Behavioural Oncology Unit at the University of Aberdeen in Scotland, where he has been evaluating psychological interventions for cancer patients in association with psychiatric and surgical colleagues. His research shows the value of including hypnotic techniques (which include guided imagery, relaxation and positive suggestions, as well as a relationship of support) in routine cancer care (Walker 1996).

## Example 4

Since 1983 I have been involved in developing a structured support service at the Department of Radiotherapy and Oncology, North Staffordshire Royal Infirmary, UK, in collaboration with medical and nursing staff of the unit. This initially involved training staff in relaxation and guided visual imagery techniques, after which two staff members (a senior registrar and a nursing sister) routinely incorporated these techniques into their medical consultations. Subsequently, a support group was established, which has met weekly in the Radiotherapy and Oncology Department. It is led jointly by myself as psychologist and by Dr Jane Williams, a doctor in radiotherapy. This is an open group for anyone wishing to explore self-help and psychological approaches to cancer. Further details of this service are given in Hegarty and Williams (1986).

I have selected these examples because they show psychologists working routinely in oncology departments alongside the medical team. In these settings, a psychological approach to treatment has become incorporated into the routine service on offer to patients. Here, psychologists are equal colleagues to doctors, offering a clinical input characterized by expertise in relaxation training, and a positive approach to the possibility of reducing patients' distress by non-drug means.

## The psychologist as colleague

The word 'colleague' comes, the *Shorter Oxford Dictionary* tells me, from the Latin word *colligare* – to join together. I asked my colleague, Jane Williams, what advantages she believed stemmed from a doctor and a psychologist joining forces in an oncology department.

First, she said, there were special techniques that a psychologist could contribute – specifically, relaxation, therapeutic visual imagery and anxiety management. She appreciated the support of a like-minded person – someone who, like herself, believed that patients needed more than medical techniques and was willing to listen and support. It was helpful to have someone share the emotional and practical demands of listening to patients and encouraging their personal resources during the weekly, 90-minute group sessions.

Of course, being a colleague is a two way thing. For me as a psychologist working in a medical environment it is essential to become acquainted with the basics of the various medical procedures, since patients often refer to them. Open communication and regular contact with doctors, radiographers and nurses are necessary to achieve this. In the group sessions, patients often wish to ask questions about treatment when the presence of a doctor with specialist knowledge is vital. Working with cancer patients psychologically is spiritually fraught and can be emotionally demanding, so having a colleague to share this with is important. Finally, a doctor brings the specialist knowledge of the treatment the person is undergoing to the psychological work of the counselling group. This particular partnership between a psychologist and a doctor meant that a new service to patients could be offered. Group meetings, stimulated by a belief that explicit help could be offered to patients who were interested 'in doing something to help themselves', and individual sessions of relaxation and counselling, began to be offered in a way which built upon the conventional medical treatment and support. It is in such partnerships, with a psychologist as equal colleague to members of the medical team, that a more holistic approach will become widely available to patients.

## Conclusions

Central to this chapter has been the personality, attitudes, thoughts and behaviour of people who have cancer. I have argued for the value of taking these into account in treatment. But is such a 'psychological approach' seen to be valuable by patients themselves?

Jim, a 45-year-old engineer with a diagnosis of terminal cancer, said, 'I knew that I needed something, that I had to do something to help myself, but I did not know what.' He found the regular contact with a therapist and the regular relaxation and other therapeutic exercises of tremendous benefit. He put on weight, was no longer depressed and found post-operative pain reduced.

Ethel, aged 60 years, had arthritis and lung cancer. Having to retire from work and experiencing severe anxiety, she started coming to group meetings. She was our most regular attender for a period of 18 months. Why did she come? 'You feel safe here,' she said. She went on to say that she could talk openly about her feelings and problems in the group, but not elsewhere.

Janette, aged 45 years, had been told there was nothing medically that could be done for her secondary cancer of the liver. Staff at the cancer care centre she visited encouraged her to build a self-help programme for herself. They helped with relaxation and support. I visited her to outline the range of opportunities and approaches that she might like to consider. Planning a programme of this kind is positive and constructive: worry, anxiety and depression are not.

The psychological approach to cancer is not easy for people. It requires hard work, a readiness to take responsibility for one's own health and, for some, a painful self-awareness. The benefits are support, help with tension, anxiety and depression and an approach to symptom control. These can be summarized as enhanced quality of life, which, whatever its length, is the ultimate goal for all people who have cancer. Psychologists are essential colleagues in helping a multidisciplinary team to achieve a structured approach to this goal for any person who has cancer.

---

### Discussion questions

1 Consider some of the difficulties of carrying out (a) retrospective and (b) prospective studies of the psychological causes of cancer.

2 Devise a plan for a controlled study of the effects of teaching patients to use a self-help, psychological approach.

3 It has been said that good medicine incorporates a caring approach to patients and encourages positive attitudes. Do you agree with this and, if so, what is the role for psychologists in medical services for cancer patients and their families?

# Further reading

Cooper, C. L. (ed.) (1991) *Cancer and Stress: Psychological, Biological and Coping Studies*. Chichester: Wiley. An edited collection of articles on psychosocial precursors of cancer, psychophysiological processes, managing psychosocial factors during treatment and methodological aspects of research studies on stress and cancer.

Guex, P. (1994) *An Introduction to Psycho-Oncology*. London: Routledge. Excellent and comprehensive introduction to the field by a French oncologist.

Simonton, O. C., Matthews-Simonton, S. and Creighton, J. L. (1980) *Getting Well Again: A Step-by-Step, Self-Help Guide to Overcoming Cancer for Patients and their Families*. New York: Bantam. A wide ranging review of available literature on stress, personality and cancer, together with a detailed account of the Simontons' self-help approach.

# References

Ader, R., Felton, D. L. and Cohen, N. (eds) (1991) *Psychoneuroimmunology*, 2nd edn. New York: Academic Press.

Bindemann, S., Milsted, R. A. V., Kaye, S. B., Welsh, J., Habeshaw, T. and Calman, K. C. (1986) Enhancement of quality of life with relaxation training in cancer patients attending a chemotherapy unit, in M. Watson, M. Greer and S. Greer (eds) *Psychosocial Issues in Malignant Disease*. Oxford: Pergamon.

Fawzy, F. I. (1994) The benefits of a short-term group intervention for cancer patients. *ADVANCES: Journal of Mind-Body Health* 10(2): 17–19.

Fawzy, F. I., Fawzy, N. W., Arndt, L. A. and Pasnau, R. O. (1995) Critical review of psychosocial interventions in cancer care. *Archives of General Psychiatry*, 52: 100–13.

Gordon, W. A., Freidenbergs, I., Diller, L., Hibbard, M., Wolf, C., Levine, L., Lipkins, R., Ezrach, O. and Lucido, D. (1980) Efficacy of psychosocial intervention with cancer patients. *Journal of Consulting and Clinical Psychology*, 48(6): 743–59.

Greer, S., Morris, T. and Pettingale, K. W. (1979) Psychological response to breast cancer: effect on outcome. *Lancet*, 2: 785–7.

Greer, S., Morris, T., Pettingale, K. W. and Haybittle, J. L. (1990) Psychological responses to breast cancer and fifteen year outcome, *Lancet*, 335: 49–50.

Hegarty, J. R. and Williams, E. J. (1986) Structured self-help for patients within a radiotherapy department, in J. R. Hegarty and R. W. DeCann (eds) *Psychology and Radiography*. Stoke-on-Trent: Change Publications.

Jones, I. (1986) Cancer following bereavement: results from the Office of Population Censuses and Surveys longitudinal study. Paper presented to the British Psychosocial Oncology Group meeting, University of Leicester, December.

LeShan, L. L. (1966) An emotional life-history pattern associated with neoplastic disease. *Annals of the New York Academy of Sciences*, 125: 780–93.

Meares, A. (1979) Meditation: a psychological approach to cancer treatment. *Practitioner*, 222: 119–22.

Rosch, P. J. (1984) Stress and cancer, in C. L. Cooper (ed.) *Psychosocial Stress and Cancer*. Chichester: Wiley.

Simonton, O. C., Matthews-Simonton, S. and Creighton, J. L. (1980) *Getting Well Again: A Step-by-Step, Self-Help Guide to Overcoming Cancer for Patients and their Families*. New York: Bantam.

Spiegel, D., Bloom, J. R., Kraemer, H. C. and Gottheil, E. (1989) Effect of psychosocial treatment on survival of patients with metastatic breast cancer. *Lancet*, 14 October: 888–91.

Temoshok, L. and Heller, B. W. (1984) On comparing apples, oranges and fruit salad: a methodological overview of medical outcome studies in psychosocial oncology, in C. L. Cooper (ed.) *Psychosocial Stress and Cancer*. Chichester: Wiley.

Walker, L. G. (1996) Psychological assessment and intervention: future prospects for women with breast cancer. *Seminars in Surgical Oncology*, 12: 76–83.

# Chapter 4

# Psychology and policing

## Jennifer Brown

This chapter discusses the role played by psychologists as colleagues when helping the police with their inquiries. In particular it charts a shift from early antagonisms between practitioners and academics to active collaboration in the development of operational and organizational procedures. The chapter concludes by assessing the status of police psychology as an area of specialist expertise, and by discussing the nature of the relationship – as colleagues – between psychologists and the police force.

## Origins and developments

Early contributions of psychologists to the criminal justice system followed two paths: the first of these was concerned with helping the police improve their investigations; the second with helping them improve their methods of selecting personnel. Examples of the first approach can be found in European experimental studies in memory. In 1879 Albert Schrenk-Notzing argued that the pre-trial publicity in a murder trial had induced 'retroactive memory falsification' on the part of witnesses. What he meant by this was that the witnesses could not distinguish between what they had seen and what had been reported in the press (Blackburn 1996). In 1908 Hugo Munsterberg published *On the Witness Stand* – a treatise drawing attention to methods for improving recall by witnesses (cited in Coolican 1996). Later, transatlantic work, such as that carried out by Elizabeth Loftus and her colleagues (Loftus and Zanni 1975; Loftus 1979; Loftus *et al.* 1987) took the experimental work of cognitive psychologists into the applied realm of investigative techniques used in eye-witness testimony and the cognitive interview (see pp. 65–7). Many of these early efforts by psychologists were resisted initially by some professional police officers, partly because the results implied criticisms of police procedures and practices. However, more recently, Robert Reiner (an academic criminologist) detected a rapprochement between the police and academe (Reiner 1994). Brewer and Wilson (1995) express current attitudes as follows:

> You can't teach an old dog new tricks, the old saying goes. Never has this been less true of policing than at present . . . The police have always had to rely on skills such as bluff, cunning, common sense, their understanding of human behaviour and communication to enforce the law. Traditionally there has been a suspicion of academic solutions, but as more police gain tertiary qualifications and confront the reality that traditional policing doesn't always work, they are looking to a range of new tools to add to their armoury. Psychological theory and research provides a number of such tools that can benefit many aspects of policing.
>
> (Brewer and Wilson 1995: ix)

Today contributions made by academic and clinical psychologists such as 'offender profiling' (see pp. 67–9) strikingly demonstrate productive collaborations between academics and police practitioners.

Examples of the second path can be seen in work carried out with police officers themselves. Here contributions range from the measurement of cognitive abilities and personality characteristics, to the support provided for officers given the potentially stressful nature of their job (Baldry 1998). The origins of such collaboration between psychologists and the police can be found in the United States, where the earliest contribution appears to have been made at the turn of the century with the use of Stanford Binet Intelligence scale to test would-be police officers (Bartol 1996). Incidentally, an IQ of 80 was set as the appropriate minimum standard (Reese 1995). In the mid-1960s, the emphasis shifted from cognitive appraisal to a search for the police personality (Bartol 1996). Such a search proved elusive, with no consistent findings. Instead it was suggested that there is a working style adopted by police officers as a result of occupational socialization (Chandler and Jones 1979).

By the late 1960s psychologists were firmly established as counsellors within US law enforcement agencies. Reese (1995) suggests that this involvement was brought about by a number of identifiable critical incidents involving police officers for which psychological expertise was actively sought because of shortcomings in police practice and knowledge.

The first incident was in 1963 when Ian Campbell and Karl Hettinger, officers from the Los Angeles Police Department (LAPD), were kidnapped and driven to an onion field out of town. Here Campbell was shot and killed whilst Hettinger managed to escape. Hettinger suffered considerable post-survival guilt, especially as he had surrendered his gun in the course of the abduction. The LAPD did not have the expertise available to help so they called in a psychologist to provide counselling. This heralded recognition of the need for psychological support and therapy in the wake of involvement in traumatic events, and it contributed to the development and routine application of critical incident debriefing (see p. 70).

The second incident occurred in 1965 when two California Highway Patrol officers were involved in a high-speed car chase and used considerable force to subdue the fleeing suspect, a black male. The suspect's capture, in a largely black, poor area of the city, was witnessed by a gathering crowd of onlookers and it sparked off wide-scale rioting and looting. In reviewing the incident later, it was acknowledged that psychological knowledge of interpersonal crisis management and crowd control might have helped to mitigate or avoid the escalation of such behaviour into a riot.

The third incident occurred in 1996 and this introduced ideas of psychological negotiation techniques into policing. A gunman, Charles Whitman, climbed the tower at the University of Texas and shot 16 people dead and wounded 20 others. A deputy sheriff eventually brought matters to a conclusion by shooting the gunman. This incident revealed a dearth of knowledge available to the police about the mental states of offenders and alternative methods to resolve such incidents.

A number of critical events also occurred in the UK that contributed to psychologists' involvement with the police. In 1983, the British Home Office issued a circular (114/83) suggesting that police officers be returned to front-line operational duties and to employ suitably qualified civilians to undertake what they called 'support functions', a process referred to as 'civilianization'. Many police forces had research departments, which were an early candidate for this, and my own involvement with the Hampshire Constabulary came about as a consequence of this process (Brown 1996). I represented an 'inside outsider' meaning that I was employed as a civilian member of the constabulary and thus working from the inside, but was not a serving police officer, and was thus an outsider. The police service is characterized by a strong informal process of socialization, sometimes referred to as the 'canteen culture'. Being a civilian, and so not part of the informal culture, had advantages and disadvantages. On the one hand, being an 'outsider' meant that I could bring a different perspective and offer new techniques of research. On the other hand, there was scepticism about how much I understood about a police officer's street experience and I needed to demonstrate my 'credibility' for my work to be seen as relevant. This I achieved by attending a briefing on Christmas Eve when other civilian members of staff had packed and gone home to start the holiday, and by participating in a public order exercise in the early hours of one morning.

A different sort of event took place in 1985 when a fire at Bradford City football stadium killed over 50 people and injured nearly 300; 40 police officers were included in the toll of the injured. Some police officers involved in the disaster showed persistent 'out of character' behaviour some days after the event. Duckworth (a psychologist) and Charlesworth (an assistant chief constable) noted the lack of police training and expertise to recognize and manage the aftermath of exposure to traumatic incidents. The chief constable took 'the unprecedented step of making available professional counselling to those officers who appeared to be suffering the psychological consequences of their involvement' (Duckworth and Charlesworth 1988). This initial step has blossomed into the wide ranging provision of supportive and preventive counselling services for the police that is now provided by a variety of in-house and external consultants. The combination of this growing awareness of the effects of exposure to traumatic incidents and my arrival at the Hampshire Constabulary as a research psychologist provided a timely coincidence in which there was a more positive attitude towards research. The chief constable granted permission for a survey of officers to be conducted that sought to profile sources of stress and the extent to which officers experienced adverse psychological consequences. This was one of the first systematic surveys into stress within the British police (Brown and Campbell 1994).

Legislation in the UK for equal opportunities in the 1970s and its implementation in the 1980s and 1990s also stimulated growth in the contributions made by psychologists. At this time I was involved in a national study of sex discrimination and sexual harassment within the police service in England and Wales (Anderson *et al.* 1993). In the aftermath of the results, which showed high levels of discriminatory behaviour by men towards women officers – together with the findings of an internal inquiry into recruitment, selection and promotion procedures by Her Majesty's Inspectorate of Constabulary (1993) and the Alison Halford sex discrimination industrial tribunal (Walklate 1996) – the police service became aware of how vulnerable it was in terms of its personnel practices. Until then, despite the attempts at civilianization, many police personnel departments were headed by senior police officers with no specialist qualifications in personnel management. Methods of recruitment and selection for specialist posts, training courses and promotion were, by and large, unsystematic and the procedures were not documented. The issues of equal opportunities and fairness in career advancement led to a growth in the professionalization of personnel departments and in the employment of occupational psychologists, who helped the police to develop and run assessment centres and to introduce systematic methods of job selection. Wigfield (1996) identifies some of the techniques the occupational psychologists introduced as:

- Work Profiling System (WPS), which uses a structured questionnaire for the purposes of analysing job task and job context information
- Critical Incident Technique, in which job holders are invited to describe incidents that have proved critical or important to their performance of the job
- Repertory Grid, by which means individuals can describe the characteristics necessary to perform a job and to differentiate between those who do so well or badly
- Focus Group Discussion, where people are asked to discuss the roles and responsibilities of particular jobs.

Psychologists were also at the forefront of developing and evaluating new methods of social skills based training for probationer constables (Bull and Horncastle 1988) and they were instrumental in designing assessment procedures for promotion and objective structured performance related examinations (OSPRE) (McGurk *et al.* 1992).

The initiatives of the then Conservative government and the Audit Commission during the 1980s in developing greater accountability for the public sector also introduced new management concepts into the police service, including performance measurement (Waters 1996). These external pushes, as well as a more internally driven ethos about quality of service, led the police to measure their own informal culture as well as public opinion, and to involve previously neglected groups – such as the gay and lesbian community – to further the interests of community policing (Mason and Palmer 1996).

## Current duties of applied psychologists

In 1968 the LAPD appointed a full-time psychologist to its staff; most major US police departments now retain the services of psychologists. Kirke and Scrivner's (1995) survey revealed that about 85 per cent of US police psychologists identify themselves as mental health care professionals providing clinical and counselling services (Kirke and Scrivner 1995). This includes treatment of post-traumatic stress disorder (PTSD), critical incident debriefing and more routine therapeutic interventions for anxiety and depressive disorders. They may also be engaged in stress-management programmes and teach relaxation and other stress reduction techniques. Around 10 per cent of US police psychologists currently identify themselves as organizational, experimental or social psychologists. They are more likely to be involved in community policing programmes or engage in organizational change. About one-third of these US police psychologists are employed full time by police departments, around one-fifth are civilian employees, and just over a half are consultants. About 7 per cent are academics and 6 per cent are also serving police officers. The services they provide include:

- screening recruits
- promotion assessment
- fitness for duty evaluations
- counselling
- stress management
- training
- organizational development
- operational support.

In a survey of psychologists who work within the police forces of England and Wales, Wainwright (1998) reports that 48 per cent are employed full time by the forces, 5 per cent are part time and the remainder are external consultants. The largest group identify themselves as occupational psychologists (29 per cent) followed by clinical (21 per cent) or crime (12 per cent) psychologists. A further 15 per cent work as crime analysts or offender profilers. Services provided for the police include:

- clinical intervention (43 per cent)
- planning and development of psychological services (40 per cent)
- research (40 per cent)
- personnel selection (36 per cent)
- training (36 per cent)
- preparation of evidence for court (17 per cent)
- crime analysis (17 per cent)
- psychological profiling (14 per cent)
- evaluation of witnesses/defendants (14 per cent).

As can be seen, this profile of areas of specialism and types of work in the UK differs in emphasis from that in the USA.

# Specific contributions to operational procedures

## Eyewitness testimony

Harrower (1998) has usefully summarized the research on our understanding of eyewitness testimony. She notes the importance of this work because of the potential for misidentification. Davies (1994) and Bull (1982) demonstrated that people do not remember faces well, and that recall is often based on stereotypes rather than memory. Kebbell and Milne (1998) suggest that police officers believe that eyewitnesses rarely provide sufficient information, although they also think that eyewitnesses are rarely incorrect. Harrower (1998) and Thompson (1995) identified the factors shown in Box 4.1 that influence reliability of eyewitness testimony.

Given these effects, which have all been demonstrated experimentally, Ainsworth (1995) itemized techniques adapted from clinical settings that may help to improve accuracy of recall. He proposes:

- providing a relaxing environment away from the noisy, perhaps sterile, police interview room
- reassuring witnesses that their testimony is not a test in which their performance is being measured
- being patient and providing gentle encouragement and reinforcement.

## Cognitive interviews

Stockdale (1993) argued that miscarriages of justice derived from weaknesses in police interviewing procedures, lack of management supervision, the drive to secure confessions rather than eliciting information, and an occupational culture that was unwilling to admit deficiencies.

The cognitive interview (CI) was developed to assist witnesses in their recall of people and events in police interviews. Fisher and Geiselman (1992), who were instrumental in introducing the technique, worked closely with law enforcement agencies in the United States in training police officers to use the CI. They claimed that the technique could double the amount of information recalled with no loss in accuracy. The original CI was developed with college students and field trials were conducted with the active assistance of police officers in the United States, Germany and Britain (Fisher and McCauley 1995). This enabled the original CI to be revised and a training programme to be implemented. As a result, police interviewers were shown to change dramatically their styles of interviewing and to elicit more information than officers using conventional interviewing procedures (Clifford and George 1996).

Harrower (1998) summarizes the four main techniques employed in the CI as:

---

*Box 4.1*   **Factors affecting witness's recall**

*Age*

Children tend to be less accurate in recalling witnessed events than adults. Elderly people may recall fewer details than younger witnesses.

*Gender*

As males are more likely to be colour blind and to experience greater acuity problems than females, women should make better witnesses than men. Research findings have not reported consistent gender differences in recall or recognition.

*Occupation*

Police officers are no more likely to recall witnessed events more accurately than other witnesses but they are more likely to be believed, especially when testimony is in dispute.

*Stress*

Recall of events can be clear and vivid under conditions of high emotion which produces a 'flash bulb' effect. This is the experience that the event has been lit up and preserved as in a flash photograph. However, 'weapon focus' is where a violent incident channels recall into details of the weapon used rather than details of the perpetrator.

*Beliefs*

Prior expectation and beliefs may result in biased recall.

*Contamination*

Information received subsequent to an event, such as the language used in questioning, may influence memory, e.g. use of the definite or indefinite article can influence recall.

*Substance misuse*

Drugs and alcohol have significant effects on memory. The effects of drink may be positive or negative depending on whether the alcohol was consumed before or after the to be remembered event.

*Source*: adapted from Harrower (1998) and Thompson (1995)

---

- reinstating the context of the incident – such as sounds or smells
- recalling events in different orders
- ignoring the relative importance of events
- recalling events from various viewpoints, e.g. the perpetrator or the victim.

Fisher and McCauley (1995) recommend from their reading of the scientific literature and careful perusal of taped interviews using the CI technique, that several factors may enhance the quality of material obtained from witnesses. They suggest the following:

- Interviewers should induce witnesses to take more active roles by asking them open ended questions and not stopping them when they appear to wander from a strict retelling of the incident.
- Interviewers should return the witness to the relevant dimensions but without dominating the interview.
- Witnesses should be encouraged to use non-verbal means to amplify responses – such as drawing or acting out movements.

The CI also follows a pre-set sequence of stages:

- introduction and rapport building
- open ended narrative guiding the witness to maximize information gain
- reviewing the accuracy of elicited information
- closing the interview by suggesting an extension to the interview should the witness later recall additional information.

After some years of using the cognitive interview, Cherryman and Bull (1996) wrote that no research had evaluated the effectiveness of the technique with suspects, but that it may be useful in cases where suspects had made admissions and there was a need to elicit corroborative information. They also noted the active involvement of psychologists in the training of British police officers in investigative interviewing. Kebbell *et al.* (in press) suggest that British police officers feel that the cognitive interview is a useful procedure that increases correct recall, but a major problem for them is that they do not often have the time to conduct a full cognitive interview.

## Offender profiling

Another significant involvement of psychological principles in police investigations has been the development of 'offender profiling'. Variously called criminal, criminal personality, psychological or behavioural profiling (Pinizzotto 1984) this too started with a dramatic event. Here the police and psychological practitioner collaborated in the apprehension of a serial bomber (see Box 4.2).

Further development of offender profiling was undertaken by the Federal Bureau of Investigation (FBI) Behavioural Science Unit who used experienced investigators with behavioural science qualifications to interview 36 convicted murderers and rapists in order to study different types of criminal personalities (Jackson and Bekerian 1997). Douglas *et al.* (1986) describe the FBI four stage approach as:

- data assimilating, in which as much information as possible is collected
- crime classification, when the type of crime is identified

---

***Box 4.2***   **Early offender profile**

During the 1950s, the New York Police Department was engaged in a massive operation to find the perpetrator of a series of bombings. Conventional investigative techniques failed to reveal the identity of the individual, who became known as the 'mad bomber'. Dr James Brussel was approached to profile the type of person who could be capable of committing the bombings. He came up with a remarkably accurate profile. The offender's characteristics were derived from deductions based on crime scene data, psychodynamic interpretation of letters written by the bomber and slashes left on the underside of theatre seats where the bombs had been secreted (Brussel 1968). For example, the letters were written in a stilted English and one chain of inference suggested the grammatical style was reminiscent of Eastern European immigrants, a majority of whom had settled in Connecticut. The duration and single mindedness of the attacks suggested an obsessive and conformist personality. George Metesky, Slavic by birth, was eventually arrested and charged with the bombings as a consequence of investigative leads provided by the profile. At the time of his arrest he was in his early 50s, living in Connecticut with two unmarried sisters and wearing a conventional double breasted suit, obsessionally buttoned up, as predicted by the profile.

---

- crime reconstruction, during which hypotheses about behaviour of victims are generated
- profile generation, describing demographic and physical characteristics of the likely perpetrator.

In Britain such profiling has benefited from collaboration between academic investigators and police officers (e.g. Canter and Heritage 1990). Their approach to profiling, as summarized by Ainsworth (1995), comprises:

- identification of the likely residential location
- criminal biography
- domestic/social characteristics
- personal characteristics
- occupational/educational history of the type of individual most likely to have perpetrated the crime(s).

Copson (1995) described thirty profilers who worked for the police. Interestingly, seven designated themselves as forensic psychologists and three as forensic psychiatrists; four were clinical psychologists and one a clinical psychiatrist; four were academic psychologists; four were police officers and one a police scientist; one was a consultant therapist; three were unclassified and the remaining two were designated as police sources. Copson also noted that detectives' expectations about the application of offender profiling were not always clear, and that not all profiles were equally well regarded. Jackson and Bekerian (1997) detected an unfortunate 'war of experts' potentially breaking out between the various academic profilers. The sources of dispute were to do with claims and counterclaims for the superiority of methods, access to databases and competition for expert status (Oleson 1996). Stevens (1997) has argued for the continued cooperation of detectives and academics so that offender profiling can become a systematized tool for use in major crime investigations.

## Specific contributions to organizational practice

### Recruitment and selection

In the aftermath of several widely publicized racial and sex discrimination cases in the police service, occupational psychologists have begun to work with police colleagues to develop better and fairer recruitment and selection procedures (Brown 1996). These involve taking a more objective approach to job selection, using techniques described on p. 63. The police have adopted a competency approach in which data are collected to profile the knowledge, skills and abilities necessary for successful job performance. Such competencies pinpoint the relevant attributes necessary for effective performance and help to place the right person in the right job (see Box 4.3).

The police service has accepted the use of assessment centres in which to conduct selection and recruitment procedures and has encouraged the evaluation of these (Feltham 1988). There has also been a willingness by the police service to incorporate the use of psychometric procedures in the selection of specialist personnel – such as the training of authorized firearms officers (Mirrlees-Black 1992).

---

*Box 4.3*  **Suggested job competencies for sergeants and inspectors**

| *Sergeant* | *Inspector* |
| --- | --- |
| leadership | taking charge |
| skill with people | motivating people |
| effective communication | communicating |
| planning and organizing | analytical thinking |
| problem analysis | decision making |
| problem solving | integrity |
| knowledge of law | drive |
| knowledge of police procedures | |

*Source*: adapted from Wigfield (1995)

---

## Stress management

The recognition of occupational stress within the police service originated with the identification of the need for stress counselling services in the aftermath of tragic events – such as the shooting of or by officers. In Britain the work of Duckworth and Charlesworth (see pp. 62–3) was instrumental in providing support for officers on duty during the Bradford City football stadium fire (Duckworth and Charlesworth 1988). The Lockerbie air disaster in December 1988 brought further recognition of the potential adverse effects of exposure to critical incidents (Walker 1997). Psychologists and serving police officers became jointly involved in research that stimulated the establishment of critical incident debriefing after a major public order event or major crime incident (see Box 4.4).

In addition to traumatic incidents as potential sources of stress, there has been a recognition that organizational mismanagement and the police occupational culture can also generate stress (Brown and Campbell 1994). Research has revealed the frequency and adverse impact experienced as a consequence of sexual harassment (Brown *et al.* 1995). Without the active cooperation of the police service and the research skills of psychologists it is doubtful that so much would have been achieved in pinpointing sources of stress and in developing methods to alleviate or support officers in distress. Psychologists, for example, work with the police to provide peer counselling support. Volunteers may be trained to 'befriend' colleagues experiencing personal difficulties and either provide a sympathetic ear or refer them to a psychologist for professional help (or both).

---

*Box 4.4*  **Critical incident debriefing (method employed by the Metropolitan Police)**

*Stage one: demobilization (occurs immediately after the incident)*

Line manager spends about 10–15 minutes with shift

1 to establish status of officers and their immediate needs
2 to identify sources of available support
3 to distribute trauma support information and contact numbers

*Stage two: defuse (occurs two to four days after the incident)*

Trained personnel meet officers for about one hour

1 to discuss incidents and any effects
2 to arrange referrals for officers in need of professional help

*Stage three: follow up (occurs five to seven days after the incident)*

Support given to officers' families if required

1 to alert partners to possible physical/psychological effects

---

There is also a growing body of research emerging as a consequence of collaborations between serving police officers and academics (Cooper and Grimley 1983; Crowe and Stradling 1993).

# Conclusions

The work of psychologists as colleagues with the police can broadly be defined in terms of practitioner (clinical and occupational) psychologists and academic (cognitive and forensic) psychologists. The practical content of the work undertaken ranges from organizing and managing staff, training, health and welfare to providing operational support such as offender profiling and witness interviewing. Research has been conducted into occupational stress and sexual harassment, and evaluations undertaken of social skills training, assessment procedures, offender profiling and investigative interviewing. Police psychology can also lay claim to an emerging theoretical literature. For example, Burke (1995) has proposed a theoretical model to account for the merging of occupational, socialization and sexual orientation in the identity construction of gay and lesbian police officers.

It is clear that distinctive methods and theory are being developed within police psychology but are they sufficient for the establishment of a sub-discipline of psychology? Coolican (1996) uses the terms criminological and forensic psychology interchangeably and gives a broad definition, i.e. the application of psychological principles to the criminal justice system. Blackburn (1996) points out that forensic literally means pertaining to or used in courts of law. He argues for a narrow definition that would exclude police psychology that deals with aspects of police officers such as the selection and training undertaken by occupational psychologists. Given that police psychology draws from a range of psychological knowledge for application within a specific forensic setting, the police component of the criminal justice system, then indeed it may be legitimate to consider this to be an emergent specialism.

So, what does it mean to be a 'colleague' working with the police? Naturally, being a colleague working inside another organization produces tensions and suspicions. From the police point of view, there are difficulties in understanding the approaches of psychologists and what they have to offer. There are stereotypes to overcome and working relationships to be built up to give confidence that something helpful and practically useful will come out of collaboration.

Working as a colleague alongside police officers involves a fine balance for the psychologist between being an 'outsider' and an 'insider'. To lean too far to one side or the other could jeopardize the role, and restrict the potential of what can be delivered (see Box 4.5). Being a colleague within the setting of another profession requires some of the skills of a diplomat to preserve the relationship. Getting this balance right sometimes involves making a judgement about which issues to fight one's corner on, and where to give way in order to keep the channels of communication open.

Generally, the role evolves over time as confidence is built up in the relationship. To achieve this necessitates continual re-evaluation and effort

**Box 4.5** 'Insider' and 'outsider' roles for the police and the psychologist

*For the police, the psychologist as 'outsider'...*

- Commands respect for impartiality, and professional ethics because of allegiance to professional body and code of conduct
- Creates expectations of objectivity and detached judgement
- Gives rights to independence, such as withholding information gained in confidence, protecting anonymity
- Demands specialized knowledge, skills and expertise to justify role
- Provides them with a more honest opinion to consider in arriving at decisions

*For the police, the psychologist as 'insider'...*

- Requires steps to build up confidence and prove oneself in order to gain acceptance
- Helps to break down barriers and gain the confidence of those you are with
- Enables them to explain their point of view and believe in a sympathetic understanding
- Involves new ways of thinking and problem solving

*For the psychologist, being an 'outsider'...*

- Can be source of security and confidence
- Provides a retreat when under pressure and support through allegiance to professional bodies
- Requires self-discipline to maintain integrity and not become too closely socialized into the 'insider' workstyles and culture

*For the psychologist, being an 'insider'...*

- Means justifying credentials and earning respect
- Gives insights into the working conditions, values, pressures and expectations that influence conduct
- Produces more understanding and sensitivity into data and its interpretation
- Means finding constructive, pragmatic and palatable ways of presenting findings from investigations while maintaining integrity

in 'selling' one's skills and tools, and disciplining oneself to deliver advice that is relevant, meaningful and pragmatic (dropping the natural academic tendency to qualify remarks) and provide more definitive conclusions. It also requires an attitude of mutual respect and humility to recognize the areas of skill and expertise that both sides have in order to foster a belief that a better outcome can be produced jointly rather than separately. For example, in offender profiling, the psychologist is able to bring powerful tools for handling data analysis and synthesis, psychological knowledge about personality and behaviour patterns, while the police have a pragmatic approach and enormous experience in running inquiries and sifting evidence, and skill in identifying prospective lines of inquiry.

---

*Discussion questions*

1 How might a police officer and psychologist collaborate in the detection and apprehension of an unknown serial rapist?

2 What are the contributions that police officers and psychologists can make to the identification and alleviation of stress in the police service?

3 What subdisciplines from psychology contribute to policing psychology? Illustrate with appropriate examples.

---

## Further reading

Bull, R. and Carsons, D. (eds) (1994) *The Handbook of Forensic Psychology in Legal Contexts*. Chichester: Wiley. This edited collection draws together much contemporary European and North American scholarship in forensic psychology.

Canter, D. (1994) *Criminal Shadows: Inside the Mind of the Serial Killer*. London: Harper Collins; Britton, P. (1997) *The Jigsaw Man*. London: Bantam. These two books provide accounts by psychologists involved in offender profiling. They illustrate the relationship between police and psychologists as well as provide some insight into the 'war of experts'.

Gudjonsson, G. and Haward, L. (1998) *Forensic Psychology: A Practitioner's Guide*. London: Routledge. This is an accessible account of the work of forensic psychologists with many case examples.

*Forensic Update* and *Issues in Criminological and Legal Psychology*, produced by the Division of Legal and Criminological Psychology of the British Psychological Society, have an excellent coverage of topics in forensic psychology including police and policing.

## References

Ainsworth, P. B. (1995) *Psychology and Policing in a Changing World*. Chichester: Wiley.

Anderson, R., Brown, J. M. and Campbell, E. A. (1993) *Aspects of Sex Discrimination in Forces in England and Wales*. London: Home Office Police Research Group.

Baldry, A. C. (1998) Is psychology 'all fangled stuff' for the police? *Forensic Update*, 53 (April): 20–6.

Bartol, C. R. (1996) Police psychology; then, now and beyond. *Criminal Justice and Behaviour*, 23: 70–89.

Blackburn, R. (1996) What is forensic psychology? *Legal and Criminological Psychology*, 1: 3–16.

Brewer, N. and Wilson, C. (eds) (1995) *Psychology and Policing*. Hillsdale, NJ: Erlbaum.

Brown, J. M. (1996) Police research: some critical issues, in F. Leishman, B. Loveday and S. Savage (eds) *Core Issues in Policing*. London: Longman.

Brown, J. M. and Campbell, E. A. (1994) *Stress and Policing: Sources and Strategies*. Chichester: Wiley.

Brown, J. M., Campbell, E. A. and Fife-Schaw, C. (1995) Adverse impacts experienced by police officers following exposure to sex discrimination and sexual harassment. *Stress Medicine*, 11: 221–8.

Brussel, J. A. (1968) *Casebook of a Crime Psychiatrist*. London: New English Library.

Bull, R. (1982) Physical appearance and criminality. *Current Psychological Review*, 2: 269–81.

Bull, R. and Horncastle, P. (1988) Evaluating training: the London Metropolitan Police recruit training in human awareness/policing skills, in P. Southgate (ed.) *New Directions in Police Training*. London: HMSO.

Burke, M. (1995) Identities and disclosures: the case of lesbian and gay police officers. *The Psychologist*, 8: 543–7.

Canter, D. V. and Heritage, R. (1990) A multi-variate model of sexual offence behaviour. *Journal of Forensic Psychiatry*, 1(2): 185–212.

Chandler, E. V. and Jones, C. S. (1979) Cynicism: an inevitability of police work. *Journal of Police Science and Administration*, 9: 209–23.

Cherryman, J. and Bull, R. (1996) Investigative interviewing, in F. Leishman, B. Loveday and S. Savage (eds) *Core Issues in Policing*. London: Longman.

Clifford, B. R. and George, R. (1996) A field evaluation of training in three methods of witness/victim investigative interviewing. *Psychology Crime and Law*, 2: 231–48.

Coolican, H. (1996) *Applied Psychology*. London: Hodder and Stoughton.

Cooper, C. L. and Grimley, P. (1983) Stress among police detectives. *Journal of Occupational Medicine*, 25: 534–40.

Copson, G. (1995) *Coals to Newcastle? A Study of Offender Profiling*. Police Research Group Special Interest Paper 4. London: Home Office.

Crowe, G. and Stradling, S. G. (1993) Dimensions of perceived stress in a British police force. *Policing and Society*, 3: 137–50.

Davies, G. (1994) Witness error still continues to convict the innocent. *The Guardian* 10 September.

Douglas, J., Reissler, R. K., Burgess, A. W. and Hartman, C. R. (1986) Criminal profiling from crime scene analysis. *Behavioural Sciences and the Law*, 4: 401–21.

Duckworth, D. and Charlesworth, A. (1988) The human side of disaster. *Policing*, 4: 194–210.

Feltham, R. (1988) Validity of a police assessment centre: a 19 year follow up. *Journal of Occupational Psychology*, 61: 129–44.

Fisher, R. and Geiselman, R. (1992) *Memory Enhancing Techniques for Investigative Interviewing: The Cognitive Interview*. Springfield, IL: Charles Thomas.

Fisher, R. and McCauley, M. (1995) Information retrieval: interviewing witnesses, in N. Brewer and C. Wilson (eds) *Psychology and Policing*. Hillsdale, NJ: Erlbaum.

Harrower, J. (1998) *Applying Psychology to Crime*. London: Hodder and Stoughton.

Her Majesty's Inspectorate of Constabulary (1993) *Equal Opportunities in the Police Service*. London: Home Office.

Jackson, J. and Bekerian, D. (eds) (1997) *Offender Profiling: Theory, Research and Practice*. Chichester: Wiley.

Kebbell, M. R. and Milne, R. C. (1998) Police officers' perceptions of eyewitness performance in forensic investigations. *Journal of Social Psychology*, 138(3): 323–30.

Kebbell, M. R., Milne, R. C. and Wagstaff, G. F. (in press) The cognitive interview: a survey of its forensic effectiveness. *Psychology, Crime and Law*.

Kirke, M. I. and Scrivner, E. M. (eds) (1995) *Police Psychology into the 21st Century*. Hillsdale, NJ: Erlbaum.

Loftus, E. (1979) *Eye Witness Testimony*. Cambridge, MA: Harvard University Press.

Loftus, E. and Zanni, G. (1975) Eyewitness testimony: the influence of wording of a question. *Bulletin of the Psychonomic Society*, 5: 86–8.

Loftus, E., Loftus, G. and Messo J. (1987) Some facts about weapon focus. *Law and Human Behaviour*, 11: 5–62.

McGurk, B., Platton, T. and Bolton, A. (1992) Perceptions of OSPRE: how does OSPRE compare with traditional examination methods? *Policing*, 8: 256–61.

Mason, A. and Palmer, A. (1996) *Queer Bashing*. London: Stonewall.

Mirrlees-Black, C. (1992) *Using Psychometric Personality Tests in the Selection of Firearms Officers*. Research and Planning Unit Paper 68. London: Home Office.

Munsterberg, H. (1908) *On the Witness Stand*. New York: Clark, Boardman.

Oleson, J. (1996) Psychological profiling: does it actually work? *Forensic Update*, 46: 11–14.

Pinizzotto, A. J. (1984) Forensic psychology: criminal personality profiling. *Journal of Police Science and Administration*, 12: 32–40.

Reese J. T. (1995) A history of police psychological services, in M. I. Kirke and E. M. Scrivner (eds) *Policing Psychology into the 21st Century*. Hillsdale, NJ: Erlbaum.

Reiner, R. (1994) A truce in the war between police and academe. *Policing Today*, 1(1): 30–2.

Stevens, J. (1997) Standard investigatory tools and offender profiling, in J. Jackson and D. Bekerian (eds) *Offender Profiling: Theory, Research and Practice*. Chichester: Wiley.

Stockdale, J. (1993) *Management and Supervision of Police Interviews*. Police Research Group Paper 5. London: Home Office Police Department.

Thompson, D. (1995) Eyewitness testimony and identification tests, in N. Brewer and C. Wilson (eds) *Psychology and Policing*. Hillsdale, NJ: Erlbaum.

Wainwright, N. (1998) Psychologists who work for the police. Unpublished MSc dissertation, University of Surrey.

Walker, M. (1997) Conceptual and methodological investigations of occupational stress. *Policing and Society*, 7: 1–17.

Walklate, S. (1996) Equal opportunities and the future of policing, in F. Leishman, B. Loveday and S. Savage (eds) *Core Issues in Policing*. London: Longman.

Waters, I. (1996) Quality of service: politics or paradigm shift?, in F. Leishman, B. Loveday and S. Savage (eds) *Core Issues in Policing*. London: Longman.

Wigfield, D. (1996) Competent leadership in the police. *Police Journal*, 64: 99–107.

## Section C

# The psychologist as expert

# Chapter 5

# Exploring how advertising works

## Alan Branthwaite

## The expert

Experts in any field are characteristically:

- knowledgeable about their subject
- experienced
- skilful in applying their knowledge and extrapolating from past experience.

The last of these is the most critical characteristic of being 'an expert'. Being skilful in applying knowledge from learning and experience requires:

- the ability to recognize similarities with past cases
- not being blinded to the special features of a new problem
- a wide perspective in considering points of similarity with previous examples
- imagination in translating from the old to the new
- inventiveness in bridging over the gaps between past and current problems.

As an expert in how advertising works, the psychologist is seeking to understand consumers and to predict the effects which ads have in influencing their ideas, attitudes, desires and behaviour. Consumer attitudes and behaviour cover a large and complex field. The study of this area stands in parallel to the psychology of work, leisure, health and education in terms of its relevance and importance in modern life. Given a choice, we buy bottled water rather than drink tap water (the water utilities do not seem to offer as attractive a product); we buy brands that cannot be distinguished in blind taste trials from cheaper, less well-known alternatives; and we are loyal users of particular brands of clothes, sports wear, supermarkets, cosmetics, and so on. Few people prefer unlabelled commodity products to familiar brands which command greater respect and offer more status to the user. Successful marketing sells products, creates jobs, expands the economy, makes profits and underpins investment and the creation of prosperity in societies. So expertise in the psychology of how to sell products that people want to buy has an important role.

In studying and analysing consumers and the effects of advertising, psychologists draw widely from studies and theories of perception, emotion, decision making, language, social influence and cultural experience. The interests of business and marketing in using the expertise of psychologists and market researchers are geared to the better understanding of consumers in order to improve competitiveness and influence buying decisions.

The role of the psychologist in this field is correspondingly pragmatic in exploiting psychology for commercial advantage. One effect of this is that psychologists working in advertising research share in the competitive and entrepreneurial spirit, and this makes them alert to changes and innovations in psychology and related disciplines. Developments in academic psychology have often been adapted by consumer researchers, who have applied and developed the theories and techniques. In turn, these applied researchers have made a contribution to academic psychology by advancing and refining the work, and discovering its practical shortcomings and limitations, before their interest and enthusiasm moves on. They have also devised specific new theories from their accumulated studies of the effects of advertising.

## Approaches to understanding consumer behaviour

What is it that advertising seeks to influence and change in consumers that will affect their choices of products? From psychological studies of human thinking and actions, certain principles (if not laws) have emerged which have shaped our approach to understanding consumer behaviour, and how to influence it. For example, it is accepted that:

- Individual, social and situation factors interact in determining behaviour.
- Attitudes and actions are influenced by an individual's subjective interpretation rather than objective reality.
- Differences in ideas, attitudes and preferences arise out of the development of individuals and their past experiences – nothing occurs in isolation but in the context of what is going on now and what has gone before.
- Unconscious factors as well as rational considerations affect consumer choices.

These principles can be contrasted with the approaches arising from other disciplines, such as economics, that emphasize rational decision making and objective financial forces (see Furnham and Argyle 1998).

Central to the psychological approach (though at times controversial) has been the principle that the causes of behaviour are not always conscious or rational, but are influenced by unconscious associations, memories and wishes. This principle has usually been aligned with Freudian psychology, but it is fundamental to explanations in other areas, such as cognition. For example, work on attention and experimental demonstrations of subliminal perception also show that stimuli are processed unconsciously in the first instance and then, depending on their significance, transferred to higher levels of consciousness for further processing (Eysenck and Keane 1995). In subliminal perception research, words are presented without awareness by displaying them very briefly, or by speaking quietly through earphones against a background of white noise to mask the sound. It has been found that words which are not consciously perceived can colour the conscious perception of other objects or events. In one experiment, the mood and imagery evoked by music were changed by words presented subliminally at the same time. In other research using different techniques, emotionally loaded words presented without conscious awareness affected both self-reported feelings and physiological measures of anxiety. So non-conscious processes do exist which influence perceptions, evaluations and conscious emotional feelings (Hill 1993).

Deliberate subliminal advertising is banned, but the subliminal perception of images and sounds occurs all the time. Research has shown that the style of music played in supermarkets can affect the choice of wines. When 'typical' German music was played, the sales of German wines increased (North *et al.* 1997).

Background music subconsciously alters the perception of ads and the interpretation of the messages about the product. In one of our research projects we tested two radically different pieces of music to accompany a TV ad for 'Lemsip Power' (a coughs and cold remedy). One version was a jazz piece while the other was a dramatic piece designed to enhance the impact of the ad. Although the visuals were the same, the effects on 150 viewers of the ad were quite different:

• The jazz music stood out more and was more noticeable as an aspect of the ad, while the dramatic music underscored the action of the visuals but in itself was not so prominent.
• The two versions did not differ in overall enjoyment, but the jazz music polarized impressions from the ad with both more likes and more dislikes. The jazz music heightened the prominence and appeal of a cat that featured in the ad, but accentuated some potential sources of confusion. This distracted attention from the explosion and mushroom cloud coming from the mug of Lemsip that were intended to signify the power of the brand, so they were noticed less often by viewers.
• The dramatic music made the ad more positively involving for viewers. The activities of the cat were less noticed and often seemed not to fit with the ad. The explosion stood out better, which enhanced appreciation of the brand's effectiveness.

This case study demonstrated the way that the creative use of music can subtly change the structure of an ad and the pattern of impressions. The music that was more in harmony with the story and intended communication, was more successful in enabling the visuals to convey the brand personality.

In analysing viewers' reactions to advertising, psychologists look for these covert, latent influences as well as for the overt and rational effects. Psychologists working in advertising research use a model of consciousness like that shown in Figure 5.1 to understand consumer behaviour.

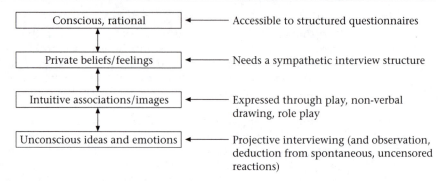

***Figure 5.1*** Layers of consciousness

Early theories about the way advertising works put great emphasis on the extreme layers in this model: either persuasion through the presentation of rational information, or stimulating unconscious motivations in consumers (Packard 1957). It is only since the 1980s that the importance of the intuitive level has been recognized as a powerful factor in consumer choices, and one that is more readily affected by ads. The intuitive level of thinking involves those hard to articulate associations, perceptions and feelings that colour our impressions about objects, ideas, people and events. Ideas at the intuitive level are not rational or easily communicated through language. This is a very rich layer of consciousness where ideas are based on imagination, personal symbols and private metaphors. Long ago, Jean Piaget characterized this type of thinking as 'autistic' (or egocentric), dealing with images and creating a dream world of imagination (Piaget 1924). We can appreciate the way this level of consciousness operates according to 'feelings', 'hunches' and associations by considering a quotation from Picasso: 'Reality lies in how you see things. A green parrot is a green salad and a green parrot. He who makes it only a parrot diminishes its reality. A painter who copies a tree blinds himself to the real tree. I see things otherwise. A palm tree can become a horse' (cited in Cohen 1970).

This kind of intuitive thought is exhibited in dreams where images are personal symbols for the objects being dreamt about, in much the same way as images are used in poetry to expand the meaning and attach particular connotations to ideas. Intuitive thought also draws on synaesthetic imagery – where sensations from different modalities become merged – as, for example, when we talk of red being 'warm', lime green as a 'loud' colour, 'hot' jazz or playing the 'blues'. It is arguable whether this intuitive layer is strictly above or below consciousness, but this does not matter much in practice, as long as there is recognition that here is a different type of thinking which inspires choices and decisions.

Advertising that is successful in the long term seeks to influence perceptions of the product by implanting intuitive associations connected to the brand. Just think of the images that come to mind when you contemplate a Cadbury's Flake bar, Coca Cola, Marlboro cigarettes, Levi jeans, Nike shoes or Esso fuel stations. We know a great deal about how this works from our understanding of theories of perception.

# How does advertising influence our thoughts and feelings? Insights from psychological concepts and theory

An American sociologist, Michael Schudson (1984), captures the task for research into how advertising works somewhat graphically. He argues that advertising is becoming more visual (both on TV and in print) and increasingly uses more 'Rococo' means of manipulation, which underlines the need to understand the processing of images, i.e. what consumers actually do with advertising. (Rococo was an eighteenth-century style of European decorative art that was highly embellished and ornamental.) The process of turning sensory experiences into meaningful perceptions involves multiple stages of processing, and various mechanisms. According to Gregory (1972) perceptions are actively constructed from 'floating fragmentary scraps of data signalled by the senses and drawn down from the brain memory banks, themselves constructions from the snippets of the past.'

What can we learn from cognitive science about the processes that operate while watching TV ads? How are they perceived, interpreted and stored in memory? It has to be admitted that when it comes to applying theories to a complex process like watching TV, our knowledge is fragmentary, and much has to be based on speculative, but hopefully expert, interpretation. Nonetheless, psychologists have identified different kinds of memory and perceptual mechanisms that are at work in processing sensory experience which have relevance for understanding advertising (Branthwaite and Swindells 1995). Briefly here we can point to two types of processing involved in the move from sensory experience to meaningful perception of advertising:

- bottom-up and top-down processing
- episodic versus semantic analysis and storage of information.

## Bottom-up and top-down processing

Everyday perception involves bottom-up and top-down processing. Perception is not an immediate, direct experience of the world around us, but a constructive process of analysis and interpretation whereby we turn physical sensations of light and sound into meaningful perceptions. Almost everything we perceive starts off with a *bottom-up process* (stimulus driven) that is triggered through one of the five senses and drives attention and perception to what is happening in the world outside of us (see Figure 5.2).

Conversely, *top-down processing* is driven by experience and 'thought', which shapes, biases or reorganizes our perception and interpretation of those sensory experiences. For example, Guinness posters have featured a number of witty sayings, as in: 'A woman needs a man like a fish needs a bicycle'. We see the marks on the paper, we notice the form of the letters and recognize the outlines that make familiar words (bottom-up). Through experience we readily decipher the meaning of the individual words. However, it requires a little thought (top-down) to go on to appreciate the paradox that gives rise to the wit and humour which makes this an advertisement, with the sign-off line that 'Not everything in black and white

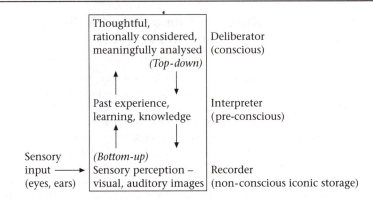

***Figure 5.2***  Bottom-up and top-down processing

makes sense' (Guinness itself being a beer with a celebrated black and white appearance).

The key point we have learnt about consumer reactions to advertising is that not all perception automatically moves up from the bottom layer to the top. We process sensory experience only so far as we need to make sense of the world at a particular moment in time and handle any reactions that are needed from us. This is true about our experience of TV advertising. We can see it as an entertaining piece of film, and we can think of it as a message about a product, but whether we go on to this higher interpretation depends on the circumstances. We do not constantly examine and rationally consider all that we see. Much that we watch is taken in simply as a collage of images. We process them so far up the chain to the point that we make sense of them – we know what we are watching – but we do not necessarily look for their relevance or implications for our lives. So we enjoy watching advertising on TV as a piece of entertainment in its own right without it influencing our decisions to buy a product at the time of viewing. But if the ad is interesting and well branded, we learn to associate images and ideas with that particular product which give it character and differentiate it from other similar makes.

## Episodic versus semantic analysis and storage of information

There are two distinct ways of processing information and experiences at the higher levels of cognitive perception: episodic knowing and semantic knowing.

*Episodic knowing* relates to the processing of everyday experiences, such as what we had for breakfast this morning, where we went on holiday, or an ad we saw on TV. Episodic knowing is experiential and autobiographical as it relates to direct, individual experience. In remembering what we had for breakfast this morning, we reconstruct the situation and play back the occasion to find the answer. Episodic knowing specializes in visual and spatial processing (faces, places, pictures) and records everyday experiences as meaningful events, images and symbols.

*Semantic knowing* is about knowledge, 'facts' and 'truths' that are abstract and generalized. Semantic knowing is learnt and more deeply processed. It is rational and held in the form of concepts and propositions, for instance:

Cornflakes are a breakfast cereal eaten with milk.

Semantic processing deals not with the observable properties of objects (their colour, shape, etc.) but with their abstract attributes and characteristics (their uses and 'inner' qualities such as whether they are edible, fragile, fashionable). It is used in the perception of verbal information, either spoken or as text.

To illustrate these two processes, consider this question:

How many windows are there in your house or apartment?

For most people, this is a novel question. We do not have the answer in semantic memory as a fact – although we could say (immediately and without thinking) what the address of our home is, which in some ways is a more complicated piece of learned information. To work out the number of windows, we use episodic memory and either count round from room to room or construct a mental image of the outside.

## Mechanisms underlying the effects of advertising

To return to Schudson's (1984) speculation about how modern advertising works, much of the way in which TV advertising is processed is episodic although this will vary according to the nature of advertising, and the frame of mind of the viewer while watching (Branthwaite and Swindells 1997).

Ads that are heavily loaded with rich imagery, and watched passively by the TV viewer as entertainment, will be episodically processed. The images and mood of the ad are associated over time with the brand being advertised to give it greater interest and status for the potential consumer. This is called the *status/interest mechanism*, by which the ad conveys and the viewer absorbs intuitive images that increase the (emotional and symbolic) appeal of the brand (see Figure 5.3). While viewing, the advertising is not consciously

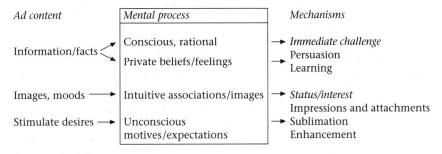

*Figure 5.3* Advertising mechanisms

evaluated for its meaning, practical relevance or immediate implications for daily living. But there is learning by which ideas, images and associations are accumulated in relation to products and services available. Through the advertising, viewers build up identities for brands in the marketplace. The effect of the advertising is to raise the profile of the brand (i.e. its status and interest). At its most basic, the advertising builds a sense of familiarity with the brand and endows it with character and identity. Mickey Mouse in the shops would be just another rag doll if not for the accumulated character and life history of this animated cartoon figure. Equally, Levis would simply be trousers without the 'Americana' images from the advertising that give them stature and identity. Advertising creates a halo in the viewer's mind of excitement, uniqueness and supremacy: it is not the product that is interesting but the consumable brand advertising.

Alternatively, ads that are loaded with information and seek to tell the viewer some facts about the product are not usually so entertaining to watch and to absorb. These ads work when the viewer has a latent problem, which they may not be directly considering while watching the TV, but is triggered by something relevant in the ad. Information loaded ads that trigger latent problem solving are processed semantically. To be effective, they have to convey 'new news' which assists with a consumer problem. This is the case especially when the buyer is already thinking, for example, about choosing a new car, a multimedia computer, or looking for a window cleaner that does not leave streaks like those they noticed with their current product. This is called the *immediate challenge* route by which ads can influence the consumer, because a conscious decision is made at the time of seeing the ad to give the product a try (see Figure 5.3).

There is a third mechanism by which ads work. Both the immediate challenge and the status/interest mechanisms set up positive expectations about what the brand will be like to own and use. These expectations produce an *enhancement effect* when the product is tried, because (as shown long ago in psychology studies) expectations lead to self-fulfilling experiences (a top-down process). So the brand of lager that promises to 'refresh the part that others cannot reach' sets up expectations that it will be refreshing and thirst quenching. When we try this chilled drink, indeed we find it does work. Over time, the successfully advertised brand can appropriate this common property of all lagers as part of its own special identity and differentiate itself from the competition. Brown and Farr (1994) demonstrated that ads for products as diverse as mint chocolates to toothbrushes used this mechanism successfully to enhance the appeal of their brands.

## Using psychological concepts and theories to develop ads

In the construction of advertising campaigns, inspiration has been found from specific concepts and theories in many areas of psychology. From the area of childhood development, the theory of object relations and transitional objects (Winnicott 1980) was instrumental in devising the ad campaign that consolidated Guinness as a modern cult drink of the 1980s. This theory argues that objects can stand for relationships with people, like the child's teddy bear which substitutes for the relationship with mother when she is not present. These objects can provide support and comfort at times of stress, and help in the transition to independence and maturity. This theory was used as an analytical tool in interpreting consumer responses and attitudes to Guinness, and it led ultimately to the development of the Genius advertising campaign, which is still in use.

Market research indicated that in consumers' perceptions, Guinness had satisfying, nourishing properties that at an inner level related to archetypal myths of power, energy and fertility (Broadbent and Cooper 1987). These features were ostensibly characterized in the dark, rich, black nature of the product, together with its creaminess and fascinating swirlingness when poured. But, at the same time, Guinness was perceived as bitter, strong and dark, with a social reputation for manliness, maturity and wit. It was argued on the basis of the research findings that Guinness, at its deepest level, was symbolically female (standing for the goodness and nurturing of mother) but this motivation for drinking it operated in the shadows of awareness. The product itself was an adult transformation of the original comforting nourishment (milk) being not only rich and creamy with a playful white head, but also black, bitter and challenging. These basic product attributes, and their symbolic associations, were believed to account for its fascination even among those who did not drink it themselves.

Advertising for Timotei hair shampoo was guided by another psychological model, this time of human relationships. The theory, known as transactional analysis (TA), examines everyday social interactions in terms of the classic roles of parent, adult and child (Berne 1968). These roles are fundamental and are inculcated in everyone through our experience of the family and social worlds through which we evolved. These roles act as templates, underpinning the ways in which we relate to other people in social exchanges (Barker 1980; Stewart and Jones 1987).

In the Timotei launch advertising, these roles were skilfully blended together in the ad to communicate messages about the product at each level (Gordon and Langmaid 1988; see Figure 5.4):

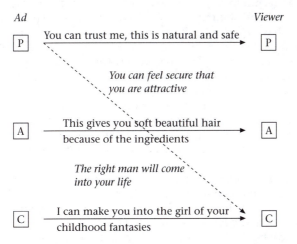

*Figure 5.4* Transactional analysis of Timotei ad

- At the *child* level (C), the commercial was a romanticized fantasy, like a fairy tale, in which a young girl blissfully communed with nature while she combed her hair. As she brushed out her long blonde hair a young man on a white horse emerged from the exact spot on the screen where her hair was falling gracefully a moment before, as if her beauty had conjured him up.
- At the *adult* level (A), the ad promised soft beautiful hair as demonstrated by the brushing action, and justified in terms of the natural ingredients described by the voice-over.
- At the *parent* level (P), the ad echoed the admiration of parents for their daughters and the beliefs they instilled that she is precious and special, so she should wait (patiently) until one day the right man will come along. At this level, the ad enabled those who wished to revisit the security and reassurance of this parental adoration, to find self-confidence from using the product.

Dissected logically like this, the ad sounds transparent and corny, but its power lies in the magic of the imagery (processed episodically) to engage emotions rather than analytical or rational thinking. These three levels in the ad connected to corresponding levels in the viewer by appealing to childish fantasies about meeting a glamorous man of your dreams, while giving rational promises that the product would deliver soft and beautiful hair because of the natural ingredients, and at the same time the 'parental' voice-over inspired trust that this was a product that could be relied upon to give you what you were looking for from a hair shampoo (either rationally or emotionally, or both).

## Combining psychology and experience in understanding ads

Psychologists as toolmakers have been instrumental in devising the basic measuring techniques used in advertising research (and much other market research, such as opinion polling). Decisions about what aspects should be measured have been refined on the basis of experience by practitioners to improve the relevance, reliability and practical performance of the tools.

In researching new advertising, we have learnt from experience (supported by the theories discussed above) that for an ad to be successful it must:

- *Be involving and engage the viewer's attention and interest.* An extensive review by the American Advertising Research Foundation concluded that 'liking of the advertising' was the single strongest predictor of advertising effectiveness. Enjoyment motivates involvement and rewards learning from the ad.
- *Contain a clear simple message that viewers can take away.* This can be either a rational claim about product values and effectiveness (semantic knowing), or intuitive images that suggest an emotional benefit from using the product (episodic knowing).
- *Be strongly branded so that the message is firmly associated with the particular product being advertised.* Ideally, for learning to be effective, what is involving

in the ad should be closely connected to the message and the brand name to tie these three elements together. So, at the point of sale when the choice of product is being made among the packs on display, the images and associations from the ad can exert their influence.

Measures of these factors have been combined in the LINK™ test developed by Millward Brown as a tool to assess advertising effectiveness (Hollis 1995). It uses as indicators of involvement viewers' ratings of enjoyment and how active or passive the ad seems to be. There are also measures of how well the ad is branded, and ease of understanding.

Taken together, these measures of an ad before it goes on air can predict its success in gaining consumer awareness when it is shown on TV, and its impact on sales (Hollis 1995). Experience has shown that when a burst of advertising for a product goes on air (lasting perhaps three weeks), attitudes to that brand do not show any immediate change. Such attitudes do not change quickly and are dependent on experiencing the product itself as well as what the ads say. What does vary is *awareness* of the advertising being shown. This stimulates consumers to try (or retry) the brand, and increases purchasing by reminding them of the product and its benefits. In this way advertising awareness is related to product sales.

## Conclusions

Psychologists as experts in advertising research draw from the other roles of psychologists, such as theoretician, detached analyst, toolmaker and colleague. The contribution of the 'expert' lies in his or her breadth of knowledge, insight into a wide range of human behaviour, practical experience and skill in application. In practice, psychologists in advertising research work in multidisciplinary teams with advertisers, designers and brand managers, each of whom has their own perspective and priorities for the advertising. The function of the psychologist in this team is to emphasize the humanity of the marketplace, draw attention to consumers' experience and the limitations on their capacity to perceive and interpret ads, mediate between the minds of sellers and buyers, and draw attention to the psychological aspects of the exchange. Advertising agency and product managers responsible for making ads can become so close to their commercials that they can no longer see what the ad will look like to an ordinary shopper, who is not so motivated to get the message or pay as much attention to the fine detail of every twist and turn in the ad. The psychologist provides a bridge between the goals of those working in marketing and consumers' interests and realities, contemporary culture, and the social significance of products and media.

In this position, the expertise of psychologists is important in unravelling the many influences that act simultaneously on consumers in a complex world. It is also important in devising solutions which can assist in achieving the aims of marketers while taking into account the real values and priorities of the consumer. For example, mystery and intrigue can motivate involvement in an ad, but too much can make the ad obscure, esoteric and a 'turnoff'. Detail can be fascinating and hold attention, but too much can obscure the theme and the intended payoff. Human reactions are almost invariably a compromise between extremes. The skill of the psychologist is in guiding the marketing and advertising decisions to strike the right balance and gain the optimum response from the consumer. In relationships with other professionals involved in producing advertising, it is important that the psychologist as expert is seen as an ally working constructively to achieving the best solution, rather than as a critic of the creative inspiration for the ad.

---

### Discussion questions

1 What are the similarities and dissimilarities between the psychologist as expert in advertising research and in sports training?

2 Examine some TV ads and consider: what psychological theories or principles might have influenced their design? What mechanisms may influence their effectiveness either positively or negatively?

3 Early in this chapter, four principles for understanding consumer behaviour were outlined, but not all of them were discussed in detail. Consider in particular the first three and try to find practical illustrations of these principles.

---

## Further reading

Foxhall, G. R. and Goldsmith, R. E. (1994) *Consumer Psychology for Marketing*. London: Routledge. A broad-based textbook covering information processing, personality and lifestyles, social contexts and the ways they affect consumer decision making.

Gunter, B. and Furnham, A. (1998) *Children as Consumers*. London: Routledge. Describes how young people have become a significant target for advertisers, and discusses the stages through which they evolve as consumers.

Martin, D. and Kelly, J. (1996) *Research Works 3: Papers from the AMSO Research Effectiveness Awards*. London: NTC Publications. One of a series of books that illustrate the usefulness of market research on a wide range of commercial topics.

## References

Barker, D. (1980) *TA and Training*. Farnborough: Gower.

Berne, E. (1968) *Games People Play: The Psychology of Human Relationships*. Harmondsworth: Penguin.

Branthwaite, A. and Swindells, A. (1995) The way forward for advertising research. *Admap*, 355: 31–4.

Branthwaite, A. and Swindells, A. (1997) Capturing the complexity of advertising perceptions. *Marketing and Research Today*, 25(2): 86–95.

Broadbent, K. and Cooper, P. (1987) Research is good for you. *Marketing Intelligence and Planning*, 5: 3–9.

Brown, G. and Farr, A. (1994) Persuasion or enhancement – an experiment. *Market Research Society [MRS] Conference Papers, 1994.* London: MRS.

Cohen, J. (1970) *Homo Psychologicus.* London: George Allen and Unwin.

Eysenck, M. W. and Keane, M. T. (1995) *Cognitive Psychology: A Student's Handbook,* 3rd edn. Hove: Erlbaum.

Furnham, A. and Argyle, M. (1998) *The Psychology of Money.* London: Routledge.

Gordon, W. and Langmaid, R. (1988) *Qualitative Market Research.* Aldershot: Gower.

Gregory, R. L. (1972) Seeing as thinking. *Times Literary Supplement,* 23 June.

Hill, A. B. (1993) Non-conscious processes and semantic image profiling. *Journal of the Market Research Society,* 35(4): 315–23.

Hollis, N. S. (1995) Liking it or not, liking is not enough. *Journal of Advertising Research,* Sept./Oct.: 7–16.

North, A. C., Hargreaves, D. and McKendrick, J. (1997) In-store music affects product choice. *Nature* 390(6656): 132.

Packard, V. (1957) *The Hidden Persuaders.* Harmondsworth: Penguin.

Piaget, J. (1924) *The Language and Thought of the Child.* New York: Humanities Press.

Schudson, M. (1984) *Advertising: The Uneasy Persuasion.* New York: Basic Books.

Stewart, I. and Jones, V. (1987) *TA Today: A New Introduction to Transactional Analysis.* Nottingham: Lifespace.

Winnicott, D. W. (1980) *Playing and Reality.* Harmondsworth: Penguin.

# Chapter 6

# Improving sporting abilities: training concentration skills

## Aidan Moran

I once heard an 'expert' described, perhaps unkindly, as anyone wearing a suit and carrying a laptop computer and laser pointer who is more than 50 miles from home. If that is so, then I am definitely a novice! But if we go beyond appearances and define 'expertise' as the growth of specialist skills and knowledge through experience in a given field, then perhaps one does not have to leave one's office to provide expert advice to people. As we shall see, such help is required increasingly in the modern world of competitive sport. To illustrate, as a research psychologist with a special interest in concentration skills, I receive many inquiries from sports performers who are having difficulty in focusing properly in athletic situations. In this chapter, I shall explore the factors which cause these difficulties and also indicate how they can be overcome using some practical psychological techniques. But to begin with, here is a brief case study to illustrate why an athlete might consult a sport psychologist in the first place.

> Several years ago, a prominent touring professional golfer came to see me with a rather unusual problem. Sitting in my office, and leaning back on his chair, he complained: 'I'm too relaxed on the course'. Naturally, I was intrigued by this remark because relaxation is more often an asset than a problem for competitive athletes. When asked to explain himself, the golfer revealed that, over the previous few months, his scores in match-play events (where the objective is to defeat a direct opponent) tended to be better than those in stroke-play competitions (where the player who achieves the best score is the winner). 'The only conclusion I can come to', he said, 'is that I relax too much when I'm playing on my own'. Odd as it may seem, a log of his scores over a number of subsequent tournaments confirmed his initial observations. It was true that

his scores in match-play were significantly better than those in stroke-play, having controlled for the number of holes completed. But what could account for this curious inconsistency in his performance? Cutting a long story short, after several weeks of analysis and on-course assessment, it emerged that his problem lay in *poor concentration* rather than in excessive relaxation. Briefly, this player had learned to focus on the task at hand only when confronted by an immediate opponent face to face rather than at other times on the golf course. Clearly, the solution lay in training him to use some practical concentration techniques both before and during his round. As we shall see, these techniques are useful not only in golf but also can be applied equally successfully to other sports.

This vignette serves as a convenient introduction to sport psychology – a discipline that is concerned with the scientific study of psychological factors affecting athletic performance (incidentally, see p. 108 for relevant Internet sites). More precisely, it illuminates three aspects of this growing field. First, it shows that athletes tend to develop informal psychological theories in order to make sense of their sporting experiences. For example, it is significant that my client did not attribute the inconsistencies in his performance to any technical flaws in his game. Instead, he ascribed them to a psychological factor – an excessively casual attitude. Second, the case study highlights the importance to sport performers of concentration, meaning the ability to focus mental effort on what is most important in any situation (Moran 1996). As we shall see, this mental skill is trainable using certain principles and techniques borrowed from the more established field of cognitive psychology. Third, the vignette suggests that once athletes have practised sufficiently to master the technical skills of their chosen sport (thereby achieving a state of 'automaticity' of performance), it is the mental side of their game which holds the key to their subsequent success. Put simply, they begin to realize that although sport is played with the body, it is *won* largely in the mind. In this chapter, I shall try to weave these three strands of thought into a single theme. Specifically, concentration is a mental skill which is vital to athletic success and which can be improved through the systematic application of certain psychological techniques.

The chapter is organized as follows. To begin with, I shall introduce the 'mental side' of sport as a familiar yet intriguing domain. Then, delving further, I shall explain what 'concentration' is and why athletes tend to 'lose it' so easily in competitive situations. After that, the theory and practice of concentration skills training will be reviewed using a variety of examples from different sports. Next, I shall explain how sports performers can be taught to focus effectively in pressure situations. Finally, the changing role of the expert sport psychologist will be considered briefly.

## What is the 'mental side' of sport?

The mental side of sport is a domain which is paradoxically familiar yet mysterious. It is familiar because almost every day, we hear about or see athletes who make uncharacteristic performance errors as a result of temporary psychological influences such as excessive anxiety. For example, in pressure situations, top soccer players often miss penalty kicks (a fact which led former England coach Glenn Hoddle to observe that penalty taking is 'at least 50 per cent mental') and expert tennis players may make elementary errors (e.g. in the 1993 Wimbledon final, Jana Novotna hit *three consecutive double faults* before losing to Steffi Graf).

Interestingly, two findings have emerged from research on such cases of performance anxiety. First, tension effects (also known as 'choking', 'icing' or the 'yips') tend to be most prevalent in sports like cricket, snooker and golf where eye–hand coordination rather than physical strength is important. Thus when anxiety strikes, bowlers (especially left-arm spinners for some strange reason) find it difficult to let go of the ball, snooker players feel as if they cannot push their cue properly and darts players struggle to release their darts when throwing. This problem was described graphically by the snooker player Steve Davis, who won the world championship six times, when he said that anxiety makes one feel as if one were 'playing with someone else's arm'. In addition, research shows that 'choking' is definitely *not* caused by a lack of motivation. In fact, if anything, it occurs ironically as a consequence of *trying too hard* to perform well. I shall return to this point later when exploring why certain kinds of thinking (e.g. placing too much emphasis on the importance of the result) can be counterproductive in sport.

Even the world's best sport performers are prone to occasional errors due to psychological influences such as performance anxiety. Yet, despite their familiarity, mental influences on athletic performance are poorly understood – largely because cognitive researchers have not taken seriously the idea that sport is a suitable domain in which to study how the mind works. As a result of this neglect, psychologists have little understanding of how sports performers acquire the skill of 'mental toughness' or the capacity to focus effectively under adverse circumstances in competition.

To illustrate this skill in action, consider the fact that during the final set of a four-hour quarter-final match against Jim Courier in the 1995 Australian Open Tennis Championship, Pete Sampras broke down in tears after he had heard that his coach was dying of a brain tumour. But astonishingly, Sampras won the match by conceding *only two points* on his serve in that final set – despite weeping openly during changeovers. This remarkable feat would have been impossible without superb powers of concentration. But what exactly is 'concentration' and why do athletes lose it so easily? How can it be improved in sport situations? What techniques do athletes use to remain focused in pressure situations? In this chapter, I shall try to provide some answers to these questions.

## What is 'concentration' and why do we lose it?

Psychologists use the term 'attention' to refer to at least two different types of mental processes. On the one hand, it denotes concentration or the ability to focus mental effort on what is most important in any situation while ignoring distractions – a skill known as 'selective attention'. On the other hand, attention also designates a form of mental timesharing whereby, as a result of extensive practice, people can learn to perform two concurrent tasks equally well. This process is also called 'divided attention'. In this chapter, we are concerned more with the former than the latter usage – in other words, with attention as concentration rather than as mental timesharing ability.

Concentration may be likened to a mental spotlight which we shine at things in which we are interested. When that interest reaches such a state of absorption that there is no difference between what we are thinking about and what we are doing, then we are truly 'focused'. For example, consider how the Irish swimmer Michelle de Bruin, a triple gold medallist Olympic champion, described this coveted state of mind: 'I was never more focused for a race. No looking about, tunnel vision all the way . . . my concentration was so intense that I almost forgot to look up to see my time after touching the finishing pads' (Roche 1995: 1). Interestingly, this type of peak experience can occur only if performers concentrate on actions that are specific, relevant to the task at hand and, above all, under their own control. This principle underlies effective concentration techniques in sport (see Moran 1996).

Unfortunately, our concentration system is rather fragile due to a combination of evolutionary and psychological factors. Thus on the one hand, our survival as a species depended on the ability to concentrate for long enough to enable us to learn new skills. But on the other hand, the capacity to switch attention rapidly is also adaptive – otherwise we would not have been able to react successfully to sudden threats from the environment. To complicate matters, our concentration span is linked to short-term (or working) memory processes which are known to be fragile. Put simply, this part of the memory system determines the amount of mental resources that are available for paying conscious attention to something. But whenever we focus on factors which are either irrelevant to the job at hand or out of our control, we use up this energy and 'lose' our concentration. As a result, our performance usually suffers. For example, in the quarter-final of the 1993 French Open tennis championship, the Argentine player Gabriela Sabatini lost a match against Mary-Jo Fernandez even though at one stage she needed only one more point for victory. Remarkably, in a post-match interview, she admitted that she had lost her concentration at that point simply because she had speculated idly about who would win the other section of the tournament.

Sabatini's experience shows us that concentration is never really 'lost', merely redirected at some target that is irrelevant to the task at hand. In everyday life, this experience happens quite regularly. To illustrate, have you ever had the experience of discovering that you have been reading the same sentence in a book over and over again without comprehension because your mind is miles away? If so, then you have distracted yourself by allowing a memory or daydream to become the target of your attention – a problem which can be overcome by writing down two or three specific study questions before you approach a textbook or notes (Moran 1997). But internal distractions are not the only threats to our concentration – external circumstances also clamour for our attention. To illustrate, notice how difficult it is to study in a room if someone else is watching television there. Apart from the obvious distractions posed by the sound and pictures, there is the added frustration of not being in control of the situation. Like students, athletes have to learn to concentrate selectively – especially when performing in front of a hostile crowd. For example, in the 1998 US Open golf tournament in San Francisco, the Scottish player Colin Montgomerie had to ignore unprecedented abuse from spectators who sneered at him and urged him to go home as he competed. Fortunately, he ignored such provocation and scored well in the tournament.

In sport, distractions fall into two main categories: external and internal (Moran 1996). External distractions consist of environmental factors such as sharp changes in noise levels, sudden movements from other people and unpredictable variations in surface or weather conditions. By contrast, internal distractions are self-generated concerns which arise from our own thoughts and feelings. Typical examples in this category include wondering what might happen in the future, regretting what has happened in the past, worrying about what other people might say or do, and feeling tired, bored or otherwise emotionally upset. Although we cannot usually alter external sources of distraction, we can learn to become accustomed to them. One way of doing this is to practise in their presence. The logic here is that by training under special conditions which simulate anticipated distractions, one can learn to habituate to or ignore them when they occur. This practice, which is known as 'adversity training', is increasingly popular among performers in both individual and team sports. For example, Darrell Pace, an Olympic archery champion, trained himself to ignore distractions by deliberately practising under noisy conditions (e.g. by setting up his target near railroad tracks or motorways). Similarly, as preparation for the 1992 Olympic Games, the Australian women's hockey team participated in simulated exercises involving potentially distracting changes in tournament rules, media exposure and transport arrangements.

So far, we have seen that the ability to block out distractions is crucial in sport. But there is more to concentration than simply ignoring irrelevant information. In fact, at least three additional skills are required by athletes. First, they must have a clear objective or target in mind (see the section on 'goal setting', pp. 100–2). Second, they must be able to break up that objective into specific 'action steps' (i.e. tasks which they can perform to take them closer to their goal). Finally, they must be able to refocus their minds periodically. To illustrate these skills in action, consider how the famous golfer Jack Nicklaus managed to stay focused under difficult conditions. At two holes down with two to play, he hit an amazing recovery shot which helped him to draw the match. When asked afterwards how he had managed to concentrate under such pressure, he uttered the immortal words: 'The ball doesn't know the score!' (Golf quotes in this chapter are taken from MacRury 1997.) Although this insight may seem trite, it conceals a wealth of Zen-like wisdom. Specifically, what it shows is that by concentrating on the immediate challenge of the situation, one can remain 'task focused' rather than 'result focused'. In other words, Nicklaus concentrated effectively by focusing on the performance of the job – not on its possible outcome – and so he avoided the mistake of wondering about what might happen in the future. Unfortunately, it is difficult to avoid thinking about results when playing any sport – especially if one has too much time available for reflection. This issue of having too much time to think raises the question of how the structure of a sport can affect its psychological difficulty.

## How does the structure of a sport affect its mental demands?

Sports vary significantly in the physical demands which they make on performers. For example, within athletics, sprinting requires a short burst of explosive power whereas marathon running demands a steady pace and great stamina. In a similar way, we can explore the possible psychological requirements of different sports. Thus, whereas some sports (like weightlifting or certain swimming events) require short periods of intense concentration for limited durations, others (e.g. road cycling) demand sustained alertness for longer periods of time. But what causes such differences?

Interestingly, the mental demands of sports are usually attributable to structural factors. For example, consider some differences between soccer and snooker. Whereas the former is a timed, physical contact, team game, the latter is an untimed, non-contact, individual sport. Not surprisingly, these sports differ considerably in their psychological demands. For example, whereas motivation, communication skills, bravery and an ability to anticipate opponents' moves are vital for soccer players, snooker performers depend more on cognitive skills like concentration and decision making. After all, a footballer can try to win the ball back off an opponent by chasing and tackling, but a snooker player can only sit and watch while the opponent is potting balls on the table. So, the structure of a sport affects its psychological requirements.

Let us now explore this idea in more detail by considering the psychological demands of another two sports – golf and tennis. To help you to discover the mental side of these pursuits, see if you can relate to the questions in Box 6.1.

If you answered 'yes' to most of the questions, then you have personal experience of the psychological demands of golf or tennis. But have you ever wondered what causes such demands? Briefly, although golf and tennis differ in obvious ways (e.g. you cannot play tennis on your own), they share several mental requirements. First, they are largely untimed activities. Therefore, if golfers and tennis players want to perform well, they cannot allow themselves to rush their shots simply because they are in a hurry to finish the match. Second, these sports place great demands on participants' concentration processes because of the discontinuous, stop–start nature of the action which they generate. To illustrate this point, consider the proportion of thinking time to playing time in a typical game of golf or tennis. Remarkably, research suggests that less than 20 per cent of total match time in these sports is spent hitting the ball. Clearly, at least 80 per cent of the time on the golf course or tennis court is devoted to such non-technical activities as walking, planning, worrying, regretting, getting distracted, becoming nervous

---

*Box 6.1*  **Exploring the mental side of your golf or tennis**

Please read the questions below and answer them with a 'yes' or 'no'.

1 Have you ever hit a poor shot early in the round or match and interpreted it as a sure sign that you were going to play badly on that day?
2 Do you find it difficult to clear your mind of negative images (such as hitting a ball out of bounds or double faulting) as you prepare to play a shot?
3 Is it difficult for you to forget about bad shots or missed opportunities while you play?
4 Have you ever made excuses to yourself about your performance before, during or after a game?
5 Do you get angry with yourself when you make mistakes?
6 Have you ever noticed that if you become too conscious of the score, you begin to play badly?

---

or even making excuses in advance of the result! This factor may explain why the golfer Sam Snead once remarked that thinking rather than acting was the 'number 1 golf disease'. A third reason why competitive golf and tennis are tough mentally is because players have to take responsibility for their own actions during a game. There are no team mates, substitutes or coaches available to help them if disaster strikes. The final source of mental difficulty in golf or tennis comes from people's natural tendency to think too far ahead – as happened so calamitously to Gabriela Sabatini (see p. 95). Unfortunately, golfers and tennis players often engage in 'fortune telling' or trying to predict what might happen in the future rather than concentrating on the present shot. For example, when asked why he had missed a 3-foot putt on the eighteenth green to win the British Open Championship in 1970, Doug Sanders replied simply: 'I made the mistake about thinking which section of the crowd I was going to bow to' (Gilleece 1997: 23). Clearly, lapses in concentration can be disastrous. In summary, golf and tennis are demanding mentally because they are untimed, discontinuous and individual games whose scoring system punishes any lapses in concentration.

In the light of these structural factors, the mental challenge for golfers and tennis players is to learn to concentrate on only one shot at a time. They have to hit the ball without thinking about themselves or the score. Psychologically, this challenge can be facilitated by learning to restructure the game in their minds not as a competition involving eighteen holes or three sets but as a series of separate contests which test their ability to play the ball accurately towards a specific target. Using this technique of cognitive restructuring, one can develop the skill of staying in the present mentally. Accordingly, one can learn to become task-conscious (i.e. aware only of the job that one has to perform right now) rather than result-conscious (i.e. worrying about the score) or self-conscious (i.e. worrying about how one appears to others). Incidentally, the hazards of becoming self-conscious when performing a sport skill have been demonstrated experimentally by Masters (1992) who studied the phenomenon of 'paralysis by analysis'. But what strategies do athletes use to help them to concentrate effectively or to become appropriately task-conscious?

## Training concentration skills in athletes

The importance of concentration skills to athletes is attested to by anecdotal reports as well as by empirical evidence. To illustrate the former, Ken Doherty, the 1997 World Snooker Champion, claimed that snooker requires 'concentration, focus – it's not just about potting balls' (cited in Doogan 1996: 8). Similarly, Teddy Sheringham, the England soccer star, revealed that he had learned from the German striker Jurgen Klinsmann that 'you have to concentrate all the time so when a chance comes you're going to take it' (cited in Lovejoy 1995: 19).

Complementing such anecdotal reports is empirical evidence derived from research on the peak performance experiences of athletes. Briefly, these studies show that athletes tend to achieve their best performances when they are totally focused on the task at hand (Jackson 1995). This state of mind was captured neatly by golfer Darren Clarke when he remarked, after a tournament victory, that his ball 'was on the club-face for so long I could almost tell it where I wanted it to go' (cited in Kimmage 1998: 29L). Another example of intense absorption in the present moment was provided by the British athlete, David Hemery, an Olympic gold medallist, who described his moment of triumph in Mexico City in 1968 in the following terms:

> Only a couple of times in my life have I felt in such condition that my mind and body worked as one. This was one of those times. My limbs reacted as my mind was thinking: total control, which resulted in absolute freedom. Instead of forcing and working my legs, they responded with the speed and in the motions that were being asked of them.
>
> (cited in Jones 1995: 10)

Given the importance of concentration, coaches have experimented with a variety of techniques to improve athletes' focusing skills. Unfortunately, some of these techniques are rather unconventional, if not unethical. For example, it is reported that when Tiger Woods was 12 years old, his father used to simulate distractions for him during a practice round so that he could learn to ignore them subsequently in competition (recall our discussion of 'adversity training' on p. 96). These distractions included such deliberate ploys as having a practice partner dropping a bag of clubs just as Tiger was preparing to play, saying loudly 'Don't hit it into the water' as he was addressing the ball, and standing in his line of sight as he was lining up a putt. But if we leave aside such questionable practices, what practical techniques can be used to improve the concentration of golfers?

Psychologists recommend at least five concentration techniques for sports performers. All of them are based on the principle that we are focused when our minds are directed at actions that are specific, relevant and under our own control (Moran 1998). These concentration techniques include:

- specifying performance goals
- using pre-performance routines
- controlling arousal
- using trigger words
- engaging in mental practice or 'visualization'.

## Specifying performance goals

Goals are targets or objectives which we strive to achieve. Without goals, our drive or energy would go to waste. For example, imagine sitting in a car that is being driven around in circles. Although energy is being expended, you are not actually going anywhere. By analogy, in order to make progress in any sport, athletes need a goal or signpost to point them in the right direction. But what if that goal is outside their control – like winning a tournament in golf? In that case, far from facilitating their concentration, the goal is likely to distract performers because it will encourage them to think too far ahead (recall what happened to Doug Sanders). For this reason, 'result goals' such as winning competitions tend to hamper rather than improve the concentration of top athletes because 'winning' is outside their control. For example, a swimmer could produce a 'personal best' time in a race but still not win the event because on the day, a rival could have swum faster. Therefore, it is a popular misconception to believe that sport psychologists teach athletes to focus on winning.

Instead, athletes are encouraged to set performance goals, or actions which are under their own control, to help them to concentrate on what they can do right now. For example, penalty kickers in soccer are trained to focus only on where they intend to place the ball rather than worrying about whether or not the goalkeeper will save the shot. Interestingly, there is some research evidence to support the value of performance goals as concentration techniques. Thus Jackson and Roberts (1992) discovered that collegiate athletes tended to give their worst performances when they were too preoccupied by result goals. Conversely, their best displays coincided with a concern for performance goals.

In general, goal setting seems to work best when it is practised according to certain rational principles. For example, Bull *et al.* (1996) recommend the SMART approach in this area (see Box 6.2). Using this approach, you can learn to concentrate more effectively in your chosen sport by asking yourself the following questions.

1 Are your goals *specific* enough or expressed in clear behavioural terms? Psychologists have found that the clearer and more specific one's goal is, the more likely one is to achieve it. For example, instead of saying 'I'd like to improve my tennis', one should say to oneself 'I'm going to work on the accuracy of my serve today with the objective of hitting six balls in a row into the service box'.

2 Are your goals *measurable*? Unless one receives feedback about the progress one is making towards one's goal, one may become discouraged and give up. The best feedback comes from keeping a log or record of one's performance over a number of practice sessions. For example, if you are training for a marathon, you could record your practice times for different

---

*Box 6.2*   **The SMART approach to goal setting**

To be effective, goal setting should follow certain principles. These principles are best explained by using the acronym SMART (Bull *et al.* 1996). Briefly, each letter of this acronym stands for a different feature of an effective goal.

*S = specific*

The clearer and more specific your goal is, the more likely you are to achieve it.

*M = measurable*

If you cannot measure your progress towards your goal, then you will quickly lose interest in it. So, it is important to keep a regular log or record of your progress towards your objective.

*A = action related*

Unless you identify a number of action steps (i.e. tasks which take you a step nearer to your goal and which involve specific actions that are under your control) for each of your goals, you may feel confused about what to do next.

*R = realistic*

Your goals should be realistic for your present level of ability.

*T = timetabled*

Most people do not begin jobs until the deadline for their completion approaches. In other words, timetables force us to concentrate on what we have to do.

*Source*: Bull *et al.* (1996)

---

distances as you build up your stamina. The importance of charting one's progress is captured neatly by the phrase 'ink it – don't just think it!'

3 Are your goals linked clearly to concrete *actions*? Research shows that goals which give rise to specific actions are more motivating than those which are more abstract. For example, saying 'I shall go for a 3-mile walk three times a week' is more likely to encourage you than is the phrase 'I wish I could become fitter'.

4 Are your goals *realistic* given your present ability? For example, you cannot expect to lower your handicap in golf unless you take lessons from a coach and practise regularly.

5 Do you have a specific *timetable* for your goals? Just as you would not plan a long journey without taking its timescale into consideration, you should develop the habit of indicating a period by which you expect to achieve certain targets in your chosen activity. For example, if you would like to

run a marathon later this year, you will have to work out a timetable by which you will run progressively increasing distances.

In summary, we have seen that sportspeople can be trained to work SMARTer rather than harder. In addition, there is evidence that performance goals can improve athletes' concentration by encouraging present focused, task relevant thinking rather than idle speculation about possible future results.

## Using pre-performance routines

Have you ever noticed that many sport stars follow systematic sequences of preparatory actions before they perform key skills? These sequences are called pre-performance routines and are used by athletes as practical concentration techniques – especially for actions (e.g. the tennis serve or the basketball 'free throw') which can be executed without interference from other people. Thus tennis players tend to bounce the ball a standard number of times before they serve and golfers take the same number of practice swings each time before they play a shot. These habits are not accidental. Instead, they reflect a deliberate attempt by athletes to focus only on what they can control, thereby minimizing irrelevant thoughts about future results.

Routines are believed to improve concentration for three main reasons. First, they encourage athletes to develop an appropriate mental 'set' for skill execution by helping them to focus their thoughts only on task relevant information. For example, golfers may concentrate only on keeping their head steady while putting. Second, routines ensure that athletes remain focused on the here and now rather than on what happened in the past or on what may occur in the future. As US golfer Paul Azinger remarked, 'Staying in the present is the key to the golfer's game. Once you start thinking about a shot you just missed or on what you have to do on the next nine to catch somebody, you're lost'. Finally, routines help players to generate appropriate discipline and moods. To paraphrase William James, 'it is easier to act your way into a feeling than to feel your way into an action'.

Different sports present different opportunities to use pre-performance routines. For example, in tennis, squash or badminton, they can be used between points or at changeovers during a match. In rugby, they can be used prior to line-outs and scrums. Soccer players can use routines before goal kicks, throw ins and free kicks. Regardless of where they are used, there is significant research evidence to support the claim that routines can improve athletes' concentration and performance. For example, Crews and Boutcher (1986) compared the performances of two groups of golfers – those who had been given an eight-week training programme of swing practice only and those who had participated in a practice-plus-routine programme for the same duration. Results revealed that the more proficient golfers benefited more from using routines than did the less skilled players.

If you would like to develop a pre-serve routine in tennis, follow the instructions in Box 6.3.

Having learned what routines are and why they reduce distractibility, it is time to consider one final issue. What is the difference between routines and superstitions? Sport psychologists believe that routines may be distinguished

---

*Box 6.3*   **Developing a pre-serve routine in tennis**

An effective pre-shot routine takes you comfortably and at your own pace from thinking to acting, or from conscious control to automatic pilot. Based on what top players do, here is a pre-serve routine which you can use to improve your tennis skills. Four steps are involved: assess the situation, get ready, visualize the serve and release it.

1 Assess the situation to decide the target and type of serve that is required. Would you like to serve to your opponent's forehand or backhand side? Are you going to go for placement, power or spin?
2 Get into the ready position, glance at your target, exhale gently and bounce the ball for rhythm.
3 Pause for a second to 'see' and 'feel' the serve that you want to play. Can you visualize it in your mind's eye hitting the target in your opponent's service box? Once you have pictured this serve mentally, glance at your target once again.
4 Clear your mind, toss the ball up high and let your body and racket do the rest.

---

from superstitions on two main grounds. First, there is the issue of control. A superstition arises from the belief that one's fate is governed by factors outside one's control. In other words, the player feels controlled by a conviction. For example, the South African golfer Ernie Els never plays with a ball marked with the number '2' because he associates 2 with bad luck. But a player is fully in control of the components of his or her pre-shot routine, and so these components can be shortened if necessary (e.g. under adverse weather conditions). Unfortunately, the opposite is true of superstitious rituals: they tend to grow longer as more and more behavioural links are added to the chain. A second criterion which may be used to distinguish between routines and rituals concerns the technical role of each behavioural step followed. To explain, whereas each part of a routine should be justifiable logically, the components of a ritual tend to seem irrational. Despite these conceptual distinctions, the pre-shot routines of many golfers are often invested with a superstitious quality.

## Controlling arousal

Peak performances in sport are usually associated with a relaxed state of mind (which is why I was surprised by the problem reported by my golfing client at the beginning of this chapter). Conversely, when anxiety strikes, people's attention span seems to narrow dramatically and they become preoccupied with worries rather than plans. This drain of mental energy leaves little attention left for concentration on task relevant actions. Not surprisingly, therefore, athletes are advised to slow down and try to lower their arousal level whenever they feel nervous. The logic here is that the more relaxed we are, the 'wider' our concentration beam becomes and the more efficiently we can perform concurrent tasks. Therefore, physical relaxation is often recommended by sport psychologists as a concentration technique. For example, archers and rifle shooters are taught to centre themselves by exhaling gently as they aim at their targets. Similarly, gymnasts are encouraged to develop awareness of their bodily feelings by focusing alternately on contracted and relaxed muscle groups while training for competition. In team sports like soccer or rugby, physical relaxation can be achieved when the ball is out of play simply by slowing down, lowering one's shoulders from time to time and by focusing on breathing deeply.

Interestingly, there is a connection between arousal control and the practice of grunting in tennis players. To explain, many coaches believe that if you exhale as you make contact with the ball, then your timing and rhythm are enhanced. The logic here is that tension causes us to hold our breath in – which, in turn, upsets the tempo of our swing. By contrast, breathing out gently as one hits the ball should improve the quality of the stroke. The increasingly noisy behaviour of tennis players is attributable, in part, to this belief in the power of synchronizing exhalation with hitting the ball.

## Using trigger words

Most sports performers talk to themselves covertly as they train or compete. For example, gymnasts may use words like 'forward' to remind themselves to push their bodies upwards while practising a floor routine. Swimmers may use a technical phrase like 'kick hard' to elicit a key movement in a certain stroke. Tennis players may cue a good service action by telling themselves to 'reach and hit'. The purpose of these instructional verbal triggers is to help athletes to refocus their minds on task relevant cues just before skill execution. For example, when standing over a putt, golfers may use phrases like 'steady head' to prevent themselves from looking up to see the result of their stroke. Unfortunately, 'trigger words' are not always helpful to athletes. Thus if they develop the habit of criticizing their own mistakes harshly, they may succeed only in distracting themselves from the task at hand. This practice is known as 'negative self-talk'.

## Engaging in mental practice or 'visualization'

The term mental practice or visualization refers to the systematic use of mental imagery in order to rehearse physical actions. It is advocated as a concentration technique by such world class athletes as Jim Courier (tennis), Michael Jordan (basketball) and Nancy Kerrigan (figure skating) and involves seeing and feeling a skill in one's imagination before actually executing it (Moran 1996).

Although mental practice has been shown to improve skilled performance (e.g. see review by Driskell *et al.* 1994), its status as a concentration technique is uncertain. However, it is possible that visualization works by helping athletes to concentrate on and 'chunk' symbolically the sequence of movements which they are trying to learn. In other words, imagery facilitates memory which, in turn, produces automaticity of the skill being rehearsed covertly. If so, then mental imagery can be useful in helping

---

*Box 6.4* **Visualizing a walk through your home**

Visualization is a powerful concentration technique because it encourages us to focus on what is under our control. Here is an exercise in which you can practise going on a mental walk through your home. Before you begin, make sure that you are sitting in a relaxed position and breathing slowly and regularly. Try to empty your mind of all distractions and concentrate on seeing, in your mind's eye, the home in which you live at present.

Imagine standing in front of your home on a warm, sunny day. Look up slowly and try to count the number of windows that are visible. Now, point to each window you can see and count the total number silently to yourself. Walk slowly up the driveway. What can you see on the left and on the right of the path? Try to hear the sound of your feet as you walk up to the front door. Look at the door very carefully and notice its colour and texture. Now, take out your door key from your pocket. Feel the weight and coldness of the key in your hand and notice how it slides gently into the lock. Turn the key slowly and feel the door opening. If you have an alarm, you'd better turn it off as it's making a high pitched beeping tone. Is the hall light on or off? Now, make sure that the front door is closed behind you. Take off your coat, hang it up and walk slowly into the kitchen. Walk over to a cupboard, open it and take down an empty glass. Then, turn on the tap and fill the glass with cool water. Notice how the water splashed over the side of the glass. Now, turn off the tap, sit down and drink the glass of water slowly. Notice how cool and refreshing it tastes. Next, walk over to the sink, rinse the glass and leave it aside. Then, walk out of the kitchen and into the living room. Sit down in your favourite chair or sofa and feel yourself begin to relax completely. You're happy to be home.

Now, using your imagination in the same way, try to visualize a situation which you will face shortly. This situation could be a meeting, a seminar presentation or a sporting encounter in which you are involved. Allow your mind to see and feel all the actions that you want to perform in this situation. Try to experience all the sights and sounds and sensations associated with this situation. Now, see yourself performing smoothly and confidently in this setting.

---

athletes to focus on task relevant information when preparing to play. In order to give you some practical experience of visualization in action, try the exercise in Box 6.4.

At least five practical guidelines arise from research on mental practice. First, visualization is a skill which improves with practice. For example, close your eyes and imagine standing in front of the house in which you live. How many windows can you see in your mind's eye? Count them. If you have difficulty with this exercise, you may need to pay more attention to the visual world around you. Transferring this skill to your favourite sport, close your eyes to find out if you can see and feel yourself performing a specific skill (e.g. a tennis serve). With practice, this type of mental rehearsal will become easier for you. Second, develop the habit of positive visualization – imagining the target you wish to hit rather than the hazard which you wish to avoid in your sport. Third, when creating a vivid mental image of your shot, try to combine as many of your senses as possible. For example, if you are a golfer, you should be able to 'see' the flight of the shot, 'hear' the sound of the club hitting the ball and 'feel' the weight of the club in your hand. Fourth, visualization works best when it is alternated with periods of physical practice. Finally, try to visualize actions rather than results – in other words, picture the shot you want to play next rather than the score that it may lead to in the future.

## How do athletes concentrate under pressure?

What does the word 'pressure' mean to you? Do you think that it is inevitable in sport? For most people, anxiety is associated with tension, fear of failure and negative thoughts. In addition, people tend to believe that pressure is inevitable simply because the purpose of competition is to determine a winner. But if we analyse where anxiety comes from, we shall discover that pressure is neither inevitable nor insuperable in sport because one can learn to turn pressure situations into enjoyable challenges. Clearly, that is what successful athletes have to do in competitive situations where fame and fortune are at stake.

At the outset, we must draw a distinction between pressure and pressure situations. To explain, pressure is a fear response to a situation which we interpret as posing a threat to us in some way. For example, soccer players might be afraid of making a mistake, losing the ball to an opponent, letting their club down, or of looking foolish in front of team mates. Although the targets of these fears are largely imaginary, they still manage to make us feel tense, pessimistic and agitated. But whereas pressure is a subjective fear-based reaction to something, a 'pressure situation' may be described in objective terms. For example, being a goal down with three minutes to play in a cup match is a stressful situation for most players. But there are some athletes who do not seem to feel pressure in such situations. Why? Because they realize that although we cannot change a pressure situation, we can change our reaction to it. In other words, by restructuring the situation differently in our minds, we can learn to interpret it as a challenge to our abilities rather than as a threat to our well-being. Hence, it becomes exciting not dreadful. For example, when Jack Nicklaus was asked if he ever got nervous on the course, he replied: 'Sure, I get nervous – but that's the fun of it – to put yourself in the position of being nervous, being excited. I never look on it as pressure. I look on it as fun and excitement. That's why you're doing it!' So, how can you turn pressures into challenges? Here is a practical exercise to test your ability to concentrate under pressure.

Think of a pressure situation that occurs in your sport or in your daily life. Now, describe the fear it causes in you by finishing the following sentence: 'I hate the pressure of . . .'. For example, you might say, 'I hate the pressure of facing a tricky 4-foot putt to halve a hole in match-play'. Or 'I hate the pressure of facing exams when I have not studied for them'.

Now, think of this pressure situation again. But this time, try to look at it differently by restructuring it in your mind. Then, use this new way of looking at the situation to finish the following sentence: 'I love the challenge of . . .' . Remember that you are not allowed to repeat the words you used previously. For example, you cannot write, 'I love the challenge of facing a tricky 4-foot putt to halve a hole in match-play' or 'I love the challenge of facing exams when I have not studied for them'.

The solution to this problem is to pick something else to focus on in your pressure situation besides the target of your fear (e.g. the possibility of missing the putt or of failing the exam). Remember that the secret of effective concentration is to focus on an action that is specific, relevant and under your own control in that situation. Usually this means concentrating on some aspect of one's preparation for the feared situation. For example, you could write 'I love the challenge of preparing in the same way for every putt – no matter how important it might be' or 'I love the challenge of using what I know to answer what I am asked in an exam'.

Successful athletes cope with pressure situations by using two key psychological principles. First, they realize that pressure is in the eye of the beholder. Therefore, they do not have to experience anxiety in a pressure situation – especially if they can identify the specific challenge which that situation poses for them. Second, they realize that feeling nervous in a pressure situation is a perfectly normal response. All it really means is that you care about what you are doing and that your body is primed and ready for action. In summary, it is possible to maintain concentration under pressure if you channel your nervous energy into actions that are specific, relevant and under your own control.

# New directions

Where do we go from here in exploring the concentration processes of athletes? At least three potentially fruitful areas for further research may be identified. First, additional research is required to investigate the nature and consequences of internal or self-generated distractions experienced by sport performers in competitive situations. Traditionally, the effect of people's own thoughts, feelings and emotions on their attentional processes has been ignored by cognitive researchers. This neglect is due partly to a methodological bias. Specifically, it proved easier to measure external influences than internal influences on people's concentration, and so the methods available for research dictated the type of questions that were studied. Perhaps that is why you will not find any discussion of internal sources of distraction in most textbooks of cognitive psychology. Fortunately, this situation is changing rapidly as researchers begin to make progress in understanding self-generated lapses in mental control. For example, consider the common

---

*Box 6.5*  **Sport psychology on the Internet**

*American Society for the Advancement of Applied Sport Psychology*

http://spot.colorado.edu/~aaasp/

*American Psychological Association – Division 47 (Sport and Exercise Psychology)*

http://www.psyc.unt.edu/apadiv47/

*North American Society for Psychology of Sport and Physical Activity*

http://grove.ufl.edu/~naspspa/

---

experience whereby the harder one tries to fall asleep, the more one stays awake. Also, it often happens that the more we try to suppress a particular thought, the more tenaciously it clings to our consciousness. In an effort to explain such ironic mental phenomena, Wegner (1994) suggested that the mind wanders *because* we try to control it. This intriguing theory, which hinges on a distinction between deliberate (intentional) and unconscious (ironic) processes, has obvious implications for sport. For example, athletes often report that in pressure situations, negative commands (e.g. 'don't double fault') are counterproductive – producing the opposite result from that which they had intended. Clearly, research is required to identify why such ironic 'rebound effects' occur in these circumstances.

A second line of investigation worth pursuing involves the task of exploring 'meta-attentional' processes in athletes – their theories about how their concentration systems work. This topic is fascinating because, as is evident from interviews with athletes, most sports performers have developed informal models of the way in which their minds work (e.g. recall the opening vignette in this chapter). Do such models become more sophisticated with increasing expertise? How accurate are they? How do they change as athletes learn to use new concentration techniques? Unfortunately, we have no answers to any of these questions.

As a third suggestion for further research, we should try to improve the measurement of individual differences in concentration processes in athletes. At present, no satisfactory psychometric test exists for this purpose. In summary, by exploring the areas I have indicated, a bridge can be built between sport psychology and mainstream psychology.

Finally, Box 6.5 lists some web sites for sport psychology.

## Changing role of the expert sport psychologist

At first glance, the opening case study shows that athletes can learn to understand and control their own mental processes (in this case, concentration skills) by seeking practical advice from psychologists. The relationship between a sport psychologist and an athlete seems to be analogous to that between a physician and a patient in the sense that an explanation and treatment are provided for the patient's problem. But closer inspection reveals several serious limitations to this medical model when applied to sport psychology (Kremer and Scully 1998). First, it puts the burden of responsibility on the 'expert' to 'cure' the problem. This situation encourages a sense of dependency in athletes which may hamper their growth towards self-reliance. Second, 'expert' sport psychologists are often on shaky ground theoretically because many of the intervention techniques which they recommend have not been validated adequately as yet. Third, the distinction between 'expert' and 'client' ignores the fact that sportspeople, including athletes and coaches, are naive psychologists. For example, recall that my golfing client already had a theoretical explanation for his performance problem when he came to see me. Similarly, coaches develop psychological theories to account for the behaviour of players. In both cases, these theories need to be deconstructed through discussion before a client can be helped.

Taken together, these three problems highlight the weaknesses of the traditional role of the expert sport psychologist. Fortunately, a new model for the delivery of sport psychological services is emerging (see Kremer and Scully 1998). Briefly, this model identifies the *coach* rather than the athlete as the primary target for psychological education. Accordingly, the role of the sport psychologist changes from that of a medical expert to that of a management consultant – somebody who works as part of a team with the coach/manager and the support staff. Of course, this new model does not eliminate the need for individual consultation. There will always be situations which warrant one-to-one interactions between athletes and sport psychologists. But what *does* change in this new approach is the expectation that sport psychologists are 'mind benders' who provide some arcane expertise to athletes who are beyond the help of their coaches. It is only when such myths are dispelled that either theoretical or practical progress is possible in sport psychology.

## Discussion questions

1 What kinds of distractions do athletes mention when they talk about the difficulties of focusing properly in their sport? Interviews with leading local sport performers will help you to answer this question. In addition, you can scan the sports sections of newspapers and make a file of relevant feature articles, quotations and match reports.

2 In what way does the efficacy of a particular concentration technique depend on the nature (e.g. individual versus team game) and structure (e.g. timed versus untimed) of a sport?

3 Do you find it difficult to concentrate effectively when you are studying? If so, which of the concentration techniques described in this chapter might be of help to you?

4 What does the word 'pressure' mean to you? Using the cognitive restructuring technique explained in this chapter, can you turn a pressure situation in your life into a challenge?

## Further reading

Cox, R. H. (1998) *Sport Psychology: Concepts and Applications*, 4th edn. Boston, MA: W. C. Brown. A recent textbook on sport psychology.

Kremer, J. and Scully, D. (1994) *Psychology in Sport*. London: Taylor and Francis. An excellent textbook which links sport psychology to mainstream psychology.

Moran, A. P. (1996) *The Psychology of Concentration in Sport Performers: A Cognitive Analysis*. Hove: Psychology Press / Taylor and Francis. A review of psychological research on concentration processes and techniques in athletes from different sports.

## References

Bull, S. J., Albinson, J. G. and Shambrook, C. J. (1996) *The Mental Game Plan*. East-bourne: Sport Dynamics.

Crews, D. J. and Boutcher, S. H. (1986) Effects of structured preshot behaviours on beginning golf performance. *Perceptual and Motor Skills*, 62: 291–4.

Doogan, B. (1996) Doherty is happier. *The Title*, 1 December: 8.

Driskell, J. E., Copper, C. and Moran, A. (1994) Does mental practice enhance perform-ance? *Journal of Applied Psychology*, 79: 481–92.

Gilleece, D. (1997) Sanders reflects on a missed putt and missed boats. *Irish Times*, 2 September.

Jackson, S. A. (1995) Factors influencing the occurrence of flow state in elite athletes. *Journal of Applied Sport Psychology*, 7: 138–66.

Jackson, S. A. and Roberts, G. C. (1992) Positive performance states of athletes: toward a conceptual understanding of peak performance. *Sport Psychologist*, 6: 156–71.

Jones, S. (1995) Inside the mind of perfection. *The Independent*, 11 December: 10.

Kimmage, P. (1998) I could almost tell the ball where to go. *Independent on Sunday*, 24 May: 29L.

Kremer, J. and Scully, D. (1998) What applied psychologists often don't do: on em-powerment and independence, in H. Steinberg, I. Cockerill and A. Dewey (eds) *What Do Sport Psychologists Do?* Leicester: Occasional Paper, Sport and Exercise Psychology Section, British Psychological Society.

Lovejoy, J. (1995) England's striking success. *Sunday Times (Sport Section)*, 3 December: 19.

MacRury, D. (1997) *Golfers on Golf*. London: Virgin.

Masters, R. S. W. (1992) Knowledge, 'knerves' and know-how: the role of explicit versus implicit knowledge in the breakdown of complex motor skill under pressure. *British Journal of Psychology*, 83: 343–58.

Moran, A. P. (1996) *The Psychology of Concentration in Sport Performers: A Cognitive Analysis*. Hove: Psychology Press / Taylor and Francis.

Moran, A. P. (1997) *Managing Your Own Learning at University: A Practical Guide*. Dublin: University College Dublin Press.

Moran, A. (1998) *The Pressure Putt* (a golf psychology audiotape). Aldergrove, Co. Antrim: Tutorial Services (UK).

Roche, P. (1995) Second gold medal for Smith. *Irish Times*, 28 August.

Solso, R. (1998) *Cognitive Psychology*, 5th edn. Boston, MA: Allyn and Bacon.

Wegner, D. M. (1994) Ironic processes of mental control. *Psychological Review*, 101: 34–52.

# The psychologist as toolmaker

# Chapter 7

# Could this be easier to read?
# Tools for evaluating text

## *James Hartley*

As you read this chapter I would like you to take a look at how much writing there is around you. Perhaps there is very little: possibly there is more than you thought? In my own office I swim against a tide of paper (see Box 7.1). If I make a journey elsewhere I see lots more. Written communication is so commonplace that, like the air we breathe, we do not often notice it.

Much of the text that we see around us – on screen as well as on paper – can be written and presented more effectively. This is certainly true of the different types of texts listed in Box 7.1. In order to help us achieve these goals, psychologists (and others) have devised numerous tools and methods for evaluating text. Schriver (1989) has grouped these different methods under three main headings: expert focused, reader focused and text focused respectively.

- *Expert focused* methods are ones that use experts to make assessments of the effectiveness of a piece of text. Subject matter experts might be asked to use checklists to evaluate the quality of an instructional textbook. Referees might complete rating scales to judge the quality of an article submitted for publication in a scientific journal.
- *Reader focused* methods are ones that involve actual readers in making assessments of the text. Readers might be asked to complete questionnaires, to comment on sections of text that they find difficult to follow, to carry out instructions, or be tested on how much they can remember.
- *Text focused* methods are ones that can be used without recourse to experts or to readers. Such measures include computer based readability formulae and computer based measures of style and grammar.

Texts can be evaluated in different ways for different purposes. For example, before you decide to buy or read a particular book, you must first consider

*Box 7.1*   **The ubiquity of text**

Text surrounds us all – not only in offices but almost everywhere we go. In my office, just looking round I can see the following items.

*Facing wall 1*

a calendar
a list of departmental phone numbers
my computer screen and keyboard
my printer with a control panel and instructions – in English and in
    French
boxes of computer disks – hand labelled
an unwrapped chocolate bar
a touch-tone telephone
my diary
the university phone book
a British Telecom phone book
a pile of printouts of recent email correspondence
a set of printouts of drafts of articles
some correspondence to reply to

*Facing wall 2*

a blackboard with scribbles on it
a noticeboard with notices varying in size, posters, lecture/reading lists,
    leaflets, postcards, messages, visiting cards, bus and train timetables,
    cartoons
files of background papers for articles in preparation
boxes of research articles updating my previous publications
a student's PhD thesis
assembled books and journals ready to go back to the library
a set of proofs for correction
a newspaper

*Facing wall 3*

a fire notice
a first aid notice
a theft warning notice
an APA Fellowship certificate

*Facing wall 4*

shelves of textbooks, workbooks, handbooks, catalogues, membership
    directories, journals, magazines
three filing cabinets full of reprints
box files full of research articles on particular topics
a computer manual
my email address book
a set of students' essays for marking

| Methods of evaluation | Areas of concern | | |
| --- | --- | --- | --- |
| | Content | Layout and typography | Suitability for readers |
| Expert focused | ✓ | ✓ | ✓ |
| Reader focused | | ✓ | ✓ |
| Text focused | | | ✓ |

**Figure 7.1**  Relationships between different kinds of evaluation and different areas of concern

its contents – how relevant is it for you? You might also consider its layout and typography – how clearly are the contents presented? And, if you do decide to buy it, you no doubt consider its cost – does it seem reasonable?

In Figure 7.1 I have tried to marry these different concerns with Schriver's different groupings listed above. You can see that expert judgements can be applied across the board, that reader judgements are often used in evaluating content (although suitability may also be important in making decisions about purchasing) and that text based measures are more limited in evaluating the suitability of a text for its intended readership.

In this chapter I shall present some examples of expert, reader and text focused methods for evaluating text – in print and on screen – and I shall conclude by showing how the applications of such measures can improve the texts that surround us.

## Expert focused methods

Experts in this context are people who have a high level of knowledge about a particular subject matter, the potential readership of a text, and the skills of writing. Such people typically use their judgement to assess texts. Teachers, for example, may want to decide if a textbook is suitable for their students. In examining a particular textbook they will be concerned whether it meets their teaching objectives and if it is written at an appropriate level. They will also be concerned with whether there are any outdated materials, important omissions or biases of any kind – academic, national, racial and sexual. They will consider the depth and breadth of the contents and how much the text may need to be supplemented by other materials.

Making such judgements is a subjective activity. However, psychologists have devised tools to help make this decision making more objective. One way to do this is to increase the number of judges. Another is to provide some sort of checklist to ensure that all the judges evaluate the same concerns. Figure 7.2 provides an example of part of such a checklist. You might like to apply it to this book.

This kind of approach is commonly used in evaluating school textbooks in countries with state-controlled school systems. Although such checklists are useful in making the judges' ratings more systematic and consistent, there are no standard tools that everyone can use. Different people with different interests tend to make up their own instruments. In one early study, for instance, it was reported that the number of items on checklists for evaluating

Please rate the book in the spaces provided on each of the items given, using a scale of 0 (very poor) to 5 (very good).

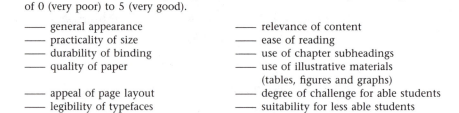

—— general appearance

—— practicality of size

—— durability of binding

—— quality of paper

—— appeal of page layout

—— legibility of typefaces

—— usability of index

—— relevance of content

—— ease of reading

—— use of chapter subheadings

—— use of illustrative materials
(tables, figures and graphs)

—— degree of challenge for able students

—— suitability for less able students

***Figure 7.2***   An excerpt from a typical checklist for judging the quality of a textbook

school textbooks ranged from 42 to 180, with an average number of 73 (Farr and Tulley 1985).

Such checklists are usually completed *before* recommending a particular textbook for use. However, this kind of information can also be collected *after* textbooks have been used by teachers and students. Information gained in this way is helpful in deciding whether or not to use a book again, and in informing authors who are planning subsequent editions. Indeed, information can also be collected from colleagues and readers concerning chapters as they are being written. The information collected in this way can be used by authors in finalizing their chapters.

## Reader focused methods

Reader based tools for evaluating text require readers to carry out some activities. Such activities can be many and varied. Schriver (1989) distinguishes between those which are *concurrent* with the reading activities and those which are *retrospective,* or come after them. Box 7.2 lists examples of reader based measures under these two headings. Here I consider three of them in more detail.

---

***Box 7.2***  **Examples of concurrent and retrospective reader-based text evaluation measures**

*Concurrent*

eye movement patterns
verbal commentaries
oral reading errors
search tasks
reading times
cloze tests

*Retrospective*

comprehension tests (including cloze)
readers' judgements of difficulty
readers' preferences
readers' feedback sheets

---

## Cloze tests

The cloze test was originally developed by Taylor (1953) to measure people's understanding of text. Here samples of a passage are presented to readers with, say, every sixth word missing. The readers are then required to fill in the missing words.

> Technically speaking, if every sixth word is deleted, then six versions should be prepared with the gaps each starting from a different point. However, it is more common ____ prepare one version and, perhaps ____ to focus the gaps on ____ words. Whatever the procedure, the ____ are scored either (a) by ____ accepting as correct those responses ____ directly match what the original ____ actually said, or (b) by ____ these together with acceptable synonyms. Since the two scoring methods (a) and (b) correlate highly, it is more objective to use the tougher measure of matching exact words. (In this case: 'to', 'even', 'important', 'passages', 'only', 'which', 'author' and 'accepting'.)

The scores obtained can be improved by having the gaps more widely dispersed (say every tenth word); by varying the lengths of the gaps to match the lengths of the missing words; by providing dashes to indicate the number of letters missing in each word; by providing the first of the missing letters; by providing multiple choice answers; or even by having readers work in pairs or small groups. These minor variations, however, do not affect the main purpose of the cloze procedure, which is to assess readers' comprehension of the text and, by inference, its difficulty.

The cloze test can be used by readers both concurrently and retrospectively. It can be presented concurrently (as in the paragraph above) as a test of comprehension, and readers required to complete it, or it can be presented retrospectively and readers asked to complete it after they have read the original text. In this latter case the test can serve as a measure of recall as well as comprehension. The cloze test can also be used to assess the effects of different textual organization, readers' prior knowledge and other textual features, such as illustrations, tables and graphs (e.g. see Reid *et al.* 1983; Couloubaritsis *et al.* 1994).

## Readers' judgements of difficulty

A rather different but useful measure of text difficulty is to ask readers to judge difficulty for themselves. One simple procedure here is to ask readers to circle on the text those areas, sentences or words that they think *readers less able than themselves* will find difficult. In my experience, if you ask readers to point out difficulties *for others* they will be much more forthcoming than if you ask them to point out their own difficulties.

An elaboration of this technique is to ask readers to give a running commentary on the difficulties they experience as they are reading or using a text. This technique has proved extremely valuable in evaluating complex text such as that provided in instructional manuals where there can be a rich interplay between text and diagrams (see Schriver 1997). Some critics of this approach suggest that talking about a task while trying to do it can cause difficulties, and this does seem to be a reasonable objection. However, such problems can be partly overcome by videotaping readers using the manuals to complete a particular task, and then asking them to talk through the resulting tape – which can be stopped at any point to allow them to make an extended commentary.

### Readers' preferences

Readers can also be asked to state their preferences for different kinds of texts, and for different layouts of a specific text (e.g. on screen). Some experts dismiss such preference judgements by readers because they think that their preferences might be based on inappropriate considerations (such as a lavish use of colour rather than the clarity of the wording). However, most people have clear views about what they like in texts, and how they expect texts to perform. So, first impressions might colour attitudes to a text. A book that looks dense and turgid is not going to encourage one to read it – no matter how important the content.

A common method of measuring preferences is to ask people to rate (or mark out of ten) original and revised texts. The results can tell you whether a revised text is preferred to the original, whether people see no difference, or whether people prefer the original version. However, one has to be careful here. For some reason or other, when people rate two things out of ten they often rate one of them 5 or 6, and the other one 8. (You might like to try this for yourself.) So it is useful to have a baseline text for comparison. The same text might be rated 5 or 8 depending on what it is being compared with.

Another useful tool to use here, if you want preference judgements for a number of texts which vary in different ways, is the method of *paired comparisons*. Suppose, for example, you have 15 designs for a poster. You could ask potential readers to judge them (overall, or on some specific aspect) and to make paired comparisons. Essentially this involves each judge comparing design 1 with design 2 and recording the preference, then 1 with 3, 1 with 4, 1 with 5 and so on, until 1 with 15 is reached. Then the judge starts again, this time comparing 2 with 3, 2 with 4, 2 with 5 and so on until 2 with 15. This procedure is repeated again, starting with 3 with 4, 5, 6, etc., 4 with 5, 6, 7, etc., until all the designs have been systematically compared. Finally, you total the number of preferences recorded for each design to see which one has been preferred the most often. And, if you are a glutton for punishment, you can ask the judges to repeat the task backwards (i.e. starting with design number 15) to see if their judgements are consistent. The method of paired comparisons thus allows you to assess preferences systematically – but it can be rather tedious!

## Text focused methods

Text based tools for evaluating text can be used without recourse to readers. These measures, too, can be applied concurrently, while one is writing the

*Table 7.1*  Two readability formulae

| Formula | British reading age |
| --- | --- |
| Gunning | 18 years |
| Flesch | 15–17 years |

text, and retrospectively, once it has been written – either by the author(s) or by others who might be thinking of using it. I shall describe two computer based tools for evaluating written text.

## Computer based measures of text difficulty

Measures of text difficulty – or readability formulae – were originally developed in order to predict the age at which children, on average, would have the necessary reading skills and abilities to understand a particular text. And this is still their main aim today, although the scope of application has widened.

Most readability formulae are in fact not as accurate at predicting this age as one might wish (and different formulae produce slightly different results), but the figures they provide do give a rough guide. Furthermore, if you use the same formula to compare two different texts, or to compare an original with a revised version, then you do get a good idea of relative difficulty.

Readability formulae typically combine two main measures to predict the difficulty of text. These are the average sentence length of samples of the text, and the average word length in these samples. One simple formula – the Gunning Fog Index – is as follows:

- Take a sample of 100 words.
- Calculate the average number of words per sentence in the sample.
- Count the number of words with three or more syllables in the sample.
- Add the average number of words per sentence to the total number of words with three or more syllables.
- Multiply the result by 0.4.

The result is the 'reading grade level' as used in US schools. (Grade 1 = 6 years old; Grade 2 = 7 years old, etc.). You can add 5 to the answer to obtain an equivalent British reading age (if you think that British and US children are similar despite the fact that British children start school one year earlier).

Most readability formulae, however, are much more complex to calculate than is the Gunning Fog Index – hence the interest in computer based methods. One computer program – the one I have on my wordprocessor – gives the results from two formulae, the Gunning Fog Index and the Flesch Reading Ease Score. (Other programs may have more.) When I ran my program on the first six paragraphs of this chapter the outcome was as shown in Table 7.1.

These results demonstrate the point made earlier – different formulae will produce slightly different results. However, a further difficulty has arisen with computer based readability formulae in that different programmers have worked out different ways of computerizing ostensibly the same formulae. Thus you might find that, for example, if you use the *Word for Windows* version of the Gunning Fog Index you will get slightly different results from using that provided by, say, *Grammatik 5*. This problem is not too serious with simple texts, but it can become more of an issue when working with complex ones (Sydes and Hartley 1997). So the moral of the tale is to use the same program when evaluating different texts, and to take the results with a pinch of salt.

To summarize: the basic idea underlying readability formulae is that the longer the sentences and the more complex the vocabulary in these sentences, then the more difficult the text will be. Clearly such a notion, while generally sensible, has its limitations. Some technical abbreviations are short (e.g. 'DNA') but difficult for people who have not heard of them. Some words are long but, because of their frequent use, become quite familiar (e.g. 'psychologist' in this context). Clearly there is more to text than just sentence and word lengths – otherwise it would be easy to make text simple by just shortening the words and the sentences (Davison and Green 1987). Indeed, many people have had fun using such techniques to produce horrendous versions of famous documents like the US Declaration of Independence. With readability formulae, the order of the words and the sentences is not taken into account and nor are the effects of other devices used to aid comprehension (e.g. typographical layout, tables, graphs and illustrations). Most importantly (unlike reader based tools) the readers' motivation, abilities and prior knowledge are not assessed.

## Computer based style and grammar checkers

Most readers who use wordprocessors will be familiar with 'spelling checkers', tools that enable you to check the spelling in your documents. Style and grammar checkers, as their name suggests, are but an extension of this idea: they aim to help you with your style and grammar. Essentially the procedure is to run these checkers over your text once you have completed it (but it can be done concurrently if you wish). The checker stops at every point where the program detects a possible stylistic or grammatical error. Box 7.3 indicates the kinds of errors picked up by *Grammatik 5*.

Early studies of style and grammar checkers focused on assessing how useful they were to writers. This research suggested that many people found them rather tedious to use, but that they did find them helpful (Hartley 1993). More recent research has focused on making comparison studies between different programs to see which is the most effective. Typically what one does here is to assemble a set of ungrammatical, or poorly written sentences or passages, and then try out different grammar checkers on them to see which errors are detected and what sort of advice is given (e.g. see Kohut and Gorman 1995). Other more theoretical research in this area concerns itself with developing more sophisticated programs than the ones currently available (e.g. see Dale and Douglas 1996).

Grammar checkers are very good at spotting the minutiae of errors in punctuation and grammar but, naturally, they cannot help with matters of content. In my experience it is best to use both computer based and human editors (experts and readers) to evaluate the effectiveness of style.

---

**Box 7.3** **Examples of different types of errors detected by *Grammatik 5***

| *Grammatical errors* | *Mechanical errors* | *Stylistic errors* |
|---|---|---|
| adjective errors | spelling errors | long sentences |
| adverb errors | capitalization errors | wordy sentences |
| article errors | double word | passive tenses |
| clause errors | ellipsis misuse | end of sentence prepositions |
| comparative/superlative | end of sentence punctuation | split infinitives |
| use | incorrect punctuation | clichéd words/phrases |
| double negatives | number style errors | colloquial language |
| incomplete sentences | question mark errors | Americanisms |
| noun phrase errors | quotation mark misuse | archaic language |
| object of verb errors | similar words | gender specific words |
| possessive misuse | split words | jargon |
| preposition errors | | abbreviation errors |
| pronoun errors | | paragraph problems |
| sequence of tense errors | | questionable word usage |
| subject–verb errors | | |
| tense changes | | |

*Note*: one difficulty with these programs as they currently exist is that you have to have a good working knowledge of grammar to understand them – and this tends to defeat the objective!

## Combining different measures

Experiments have been carried out to see if the information provided from different sources is equally effective or not in improving texts. De Jong and Lentz (1996), for instance, compared the usefulness of expert versus reader feedback in assessing the effectiveness of a public information brochure about rent subsidies. Here the criticisms of 15 expert technical writers were compared with those of 15 members of the public. The main conclusions of this study were that criticisms of the two groups were very different. The readers pointed out significantly more problems associated with the typographic design of the brochure and with their understanding of it. The technical writers pointed out significantly more problems with the use of appropriate expressions and conventions, and with matters of writing style.

In another study, Weston *et al.* (1997) gave suggestions from experts, readers and instructional designers for rewriting a six-page instructional unit on diet and cancer to a new set of instructional designers. These new designers most frequently used the suggestions from the readers and the previous instructional designers in making their revisions. However, subsequent comprehension tests showed that the most important information for improving the comprehension of the passage came from the readers' earlier comments.

In a third study, Wilson *et al.* (1998) reported, among other things, the responses of general practitioners (GPs) and patients to questions concerning the content and usefulness of patient information leaflets. Both the GPs and the patients thought that the leaflets were useful, but they had widely disparate views about the content. Thus, for example, 80 per cent of the GPs responded 'No' and 75 per cent of the patients responded 'Yes' to the question, 'Is there anything you feel is essential to include but is omitted?' Similarly, 86 per cent of the GPs responded 'No' and 46 per cent of the patients responded 'Yes' to the question, 'Is there anything you feel should be left out that is included?' Finally, 86 per cent of the GPs responded 'No' and 50 per cent of the patients 'Yes' to the question, 'Is there anywhere where you feel the style of the language is not appropriate (e.g. patronizing/confusing)?'

A different kind of study (Hartley and Benjamin 1998) showed how making multiple measures could be more informative than making single ones. Here comparisons were made between traditional abstracts (summaries) of journal articles and what are called *structured* abstracts. (These contain subheadings, such as 'background to the study', 'aims', 'methods', 'results' and 'conclusions'.) In this investigation the effects of these changes were assessed in five ways. The results showed that:

- In terms of *length* the structured abstracts were significantly longer.
- In terms of *information content* the structured abstracts were significantly more informative – as assessed by readers.
- In terms of *readability* the structured abstracts were significantly more readable – as assessed by computer based readability formulae.
- In terms of *searchability* the readers were able to find information more quickly with the structured abstracts.
- In terms of *preferences* the authors of the abstracts were almost unanimous in their preferences for the structured versions.

The results from combining these measures suggested that the structured abstracts were more effective than the traditional ones – but that they took up more journal space to achieve this. The use of several evaluation methods – rather than just one – strengthened this conclusion.

Studies such as these (and others reported by Schriver 1997) point to the usefulness of combining different sources of evaluation and using different – complementary – tools. This is an important consideration that applies to almost all evaluation studies.

## Cyclical testing and revision

However, we may not always be interested in testing to see whether, say, one text is easier to use than another. We may be concerned with using a selection from the tools described above to *improve* a text. One of the most useful approaches here involves *cyclical* testing and revision. This approach requires testing the first version of a text with appropriate tools, revising it on the basis of the results obtained, testing this revised version again, revising it, retesting and so on, until the text obtains its objectives.

Examples of this approach are described by Komoski and Woodward (1985) and Waller (1984). Waller describes how he and his colleagues used this iterative or cyclical approach to improve a form published by the then Department of Health and Social Security (DHSS). This form, used by unemployed people claiming supplementary benefits in the UK, was attractive to look at but difficult to complete. In fact only 25 per cent of the forms were completed satisfactorily. Such a high error rate had enormous costs for the DHSS – forms had to be returned for correction, or respondents had to be followed up in some way before an assessment of benefit could be made.

In order to improve the form, a revised prototype was first tested with small groups of appropriate people. Part of this assessment included the use of an eye movement recorder to assess which pieces of text were read and in what order. The aim of this first assessment was to isolate the main causes of difficulty, and to collect data against which the final version of the form could be compared. The investigators concluded from this first test that the form was not asking the right questions to obtain the information that was needed, and that many of the questions were ambiguous.

Thus a redesigned form was prepared. The emphasis now was on making clearer the language of the form and its sequencing. This version was again tested with small groups of appropriate people. It was clear that improvements had been made, but that more could be done. So a third version was prepared. Headings were added to make clearer the different sections of the form, and the routing instructions were further clarified.

The testing of this third version showed that this had solved most of the problems. So a fourth and final version was prepared. This version introduced colour coding for the main headings (the earlier versions had been in black and white), a larger page size and yet another resequenced order. This final version was tested with larger groups of appropriate people. Now about 75 per cent of the forms were completed satisfactorily. These results, although not perfect, ensured massive cost savings for the DHSS.

## Concluding remarks: the psychologist as toolmaker

In this chapter I have discussed a number of tools used by psychologists to evaluate the effectiveness of text, whether presented on screen or in written form. Although some of the tools I have described may seem deceptively simple and easy to use (e.g. the cloze test and reader preferences) each has a whole technology behind it, and a research literature debating its advantages and limitations. It is for reasons such as these that many psychologists are reluctant to 'give these tools away'. Psychologists, being more familiar with the technicalities of the measures, are happier for them to be employed with expert guidance rather than have them used by non-psychologists who do not fully appreciate their complexities.

Perhaps the best indication of how a tool can be misused in this context is provided by the (mis)use of readability formulae by some publishers and authors of young children's textbooks. Such people appear to argue that, if high readability results from short sentences and simple wording, then it is a relatively simple task to produce readable textbooks. All one has to do is to shorten the sentences, simplify the text, put a readability label on the cover and advertise it as suitable for a particular age group. In fact such procedures serve only to produce 'choppy' text which might be more rather than less difficult for young children to understand (see Box 7.4).

---

**Box 7.4   Changing readability scores by shortening sentences**

It is possible to make marked changes in the results from a readability formulae simply by shortening sentences. The first passage has a Flesch reading age of 15–17 years. The second passage has one of 13–14 years.

*Version 1*

Scientists divide the different forms of life into two main groups. There are animals called *vertebrates* that have backbones, and there are animals called *invertebrates* that do not. *Vertebrates* can be divided into several sub-groups. There are *reptiles* such as snakes and crocodiles; *amphibians*, such as frogs and toads; *fish*, such as salmon and sharks; *birds*, such as sparrows and eagles; and *mammals*, such as dogs, horses and people.

*Version 2*

Scientists divide the different forms of life into two main groups. There are animals called *vertebrates* that have backbones. There are animals called *invertebrates* that do not. *Vertebrates* can be divided into several sub-groups. There are *reptiles* – such as snakes and crocodiles. There are *amphibians* – such as frogs and toads. There are *fish* – such as salmon and sharks. There are *birds* – such as sparrows and eagles. And there are *mammals* – such as dogs, horses and people.

---

It is perhaps going too far to say that the tools invented by psychologists are dangerous instruments when they are used by non-psychologists but I, for one, am impressed by how experts use tools far more professionally than novices.

---

*Discussion questions*

1 If you could use only one tool to measure the effectiveness of text, which one would you choose, and why?

2 When typography looks a mess (see if you can provide examples) what has gone wrong?

3 How far do tools depend on experts to be useful?

---

# Further reading

Hartley, J. (1994) *Designing Instructional Text*, 3rd edn. London: Kogan Page. A practical guide to producing instructional text based upon a critical reading of the research literature.

Hartley, J. (1998) Return to sender. Why written communications fail. *The Psychologist*, 11(10): 477–80. This article examines numerous features of academic and promotional texts in order to show how both genres, in their way, fail their readers, and how they can learn from each other.

Schriver, K. A. (1997) *Dynamics in Document Design: Creating Text for Readers*. New York: Wiley. This text looks at what readers need from documents, how they respond to them, and how designers can take these issues into account.

# References

Couloubaritsis, A., Moss, G. D. and Abouserie, R. (1994) Evaluating curriculum materials: do Greek children understand their history textbook? *Education Training and Technology International*, 31(4): 268–75.

Dale, R. and Douglas, S. (1996) Two investigations into intelligent text processing, in M. Sharples and T. van der Geest (eds) *The New Writing Environment: Writers at Work in a World of Technology*. London: Springer.

Davison, A. and Green, G. (eds) (1987) *Linguistic Complexity and Text Comprehension: A Re-Examination of Readability with Alternative Views*. Hillsdale, N. J.: Erlbaum.

de Jong, M. D. T. and Lentz, L. R. (1996) Expert judgements versus reader feedback: a comparison of text evaluation techniques. *Journal of Technical Writing*, 26(4): 507–19.

Farr, R. and Tulley, M. A. (1985) Do adoption committees perpetuate mediocre textbooks? *Phi Delta Kappan*, 66(7): 467–71.

Hartley, J. (1993) Writing thinking and computers. *British Journal of Educational Technology*, 24(1): 22–31.

Hartley, J. and Benjamin, M. (1998) An evaluation of structured abstracts in journals published by the British Psychological Society. *British Journal of Educational Psychology*, 68(3): 443–56.

Kohut, G. F. and Gorman, K. J. (1995) The effectiveness of leading grammar/style software packages in analyzing business students' writing. *Journal of Business and Technical Communication*, 9(3): 341–61.

Komoski, P. K. and Woodward, A. (1985) The continuing need for learner verification and revision of textual materials, in D. H. Jonassen (ed.) *The Technology of Text, Vol. 2*. Englewood Cliffs, N. J.: Educational Technology Publications.

Reid, D. J., Briggs, N. and Beveridge, M. (1983) The effects of pictures upon the readability of a school science topic. *British Journal of Educational Psychology*, 53: 327–35.

Schriver, K. A. (1989) Evaluating text quality: the continuum from text-focused to reader-focused methods. *IEEE Transactions on Professional Communication*, 32(4): 238–55.

Schriver, K. A. (1997) *Dynamics in Document Design: Creating Text for Readers*. New York: Wiley.

Sydes, M. and Hartley, J. (1997) A thorn in the Flesch: observations on the unreliability of computer-based readability formulae. *British Journal of Educational Technology*, 28(2): 143–5.

Taylor, W. L. (1953) Cloze procedure: a new tool for measuring readability. *Journalism Quarterly*, 30: 415–33.

Waller, R. (1984) Designing a government form: a case history. *Information Design Journal*, 4(1): 36–57.

Weston, C., Le Maistre, C., McAlpine, L. and Bordonaro, T. (1997) The influence of participants in formative evaluation on the learning from written instructional materials. *Instructional Science*, 25: 368–86.

Wilson, R., Kenny, T., Clark, J., Moseley, D., Newton, L., Newton, D. and Purves, I. (1998) Ensuring the readability and understandability and efficacy of patient information leaflets. *Prodigy Publication no. 30*. Sowerby Centre for Health Informatics, Newcastle University.

# Chapter **8**

# Are women better drivers than men? Tools for measuring driver behaviour

## *Michelle Meadows and Stephen Stradling*

Are women better drivers than men? As applied social psychologists working in the area of driver behaviour this is a question we often get asked. How should we go about answering it? Answering what – at first sight – appears a straightforward question requires a range of different tools (Meadows and Stradling 1995). These include:

- analyses of accident statistics
- questionnaire/survey studies of drivers
- performance studies using driving simulators, instrumented vehicles, videotaped driving behaviour or on-road observation
- statistical procedures for summarizing data, exploring interactions between different variables and finding patterns in the data
- deriving models for organizing concepts and findings which suggest hypotheses for future research.

In this chapter we shall present information derived from using a number of these tools, mostly analyses of data from accident statistics, surveys and questionnaires, and conclude with a summary model of factors influencing the behaviour of drivers.

So – are women better drivers than men? Well, that depends what you mean by 'better'. The first thing is to decide what counts as being a 'good' driver? Should it be:

- Passing the driving test first time?
- Setting a lap record in a Formula 1 racing car?
- Forfeiting the least penalty points over forest tracks in a prepared rally car?
- Passing, with distinction, a police Class 1 driving course?
- Achieving the maximum 'no claims bonus' on your insurance premium?
- Driving for 60 years on the road and never having an accident?
- Getting to the airport through rush hour traffic without losing your temper or missing your flight?
- Ferrying the children safely to and from school, yourself safely to and from work, and the shopping safely home without unduly inconveniencing any other road user?
- Being able to drive home drunk without attracting the attention of the police?

As bases for comparison between men and women each of these has advantages and disadvantages, so let us look now at just the first one.

Since a practical driving test was introduced in the UK in 1935, the overall first time pass rate has varied between 45 per cent and 55 per cent with that for women some 10 per cent below that for men throughout this period (Cameron 1998). But does this tell of permanent and pervasive differences in driving competence between males and females, or of differences in the proportions of males and females properly prepared and ready for the test, or of even bias on the part of the (largely male) examiners? And, as the test involves a brief, daytime drive on urban roads, is it an ecologically valid assessment of the competence currently needed, given the amount of motorway, night-time and long distance driving the modern motorist undertakes (though female drivers tend to do less of each of these)? Answering our question, as we shall see, is one of attempting to tease apart a host of interacting or what we technically called 'confounded' variables.

## What do accident statistics tell us and how should we interpret them?

Driving is a skill-based, rule-governed, expressive activity. Becoming a driver involves:

- mastering the technical skills of vehicle handling and positioning
- learning the rules (both formal and informal) in order to 'read the road' and anticipate hazards
- resisting self-serving impulses that bring immediate gratification but might place others at risk.

Perhaps the most important single indicator of the extent to which drivers manage to master each of these skills is the extent to which they remain crash free. Keeping clear of accidents benefits both the individual driver and the society which has to meet the costs of crashes (which in fiscal terms alone is currently estimated at around £1 million per fatality in the UK).

*Table 8.1*  Numbers of injury accidents for female and male car drivers in Great Britain, 1993/5

|                | All injury | KSI*  | Killed | Killed/day |
|----------------|-----------|-------|--------|------------|
| Female drivers | 56,443    | 5,240 | 249    | 0.68       |
| Male drivers   | 72,416    | 9,770 | 897    | 2.46       |
| F/M as %       | 78%       | 54%   | 28%    | (28%)      |

*Note*: *KSI = killed or seriously injured
*Source*: data from UK DETR (1997a: Tables 5a and 5b)

The basic facts about accident frequency and accident severity seem, initially, fairly straightforward:

1 Overall there are more serious crashes involving male than female car drivers. The most recent figures are shown in Table 8.1. In 1996, more male car drivers were killed, seriously injured, or injured than female car drivers. Dividing the figures in column four of Table 8.1 by 365 gives the average number of female and male car drivers killed each day on the roads in Great Britain (column five).
2 Male drivers have a higher fatality rate. The fatality rate also varies substantially with driver age, but this sex difference remains relatively stable right across the age range (McKenna *et al.* 1998).
3 In identical impacts a female driver will probably be more severely injured than a male (though this difference in anatomical vulnerability is not as large as that between older and younger drivers).

But if we refocus our question as 'Who are the least dangerous drivers – men or women?', this will require more than examining aggregate crash statistics. We must consider a number of other variables.

## Proportions of men and women drivers in accidents

As noted above, there are more accidents involving men than women drivers on UK roads. But there are also a number of other documented differences between men and women drivers that may contribute to this, and these differences may act as 'confounding variables'. For example, there are more male than female drivers on the roads and thus more males are exposed to the risk of being crash involved. Table 8.2 gives the figures for the numbers and proportions of female and male full licence holders in Great Britain during 1993/95 and, in the final column, we have calculated for each age band the number of females as a percentage of the number of males.

At present, around 80 per cent of eligible males in the UK population are registered drivers, compared to around 55 per cent of eligible females. The proportion for males now appears to have reached a peak and seems unlikely to get much higher, whereas that for females is continuing to rise. Of the 30 million registered drivers in the UK in 1993/95, 42 per cent were female and 58 per cent were male, but these overall figures mask large age-related

*Table 8.2*  Numbers of female and male registered drivers by age band in Great Britain, 1993/95

| Age band | Female* | Male* | F as % of M |
|----------|---------|-------|-------------|
| 17–20 | 0.55 | 0.69 | 80 |
| 21–29 | 2.62 | 3.29 | 80 |
| 30–39 | 3.09 | 3.83 | 81 |
| 40–49 | 2.77 | 3.40 | 81 |
| 50–59 | 1.79 | 2.66 | 67 |
| 60–69 | 1.10 | 2.08 | 53 |
| 70+ | 0.74 | 1.47 | 50 |
| Total | 12.66 | 17.42 | 73 |

Note: *millions of persons
*Source*: data from UK DETR (1997b); Cuerden and Hill (1997)

differences as shown in Table 8.2. Among drivers aged 17–49 there were five males for every four females (or 1.25 males for every female). At the top of the age range, though, among the over 70s, there were two registered male drivers for every female driver.

The proportion of female to male drivers thus varies historically: the number and hence the proportion of female drivers on UK roads is inexorably increasing. It also varies geographically – for example, the proportions of female drivers are much higher in northern than in southern European countries.

## Mileage differences

An important further part of the gender difference in crash involvement – and a further confounding variable – is that the average male driver drives a higher annual mileage than the average female driver. This increases men's level of exposure to crash risk. In the UK the average annual mileage is around 12,000 miles per year (*c*.19,000 kilometres) for males and 8000 miles (*c*.13,000 kilometres) for females, although this difference is continually reducing. Furthermore, not only do male drivers have a higher annual mileage than female drivers, but also the size of this 'exposure differential' increases with increasing age. The number and proportion of 'dormant drivers' – those who hold a full driving licence but rarely venture behind the wheel – is highest among elderly women.

## Journey differences

There are further differences in the types – and hence times, places and purposes – of journeys made by male and female drivers. For example, more 'school runs' on urban roads in the latter part of the morning rush hour and in the mid-afternoon are made by female drivers; more male drivers are sales representatives, service engineers and delivery drivers who hurry from call to call, on motorways or through city centres. Thus gender differences are confounded not only with the distance covered but also with the types of journeys made.

## Road differences

Where you drive is important in accounting for the extent of crash involvement. As Maycock notes

> To take an extreme example, speeds are higher on motorways than on urban roads, but despite the higher speeds, accident rates [*accidents per mile*] are much lower on the former than on the latter. Unless the two road types are considered separately, therefore, an overall [*system wide*] speed–accident relation would show a strong negative relation – lower speeds, higher accident rates.
>
> (Maycock 1997: 166)

This would clearly misrepresent the well documented finding (e.g. Horswill and McKenna 1997; Maycock 1997) that speed is positively related to crashes, both their frequency (by reducing safety margins) and their severity (at higher speeds the laws of physics dictate that there is greater energy to be absorbed at impact).

## National differences

These patterns of social change outlined above have been reported for the US as well as for the UK:

> Over the last two decades, there have been major changes in life style for women, with corresponding changes in their driving behaviour. Women are increasing in both their rate of licensure and in the amount of driving that they do. They are also driving at times and places where they previously did not drive. In the US, women now account for about half of all new cars sold.
>
> (Waller 1997: 207)

## Age differences

So far we have noted that sex and exposure (amount and type) are related to crash involvement. The age of the driver also makes a big difference. Young drivers are more crash involved. In the UK, for example, drivers aged 17–21 comprise 10 per cent of the driving population yet are involved in 20 per cent of the road traffic accidents and make up 25 per cent of the road deaths. But there are also confounds here: young drivers tend to drive older and smaller – and hence less crash resistant – vehicles, and to do more night driving. Males have a higher proportion of their crashes on bends, while overtaking, and during the hours of darkness than females – and these gender differences are largest among younger drivers (McKenna *et al.* 1998).

***Table 8.3*** Mean accidents per driver per year for experienced female and male drivers by age band and annual mileage

| *Accidents per driver per year* | *Female* | | | *Male* | | |
|---|---|---|---|---|---|---|
| *Annual mileage* | *Low (0–5K)* | *Med. (5–12K)* | *High (12K+)* | *Low (0–5K)* | *Med. (5–12K)* | *High (12K+)* |
| Age band | | | | | | |
| 21–25 | 0.113* | 0.167 | 0.147 | 0.173 | 0.163 | 0.223 |
| 26–39 | 0.073 | 0.093 | 0.080 | 0.127 | 0.110 | 0.143 |
| 40–70 | 0.070 | 0.133 | 0.097 | 0.093 | 0.137 | 0.103 |

*Note*: *interpret this figure as: female drivers aged 21–25 years who drove less than 5000 miles a year had an annual probability of involvement in a road traffic accident of 0.113 i.e., in the previous three years, 11.3% × 3 = 34% of them reported at least one road traffic accident.
*Source*: data from Meadows (1994)

Table 8.3 gives figures from one of our studies at Manchester (Meadows 1994) from which a complicated but comprehensive picture emerges. We asked a large, national sample of experienced drivers to tell us how many road traffic accidents of all kinds they had been involved in over the previous three years. For the purposes of comparison we have divided age and annual mileage into three bands to create equivalent groups of female and male drivers and express the accident figures as annual probabilities. All three factors – sex, age and mileage – make a difference to the extent of crash involvement. Overall, male drivers reported more crashes and, for both females and males, younger drivers tended to report more and low mileage drivers tended to report fewer accidents.

Waller (1997) notes similar findings from US studies. 'If you look at low-mileage women compared with low-mileage men or high-mileage women compared with high-mileage men, the women do at least as well as the men and possibly a little better' (Waller 1997, quoted in Faith 1997: 131).

## Novice and expert drivers: survey data

We know that young drivers are particularly accident prone during the early years of their driving careers. Do gender differences in crash rates also hold for these inexperienced, novice drivers? A large cohort of recently qualified drivers was extensively surveyed by the UK Department of Transport (Forsyth *et al.* 1995; Maycock 1995). Drivers reported on the number of accidents that they had experienced in their first, second and third post-qualification years. Arranging the results by age at which they started driving, Maycock (1995) showed:

- that accident frequency was higher for the drivers who started when younger
- that for all age groups accident frequency decreased with added driving experience (i.e. from Year 1 to Year 3 post driving test)
- that women drivers were involved in fewer accidents per year than men drivers equivalent in age and experience – though 'their annual mileage is only 55–60% of that of the male drivers' (Maycock 1995: 1).

*Table 8.4*  Mean accidents per driver per year

| Accidents per driver per year | Female (F) | Male (M) | F/M × 100% |
|---|---|---|---|
| Age 17–19 | | | |
| Year 1 | 0.202 | 0.317 | 64 |
| Year 2 | 0.142 | 0.190 | 75 |
| Year 3 | 0.128 | 0.141 | 91 |
| Age 20–24 | | | |
| Year 1 | 0.177 | 0.203 | 87 |
| Year 2 | 0.111 | 0.146 | 76 |
| Year 3 | 0.096 | 0.145 | 66 |

*Source*: data from Maycock (1995: Table 1)

Table 8.4 shows mean number of accidents per driver per year for the two youngest age groups separately for female and male drivers. If annual mileage were the sole determinant of accident frequency, then we would expect the ratio of female to male accidents per driver per year to be around 55–60 per cent – the same as their annual mileage ratio. In fact, when we calculate this ratio for all comparisons the ratio is greater than this and, for most comparisons, it is considerably so (see the final column of Table 8.4). Thus young, recently qualified female drivers report fewer accidents per year than males equivalent in age and experience, but more than would be expected on the basis of their reported lower mileage. Part of the reason for this is that accident rate (crashes per mile) is higher for all low mileage drivers – the relationship between crash rate and exposure is not a simple linear one (Maycock 1995). But part of it may also be that young females have particular difficulties in learning to drive.

In an intriguing set of analyses conducted on data from the Department of Transport cohort of recently qualified drivers, driving examiners' scores relating to particular types of errors on test were used to estimate post-test crash liability (Maycock 1995). Of course, in so far as they had passed their driving tests, the type and severity of errors reported on the test were necessarily minor ones. 'A candidate fails the test if he or she commits one or more [*of the 46 different types of*] errors judged by the examiner to be either serious or dangerous. Any number of minor errors can be committed on test without the candidate failing' (Maycock 1995: 5).

Maycock reported that, for both men and women, the more 'errors of awareness and anticipation' they committed on the driving test the more likely they were to be involved in an accident in the three years after passing their driving test. Falling under this heading were matters such as:

- inadequate observation at junctions and while reversing and turning in the road
- not showing due regard for approaching traffic
- failing to take precautions of various kinds
- failure to act on the signals of other road users and to anticipate their actions.

These are all aspects of 'reading the road' and problems here seem to raise the accident liability of both male and female drivers. Comparing drivers who made four or more errors of this kind with those who made none showed an elevated accident liability of 24 per cent for men and 19 per cent for women.

Peculiar to female drivers, though, was an additional category of difficulties. Female novice drivers had problems – albeit minor – with what Maycock (1995) called 'manoeuvres'. These involved

- moving off
- reversing
- turning in the road
- stopping in an emergency.

'Women drivers who committed three errors of this kind *[while on test]* had an accident liability which was 26% higher than those who did not make these errors' (Maycock 1995: 6).

Overall, from the 'cohort' study, Maycock (1995) concluded, *inter alia*,

- that there are some women learner drivers who take extensive tuition before finally passing
- that for women learner drivers, (minor) 'manoeuvres' errors made while passing the test are predictive of elevated accident involvement in the following three years
- that women learner drivers tend to have more difficulty with vehicle control skills.

However, we need to remember that 'young male drivers still have considerably higher accident rates than young women drivers' (Maycock 1995: 7). So we need to look beyond car control for the full picture.

# Speeding

Vehicle speed has two consequences for crashes, increasing both crash frequency and crash severity. What differences are there between female and male drivers in their speeding behaviours and in their attitudes to speeding? Box 8.1 summarizes some illustrative findings extracted from several of the survey studies of UK drivers that the Manchester Driver Behaviour Research Group has conducted in this area. All the studies involved large numbers of experienced female and male drivers completing questionnaires concerning various aspects of their driving attitudes and driving behaviour.

Greater proportions of male drivers are likely to have been stopped for speeding by the police, to report speeding behaviour, to nominate higher speed preferences and to endorse pro-speeding attitudes. Consistent with this pattern of gender differences, greater proportions of female drivers deem adverse consequences of speeding as more likely.

**Box 8.1** Comparisons of speeding behaviours and attitudes of female and male drivers

|  |  | Female | Male |
|---|---|---|---|
| *Speeding offences* |  |  |  |
| Stopped for speeding in the last 12 months | 'Yes' | 11% | 21% |
| *Self-reported speeding* |  |  |  |
| 'I disregard the speed limits late at night or very early in the morning' | Agree | 8% | 22% |
| 'I am always speeding' | Agree | 8% | 17% |
| *Preferred speed* | *Mean* |  |  |
| 'At what speed do you prefer to drive on . . .' | mph |  |  |
|    a busy High Street? |  | F = M | |
|    a road through a residential area? |  | F = M | |
|    winding country lanes? |  | F < M | |
|    motorways? |  | F < M | |
| Persistent speeders (High on all four of the above) |  | 7% | 15% |
| *Attitudes to speed* | *Strongly:* |  |  |
| 'I find travelling at high speed no thrill at all' | Disagree | 20% | 32% |
| 'I really enjoy the feeling of accelerating hard' | Agree | 8% | 23% |
| 'It is completely unimportant who is first away from the traffic lights' | Disagree | 11% | 15% |
| 'It is important to me that driving is exciting' | Agree | 4% | 12% |
| *Consequences of speed* |  |  |  |
| How likely is it that disregarding the speed limit: |  |  |  |
|    will cause an accident? | Likely | 39% | 26% |
|    will give offence to other road users? | Likely | 50% | 33% |
|    would make me feel sorry and/or guilty? | Likely | 41% | 28% |

## Attitudes to driving and their importance

To understand fully the differences between male and female drivers we need tools to go beyond the statistics of observable driving behaviour. It is important to address drivers' attitudes and frames of mind – both those they hold while driving, and those with which they approach the whole business of driving generally.

Many of the attitudinal differences between males and females are in place even before reaching the road. Boys in a Manchester study of pre-drivers (Stradling 1991) reported more interest in cars, anticipated more thrill seeking

---

**Box 8.2**   **Examples of skill and safety items from the *Driver Skill Inventory* (DSI)**

|  | *Below average* |  |  | *Above average* |
|---|---|---|---|---|
| 'Please estimate how you compare on each of the following aspects of driving' | 0   1 | 2 | 3 | 4 |

*Skill items*

Fluent lane changing in heavy traffic
Overtaking
Driving in the dark
Driving in a strange city

*Safety items*

Keeping sufficient following distance
Adjusting your speed to the conditions
Tolerating other drivers' blunders calmly
Conforming to the traffic rules

---

when they came to drive, rated current speed limits as 'too slow' and anticipated that driving would give them 'a way of expressing themselves' more than did the girls. Girls rated a range of traffic offences as both more serious and more dangerous than did the boys. Most of these differences were present from age 11 (the youngest group questioned).

Almost all drivers – males and females – will, if asked to rate their abilities as drivers, indicate that they think of themselves as 'average or above average'. In reality, this cannot be the case. Lajunen and Summala's (1995) *Driver Skill Inventory* (DSI) gives drivers the opportunity to rate themselves on a wide range of driving competencies and tendencies. These divide into two main dimensions, one concerned with perceptual and motor *driving skills*, the other with *safety mindedness* on the roads. Box 8.2 gives some examples of the scale items and the method by which they are measured (a five-point Likert type scale).

In one Manchester study almost 300 drivers completed the DSI (Lajunen, Parker and Stradling 1998). Figure 8.1 graphs the mean scores on the two scales – skill and safety – for female and male drivers. The mean safety orientation scores for female and male drivers did not differ, but those for skill did, with the males rating themselves significantly more skilful than did the females. However, the figure shows an interaction effect which suggests a further difference between the two groups: that the average male driver thinks he is more skilful than safe, while the average female driver thinks she is more safe than skilful. Computing a safety:skill ratio score for each driver (dividing their safety score by their skill score) and comparing female and male means on this measure yields a statistically significant value on a *t*-test, with females scoring higher.

There are many other attitudinal factors where sex differences between female and male drivers have been reliably demonstrated. For example, Rolls

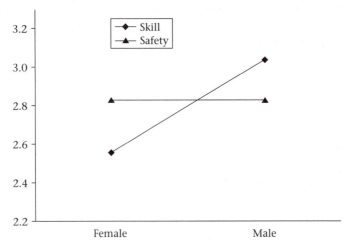

*Note*: Scale range: 0 = below average to 4 = above average

***Figure 8.1***   Skill and safety orientation scores for UK female and male drivers

*et al.* (1991) asked young drivers to rate the importance they attached to a number of factors in current car choice and ideal car choice. Males placed more importance on the appearance of their current car, while females were more concerned with its reliability. When the researchers looked at the ratings for an ideal car they found not only that preferences for speed, acceleration and engine size were higher for the young male drivers, and that preferences for safety and reliability were higher among the young females, but also that preferences for speed, acceleration and engine size correlated positively, and preferences for safety and reliability correlated negatively with actual accident involvement.

## Behaviour on the road: lapses, errors, violations and crashes

At Manchester we have conducted a number of survey studies asking drivers to rate how often when driving they experience departures from normative, reference driving behaviour (Rothengatter 1997). These driving behaviours group into three basic types: lapses, errors and violations (Reason *et al.* 1990; Meadows 1994; Parker *et al.* 1995a, 1995b). This basic threefold typology has been replicated by studies in Australia (Blockley and Hartley, 1995) and in Sweden (Aberg and Rimmo 1998). Box 8.3 gives examples of each type.

- *Lapses* are potentially embarrassing and may be a source of inconvenience to the driver, but are not usually life threatening. They are more commonly reported by female drivers and by older drivers.
- *Errors* are an example of 'the failure of planned actions to achieve their intended consequence' (Reason *et al.* 1990: 1315) and include both failures of observation and misjudgements.

---

*Box 8.3* **Examples of lapses, errors and violations**

*Lapses*

How often* do you:

- Try to pull away from the traffic lights in third gear?
- Switch on one thing when you meant to switch on another?
- Take the wrong lane approaching a roundabout or junction?
- Forget where you left the car in the car park?

*Errors*

How often* do you:

- Fail to see a 'Stop' or 'Give Way' sign and narrowly avoid colliding with traffic having right of way?
- On turning nearside, fail to see a cyclist who has come up on your inside?
- Underestimate the speed of an oncoming vehicle when overtaking?
- Brake too quickly on a slippery road, or steer the wrong way in a skid?

*Violations*

How often* do you:

- Disregard the speed limits late at night or very early in the morning?
- Cross a junction knowing that the traffic lights have already turned against you?
- Drive especially close to the car in front as a signal to its driver to go faster or get out of the way?
- Drive even though you realize you may be over the legal blood-alcohol limit?

*Note*: *rated on a six-point scale from 'Never' to 'Nearly all the time'

---

- *Violations* are defined as 'deliberate ... deviations from those practices believed necessary to maintain the safe operation of a potentially hazardous system' (Reason *et al.* 1990: 1316). These are to be distinguished from the US usage of the term, where a driver's traffic violations are an official record of the number of times he or she has been apprehended for breaches of the road traffic regulations.

In terms of violations, our analyses show speeding to be the *most* frequent and drink-driving (these days) to be the *least* frequent. Drivers who committed one type of violation were more likely to commit other types. Typically in our studies at Manchester it was those drivers who scored high on violations, and not those who scored high on lapses or errors, who were statistically more likely to have been involved in accidents in the past and to be accident involved (again) in the future.

---

***Box 8.4*  Psychological characteristics of high violators**

*High violators tend to*

- consider themselves (even) better drivers than do others
- report stronger intentions to speed across five different road types (residential road, shopping street, country lane, dual carriageway, three-lane motorway)
- overestimate the number of other drivers who speed, drive too close, etc.
- rate the potential adverse consequences of their actions (e.g. having an accident, being stopped by the police) as less *likely*, and as less *bad*
- believe that their significant others are less likely to disapprove
- think that other drivers will be less upset by the bad behaviour
- are more likely to experience immediate, positive affect ('feel good') *while* violating
- are less likely to anticipate feeling regret *after* violating
- believe that refraining from the behaviours would be more difficult and thus that they are less in control of their behaviour
- show greater outward irritability (anger directed towards others)

---

When we divided drivers into high, medium and low violators we found that

- around 40 per cent of male drivers were high violators as opposed to 20 per cent of female drivers
- over 50 per cent of male drivers aged 17–25 and approaching 40 per cent of female drivers aged 17–25 were high violators.

Thus male drivers and young drivers are over-represented in the high violator group. However, we should bear in mind that

- not all high violators are young and male (around 10 per cent of female drivers over the age of 35 years are)
- not all young male drivers are high violators (around 20 per cent are low violators).

Therefore persuasive materials (e.g. road safety campaigns) aimed solely at young male drivers will miss some targets and may antagonize others who should be role models, not targets.

In a series of studies at Manchester, looking at a range of particular violations, high violators were shown to differ from other drivers in a number of ways. Box 8.4 summarizes these findings.

## Different kinds of crashes and their correlates

At this point we turn to look at the effects that all these different factors have on accident records and ask, do female and male drivers have different

***Box 8.5*  Active crash involvement: separate effects***

|  | | Overall: | 18% | | | |
|---|---|---|---|---|---|---|
| Annual mileage | <7000 | 14% | 7000–16,000 | 25% | >16,000 | 15% |
| Gender | Female | 14% | | | Male | 21% |
| Age | 18–30 | 23% | | | 31–70 | 14% |
| Violation score | Low, medium | 15% | | | High | 25% |

*Note*: *all of which are statistically significant (chi-square) at $p < 0.05$
*Source*: data from Meadows (1994)

kinds of crashes? Pioneering work by West (1995) classified crashes into a number of different types, including the following:

- *Shunts*: one vehicle hits another on the same carriageway from behind (around 30 per cent of self-reported crashes overall).
- *Right of way contraventions*: a vehicle pulls on to or across a carriageway without having right of way (around 20 per cent of crashes overall).
- *Loss of control*: a driver fails to control the direction of a vehicle and keep it on the carriageway (around 10 per cent of crashes overall).

Younger drivers are more likely to be killed in single vehicle, rollover crashes (loss of control) (Evans 1991); older drivers are at greater risk of injury from multi-vehicle side impact collisions (right of way contraventions) (Viano *et al.* 1990).

For most crashes it is also possible to characterize them as:

- *active* crashes – where the reporting driver's vehicle runs into another or off the road
- *passive* crashes – where the reporting driver's vehicle is struck by another.

Box 8.5 shows the separate main effects for annual mileage, gender, age and violation score (categorized into low, medium or high thirds) on the frequency of reported *active* crashes in the previous three years.

Overall, 18 per cent of drivers in this sample of 1000 drivers aged 18–70 with at least four months' post-test driving experience reported one or more active crashes in the previous three years. Box 8.5 shows that variations in reported annual mileage, gender, age and violation score each made a significant difference to active crash frequency when they were considered separately.

However, when the combined effects of all four variables were tested together, the optimum solution for *active* crashes was as shown in Figure 8.2. Here violation score proved to be the best single predictor of variation in active crash frequency. There was also a gender by violation interaction effect: 12 per cent of female low or medium violators reported one or more active crashes in the previous three years, compared to 18 per cent of male low or medium violators and 25 per cent of high violators. Thus male drivers

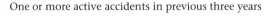

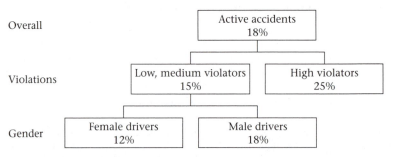

*Figure 8.2* Active crash involvement: interactive effects

---

**Box 8.6**   Passive crash involvement: separate effects*

|                 | Overall:  17%       |              |        |
| --------------- | ------------------- | ------------ | ------ |
| Annual mileage  | <11,000   14%       | >11,000      | 21%    |
| Gender          | Female = Male = 17% |              |        |
| Age             | 18–55     18%       | 56–70        | 8%     |
| Violation score | Low       13%       | Medium, high | 19%    |

*Note*: *three of which are statistically significant (chi-square) at p < 0.05

---

who drove carefully were 50 per cent more at risk of active crashes than female drivers with the same driving style (18 per cent v. 12 per cent). But a high violating manner of driving doubled the active crash risk for female drivers (12 per cent to 25 per cent) and increased by a half that for male drivers (18 per cent to 25 per cent). For high violators, whether the driver was male or female made no difference to the frequency of active crash involvement, they were equally at risk.

The picture was intriguingly different for *passive* crash involvement. Box 8.6 shows that three of the four measures had a significant effect here. Male and female drivers in this sample experienced the same number of passive crashes in the previous three years, but there was a difference between lower and higher mileage drivers, between drivers below and above age 55, and between low violators and high and medium violators.

Figure 8.3 charts the best combined solution. High mileage drivers were more at risk of passive crashes – having other road users run into them – simply by virtue of their greater exposure (24 per cent v. 14 per cent). But there was an interaction between mileage and frequency of committing violations. Here careful and considerate driving – low violating – protected high mileage drivers, reducing their risk (13 per cent) to the same level as that of low mileage drivers (14 per cent).

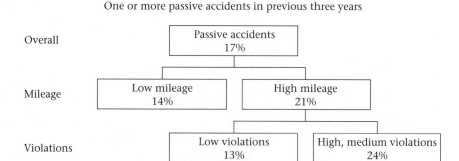

*Figure 8.3* Passive crash involvement: interactive effects

The female and male drivers in this study differed in their mean annual mileages (men driving more than women) and in their mean violation scores (men scoring higher than women), but not in their mean age. The statistical software used for these analyses (SPSS CHAID) takes account of such relationships between predictor variables when producing the solutions of Figures 8.2 and 8.3. We may thus confidently conclude that, when the other factors – possible confounding variables – had been taken into account statistically, there remained a significant tendency for female low and medium violators to have fewer *active* accidents than equivalent male drivers, but that there was no gender effect for passive accidents. Thus:

- Among 'careful' drivers (low, medium violators) active crash involvement was higher for males than for females.
- Among high violating drivers, women and men had the same (elevated) level of active crash involvement.
- The passive crash involvement of both female and male drivers was determined by how much and how badly they drove (exposure and violation tendency), not by what gender they were.

## The contribution of gender differences to crash involvement: a model

Most drivers 'drive as they live' (Beirness 1993). Female and male drivers can be considered as just women and men who are driving. The findings we have sketched in this chapter mirror those from studies of gender differences in other areas of risk-taking behaviour.

> Most typically, though not universally, studies find males take greater risks and risk taking decreases with age. Such results are primarily descriptive: . . . In fact, gender differences [*in risk taking*] may be spurious, that is they can be attributed to situational variables which are gender-linked.
>
> (Bromiley and Curley 1992: 121–2)

We have seen that women and men behind the wheel differ not only in the detail of the amount and type of their crash involvement, but also in a large number of other aspects of driving behaviour, namely:

- in how much, where, when and how they drive
- in the views they hold about and the satisfactions that they seek from driving
- in particular, in the extent to which they commit driving violations.

All of these factors have demonstrable links to crash involvement.

Figure 8.4 (adapted from Lajunen 1997: 32) provides a descriptive model or outline framework which attempts to summarize the various routes of influence from demographic differences (such as female versus male) to crash involvement. The top two rows of the model refer to *driver* differences, subsequent layers to *driving* differences. Generally the factors above influence the factors below – though a full model would need to specify the plethora of interactions and feedback loops to do justice to the complexity of human behaviour on the road. Age and gender make documented differences to the factors below them. Age and gender *and* all the factors below them have documented links to crash involvement (e.g. Maycock *et al.* 1991; Beirness 1993; Elander *et al.* 1993; Parker *et al.* 1995a, 1995b).

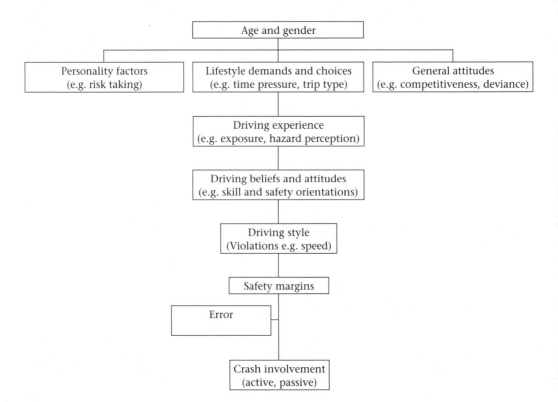

***Figure 8.4*** Outline model of the distal influence of age and gender on crash involvement
*Source*: adapted from Lajunen (1997: 32)

# Conclusions

> . . . are men and women equal with regard to traffic risks? In conclusion it can be stated . . . that if men are more exposed to risk, this is obviously not only because they use their car differently, but also because they are more attracted to risk – in accordance with their social stereotype – and because risky behaviour is made possible by the condition of the traffic system as such.
>
> (Barjonet 1988: 137)

We regard driving as an expressive activity. Male and female drivers – and, indeed, younger and older drivers – express themselves in different ways on the road. We believe that these different ways have consequences for their crash involvement.

So are women better drivers than men? Women are more successful than men in limiting the frequency and – especially – the severity of their crash involvement. Men are – on average – more skilful *and* more dangerous. The proximal cause of road traffic accidents is driving with reduced safety margins. The extent to which drivers adopt reduced safety margins is a function of their driving style. Driving style is affected by the particular beliefs and attitudes a person holds about driving. Unsafe attitudes and beliefs are more frequently – but not exclusively – held by young male drivers. Psychologists have methods for studying and techniques for changing a driver's values, beliefs, attitudes and motivations in order to influence the manner in which that person drives. Short of banning cars or removing discretionary decision making from drivers, it is in changing attitudes that the best hope lies of reducing the carnage on the roads that has seen upwards of 20 million persons across the planet killed by automobiles during the twentieth century (Faith 1997).

---

*Discussion questions*

1 Summarize the differences in crash involvement between female and male car drivers.

2 What potential confounding variables need to be taken into account when looking at gender differences in crash involvement?

3 Given what you have learned about the correlates of crash involvement, what road safety countermeasures would you recommend, and for whom?

4 What other tools used by psychologists can you think of that would be useful in furthering our understanding of the different driving patterns of males and females?

## Further reading

Elander, J., West, R. and French, D. (1993) Behavioral correlates of individual differences in road-traffic crash risk: an examination of methods and findings. *Psychological Bulletin* 113: 279–94. This article provides a state-of-the-art academic overview of the types of people that psychologists have linked to crash rates, and of the kinds of research methods that have been used.

Faith, N. (1997) *Crash: The Limits of Car Safety*. London: Boxtree. A tie-in with the 1997 UK Channel 4 television *Crash* series, this book provides a very readable account of the first 100 years of our love affair with the automobile and some of the havoc it has caused. The first half examines vehicle safety, the second half looks at 'the nut behind the wheel'.

Rothengatter, T. and Vaya, E. C. (eds) (1997) *Traffic and Transport Psychology: Theory and Application*. Amsterdam: Pergamon. The most up-to-date textbook in the field which, while expensive, provides a compendium of research on driver behaviour illustrating the breadth of the field and the multidisciplinary mix of theory and methods.

## References

Aberg, L. and Rimmo, P-A. (1998) Dimensions of aberrant driver behaviour. *Ergonomics*, 41: 39–56.

Barjonet, P. (1988) Sex differences in risk exposure and risk perception, in T. Rothengatter and R. de Bruin (eds) *Road User Behaviour: Theory and Research*. Maastricht: Van Gorcum.

Beirness, D. J. (1993) Do we really drive as we live? The role of personality factors in road crashes. *Alcohol, Drugs and Driving*, 9: 129–43.

Blockley, P. N. and Hartley, L. R. (1995) Aberrant driving behaviour: errors and violations. *Ergonomics*, 38: 1759–771.

Bromiley, P. and Curley, S. P. (1992) Individual differences in risk taking, in J. Frank Yates (ed.) *Risk-Taking Behavior*. Chichester: Wiley.

Cameron, K. (1998) Driver testing and training – is it relevant in today's conditions?, in *'Drivers: Licensed to Kill?'* Proceedings of the RoSPA 63rd Road Safety Congress. Birmingham: Royal Society for the Prevention of Accidents.

Cuerden, R. and Hill, J. (1997) Collision types and risk of injury for different driver characteristics, in *'Drivers: Licensed to Kill?'*, Proceedings of the RoSPA 63rd Road Safety Congress. Birmingham: Royal Society for the Prevention of Accidents.

Elander, J., West, R. and French, D. (1993) Behavioral correlates of individual differences in road-traffic crash risk: an examination of methods and findings. *Psychological Bulletin*, 113: 279–94.

Evans, L. (1991) Airbag effectiveness in preventing fatalities predicted according to type of crash, driver age, and blood alcohol concentration. *Accident Analysis and Prevention*, 23: 531–41.

Faith, N. (1997) *Crash: The Limits of Car Safety*. London: Boxtree.

Forsyth, E., Maycock, G. and Sexton, B. (1995) *Cohort Study of Learner and Novice Drivers, Part 3: Accidents, Offences and Driving Experience in the First Three Years of Driving*. Project Report PR111. Crowthorne: Transport Research Laboratory.

Horswill, M. S. and McKenna, F. P. (1997) Measuring, manipulating and understanding drivers' speed choice, in G. B. Grayson (ed.) *Behavioural Research in Road Safety VII* (PA 3296/97). Crowthorne: Transport Research Laboratory.

Lajunen, T. (1997) Personality factors, driving style and traffic safety, PhD thesis, Faculty of Arts, University of Helsinki.

Lajunen, T., Parker, D. and Stradling, S. G. (1998) Dimensions of driver anger, aggressive and Highway Code violations and their mediation by safety orientation in UK drivers. *Transportation Research Part F: Traffic Psychology and Behaviour*, 1: 107–21.

Lajunen, T. and Summala, H. (1995) Driving experience, personality, and skill and safety–motive dimensions in drivers' self-assessments. *Personality and Individual Differences*, 19: 307–18.

McKenna, F. P., Waylen, A. E. and Burkes, M. E. (1998) *Male and Female Drivers: How Different are They?* Basingstoke: AA Foundation for Road Safety Research.

Maycock, G. (1995) Novice driver accidents in relation to learning to drive, the driving test and driving ability and behaviour, in G. B. Grayson (ed.) *Behavioural Research in Road Safety V* (PA3081/95). Crowthorne: Transport Research Laboratory.

Maycock, G. (1997) Speed, speed choice and accidents, in G. B. Grayson (ed.) *Behavioural Research in Road Safety VII* (PA 3296/97). Crowthorne: Transport Research Laboratory.

Maycock, G., Lockwood, C. R. and Lester, J. F. (1991) *The Accident Liability of Car Drivers*. TRRL Report RR315. Crowthorne: Transport and Road Research Laboratory.

Meadows, M. L. (1994) Psychological correlates of road crash types. Unpublished PhD thesis, University of Manchester.

Meadows, M. L. and Stradling, S. G. (1995) Large-scale questionnaire research on drivers, in J. T. Haworth (ed.) *Psychological Research: Innovative Methods and Strategies*. London: Routledge.

Parker, D., Reason, J. T., Manstead, A. S. R. and Stradling, S. G. (1995a) Driving errors, driving violations and accident involvement. *Ergonomics*, 38(5): 1036–48.

Parker, D., West, R., Stradling, S. G. and Manstead, A. S. R. (1995b) Behavioural traits and road traffic accident involvement. *Accident Analysis and Prevention*, 27(4): 571–81.

Reason, J. T., Manstead, A. S. R., Stradling, S. G., Baxter, J. S. and Campbell, K. A. (1990) Errors and violations on the road: a real distinction? *Ergonomics*, 33: 1315–32.

Rolls, G. W. P., Hall, R. D., Ingham, R. and McDonald, M. (1991) *Accident Risk and Behavioural Patterns of Younger Drivers*. Basingstoke: AA Foundation for Road Safety Research.

Rothengatter, T. (1997) Errors and violations as factors in accident causation, in T. Rothengatter and E. C. Vaya (eds) *Traffic and Transport Psychology: Theory and Application*. Amsterdam: Pergamon.

Stradling, S. G. (1991) Age and gender differences in attitudes of pre-drivers, in G. B. Grayson and J. F. Lester (eds) *Behavioural Research in Road Safety I*. Crowthorne: Transport and Road Research Laboratory.

UK Department of the Environment, Transport and the Regions (DETR) (1997a) *Road Accidents Great Britain: 1996. The Casualty Report*. London: Stationery Office.

UK Department of the Environment, Transport and the Regions (DETR) (1997b) *Directorate of Statistics: National Travel Surveys*. London: Stationery Office.

Viano, D. C., Culver, C. C., Evans, L., Frick, M. C. and Scott, R. (1990) Involvement of older drivers in multivehicle side-impact crashes. *Accident Analysis and Prevention*, 22: 177–99.

Waller, P. (1997) Future possibilities for behavioural research, in G. B. Grayson (ed.) *Behavioural Research in Road Safety VII* (PA 3296/97). Crowthorne: Transport Research Laboratory.

West, R. (1995) *Accident Script Analysis*. Contractors Report CR343. Crowthorne: Transport Research Laboratory.

# The psychologist as detached investigator

# Chapter 9

# Do fire-fighters suffer from stress?

## John McLeod

One of the major areas of research and practice in applied psychology since the 1960s has been concerned with the topic of *stress*. The research literature amounts to many thousands of articles and book chapters. Studies of stress in non-occupational settings have largely focused on the impact of discrete life-events such as bereavement, divorce and moving house. As we saw in Chapter 2, studies in occupational settings have established the effects on the health and well-being of employees of many aspects of organizational life, such as workload, change, interpersonal conflict and shift systems. Some of these stressors have generally been conceptualized as 'daily hassles', or dimensions of work pressure which persist over substantial periods of time (Cooper and Payne 1988). A third tradition in stress research has been to explore reactions to traumatic incidents, using the post-traumatic stress disorder (PTSD) syndrome as a general framework (Hodgkinson and Stewart 1991). PTSD comprises a pattern of symptoms which occur in response to exposure to a dangerous or horrific event, and which may include intrusive remembering and reliving of the scene (flashbacks), high levels of anxiety, emotional numbness, sleep problems, feelings of detachment, and consequent damage to relationships and work performance (van der Kolk 1987).

There are some occupations which involve significant and repeated exposure to traumatic events as well as to ongoing organizational pressures and everyday life-events. People working in the emergency services (police, fire, ambulance, emergency medical teams, mountain rescue) routinely encounter death, tragedy and horror. They are required not only to deal with people in pain and distress but also to handle dead bodies (Taylor and Frazer 1982; Jones 1985; Duckworth 1986). Emergency services workers may also be exposed to situations in which they themselves are in personal danger of injury. Fire-fighters represent an occupational group exposed to a broad range of organizational and operational stressors. Previous studies of fire-fighter stress have mainly looked at the effects of dealing with large-scale disasters and one-off extreme events (e.g. Markowitz *et al.* 1987; McFarlane 1989; Markowitz 1989; Fullerton *et al.* 1992).

There has been very little research into stress in the UK Fire Service, which is surprising given the distinctive nature of its organizational structure and culture, and the considerable emotional demands placed on its personnel. Within the Fire Service there are a number of different work patterns which result in contrasting levels of exposure to different types of stress. Fire-fighters (the generic term for all operational staff) are employed according to a number of different work patterns:

- *Watch* fire-fighters are employed full time on a shift system (two days and two nights on followed by four days off).
- *Senior officers* are on call on a flexible duty system.
- *Day manning* fire-fighters live close to their station and are on call outside of normal working hours.
- *Retained* or part-time fire-fighters, mainly based in rural areas, live and work close to the station and respond to a pager when there is a fire call.

The various ranks of fire-fighter within the service are also associated with different types of stress. Junior officers (leading firemen/women and sub-officers) have first-line management and supervisory responsibilities. Firemen/women, leading firemen/women and sub-officers usually constitute the crews of fire appliances (although station officers in larger stations may also ride appliances). Senior officers (station officers, divisional officers and brigade officers) have a more managerial and administrative role, but are on call to take command at more serious incidents. All fire-fighters, even at the most senior command level, have operational responsibilities and must maintain levels of fitness and training sufficient to undertake operational duties.

All fire-fighters undergo three-yearly medical checks after the age of 40; there is a significant proportion of early retirements on health grounds before the normal retirement age of 55. The Fire Service recruits only at basic fireman/woman level, so all officers have had substantial experience of routine duties. The work of fire-fighters encompasses not only responding to fires, but also fire prevention and safety, rescuing victims of road traffic accidents (RTAs) and cleaning up chemical spills. These latter two areas of work are becoming increasingly important. Fire-fighters are therefore gaining much more exposure than ever before in their everyday work to dealing with the badly injured, maimed or dying victims of car crashes and industrial accidents.

## A study of stress and fire-fighters

As an applied counselling psychologist, I first became interested in stress in fire-fighters when I was invited by a fire and rescue service, as a neutral observer, to carry out a survey of levels of stress in their operational personnel. Both the management and union representatives in this brigade had become concerned about the number of fire-fighters seeking early retirement on grounds of stress, and had been influenced (as had the whole UK Fire Service establishment) by the experiences of various groups of emergency service workers who had reported PTSD symptoms following participation in the tragic series of events which Britain experienced in the 1980s – for example at the Lockerbie air disaster, the Hillsborough (Sheffield) and Bradford City football stadiums, Manchester airport and at King's Cross tube station in London. Both the brigade management and the union wished to know how serious the problem of stress was within their workforce, and, if it was serious, what they might do about it. At this time, managers in the Fire Service (and many other organizations) were being regularly visited by representatives seeking to sell them different kinds of counselling and critical incident debriefing services. But how big was the problem? What was the most cost-effective way of responding to stress? Should they buy into a commercial counselling scheme? Would they be liable under health and safety legislation if they failed in their duty of care to service personnel if they provided nothing? These were some of their very real concerns which led them to commission research by an independent observer.

It is perhaps worth mentioning here that the decision of this particular brigade to undertake this study took an act of some courage. The Fire Service is a very male-dominated organization, and it places high value on the capacity of the individual to cope with danger and to work effectively under pressure. A study which explored the experience of vulnerability and *not* coping was made possible only by the openness and awareness of senior figures within the brigade.

## The design of the study

A key feature of the research design was its emphasis on basing its findings in the experiences and constructs of fire-fighters themselves. The participants in the study included all operational personnel, encompassing more than 800 fire-fighters. Initial group interviews were carried out with groups of officers and fire-fighters in 21 stations, selected to reflect the different work groups and geographical locations through the brigade. We intentionally conducted these interviews in an open-ended way, using the material that emerged to identify areas of stress and coping for further study. The themes elicited in the group interviews were then further explored in a series of 60 in-depth (two-hour) individual interviews with a sample of officers and men randomly selected to represent different ranks and work groups. Finally, to test the generalizability of the interview material, a 247-item questionnaire was then constructed and piloted on a small group of fire-fighters, and then distributed to all members of the brigade (N = 800). This questionnaire included items on stress factors identified in the interviews, along with a number of standard measures of stress and coping, including the Holmes and Rahe (1967) Life-Events scale (see Box 2.3, pp. 36–7), the Maslach and Jackson (1981) Burnout scale, the Horowitz *et al.* (1979) Impact of Event Scale – a measure of PTSD symptoms – and the Goldberg and Williams (1988) 28-item version of the General Health Questionnaire (GHQ) – a measure of general levels of stress. Other sections of the questionnaire covered work group supportiveness, coping strategies and attitudes to counselling.

Throughout the study, my researcher colleague Dee Cooper and I met regularly with an advisory group drawn from all ranks, which provided feedback on the phrasing and appropriateness of interview and questionnaire items, and on the general interpretation of data. We attended a limited number of incidents, to observe the work of fire-fighters at first hand, and we were able to discuss brigade stress management procedures with occupational health and senior management staff. We also carried out a series of interviews with the wives and partners of fire-fighters.

We used elaborate procedures to guarantee the confidentiality of all the informants, and to ensure that those who participated in the study did so on a voluntary basis and felt safe to be honest about how stress had (or had not) affected them. The research generated a large amount of both quantitative and qualitative information. This allowed us to engage in method 'triangulation' (i.e. comparing data and conclusions derived from different sources).

## The findings of the study

The main theme to emerge from the fire-fighters' 'stress stories' gathered in group and individual interviews was the interpenetration of operational and organizational factors in their experience of situations which caused them distress. For example, fire-fighters working under great pressure, or attending traumatic or horrific incidents involving dead or dying victims, usually employed a professional 'armour' to distance themselves from the scene. However, underneath this professional role, they would have strong feelings about what was happening. These feelings would be channelled in directions shaped by a hierarchical, male-dominated organizational culture. The 'adrenalin high' of an incident might be dissipated by volleyball. Anger was sometimes expressed toward ineffective colleagues or bystanders. 'Black humour' was widely used to release emotional tension and reinforce group solidarity. Few fire-fighters would openly shed tears of distress after harrowing operational incidents.

It was striking that in group settings, for example during workshops or in group interviews, most fire-fighters claimed that they were unaffected by operational incidents (see Box 9.1). In individual in-depth interviews, by contrast, almost all were able to describe, in vivid detail and with considerable feeling, traumatic incidents in which they had been involved. Some informants reported that they had never previously spoken to anyone about these episodes. This phenomenon indicates the gap between an organizational culture which on the whole denies that fire-fighters are affected by their work, and a private reality that is quite different.

---

**Box 9.1  Experiences of stress**

Fire-fighters were asked what event they had found most stressful during their time in the job. The statements presented below have been edited to preserve anonymity.

On nights we'd had a run of malicious calls. I remember thinking this was another. Then we see it is well alight. That was a sudden shock.

Pull up and neighbours and relatives screaming that he's in there. Suddenly faced with it. Adrenalin and hearts going. Very fine line between your own safety and to try and find him. Knowing what's expected. Public expect you to save people . . . this was my first real goer. I was with an experienced man. He just seems to float through rooms. I was scared, frightened. I'm not one for pain. He whipped in and out. I was on hose reel . . . In training school you're told to stick with buddy but in reality don't. One goes for fire, one goes for casualties. I was torn between reality and training trying to do both. Only when he screamed at me 'put the fire out'. Man in kitchen was dead. They tried to revive him all way to hospital . . . I could feel my legs literally shaking under my body I was so hyped up. Fortunately I was working with a good bloke. Difficult to take it all in in one go. So much going through your mind. I felt physically drained after. I felt very nervous for ages. Because I felt I'd let the side down. I hadn't performed to my ability. I should have known better. Disappointed with myself. Let other man down. Nothing is ever said. It wasn't a disaster but you don't talk about it. Only if something drastic goes wrong then you say.

She died later that day. My wife said that one affected me. I felt sorry for her. I talked about it. It played on my mind so it came out in conversation. I talked to the wife and at work but you talk differently. At work you put a bit more of the macho image to the conversation but the actual things you are saying are the same. I wasn't horrified at what I'd seen – the serious injuries were internal. But I felt for her. I wouldn't say I've got over it now 'cos you still remember it. The feeling of sorrow has gone now it's something that has happened . . . It wasn't a, just a job, I really felt for her but you just accept it in the end that people do die in cars . . . I don't know how long it took. It didn't create any problems. I might have thought about her at night but I didn't lose sleep.

Several years ago I went through a period of utter dread of going on duty. We had a lot of paraffin heater fires and every job we went on there was a stiff or multiple stiff. I got to the stage where I physically just didn't want to go on duty. I was fed up with seeing bodies, dragging out bodies. Feelings of dread. Wanted to stay at home but if you didn't go the machine would not go on the run. It eased off – a couple of jobs where we didn't have bodies and straightaway the pressure was off and there were other incidents so these began clouding . . . awful period . . . Wasn't talking to my wife about it, she can't take that sort of thing. I could never release any of that with my wife and why should you lay something like that on someone else? You can't talk to people outside the job. Persuaded myself to go to work because it was my duty but still with the dread. At that time my children were babies so I was preoccupied when I got home. There was a very real dread.

You remember every death.

The culture of the Fire Service is characterized by tendencies to criticize or belittle personnel who do not live up to expectations. When asked to describe experiences that were highly stressful to them, several fire-fighters reported episodes in which they felt that senior officers publicly humiliated them at incidents, through an imposition of heavy-handed or persecutory disciplinary authority. The special impact of these episodes appeared to arise from the fact that they occurred at moments when the fire-fighters were most deeply acting out their core occupational identity of being a competent rescuer. The actions of senior colleagues here represented a wounding threat to that occupational identity.

Another theme in the interview material concerned the relationship between operational incidents and family life. The role of fire-fighter involves a high level of reciprocal impact between work and home. All fire-fighters either work shifts or are on call while at home. There is, therefore, significant potential for disruption to domestic routines. At the officer level, training is carried out through lengthy residential courses and promotion will often involve the necessity for moving house. The incidents which most affected fire-fighters were those that made them aware of the vulnerability of their own children. Conversely, exposure to these incidents at work led them to be highly safety conscious at home. Despite this intimate link between work and family life, very few of the informants chose to disclose to their wives or partners their true feelings about the disturbing aspects of their jobs, although interviews with wives/partners indicated that the latter were generally aware when something had happened. One way of making sense of these observations is to hypothesize that fire-fighters were internalizing their occupational identity to such an extent that being competent and able to cope with anything played a prominent role in their private as well as in their work life.

Many of the themes and trends apparent in fire-fighters' personal accounts also emerged from analysis of the results of the quantitative questionnaire, which was completed by 480 fire-fighters (a response rate of about 60%); all but one of these respondents was male.

The survey questionnaire included questions about the impact of an array of organizational, operational and domestic stressors. Fire-fighters as a whole reported that what they found stressful about the organization was the lack of consultation and communication, pressure caused by inspections, and the amount of criticism. In addition, senior and junior officers perceived themselves as overworked because of staff shortages and the amount of paperwork. Junior officers viewed their personal beliefs and values conflicting with those of the Fire Service and, along with many watch and day manning fire-fighters, they experienced stress from the pressure of the examinations necessary to secure promotion. Retained fire-fighters emerged as perceiving themselves to be significantly less affected than their full-time colleagues by the demands of the organization.

In the domain of operational stress, fire-fighters as a whole reported that driving to incidents, not having enough personnel to deal with an incident and uncertainty over what to do on the incident ground were all stressful. Events characterized by death and suffering, particularly when there might be children or colleagues injured, were also generally stressful. Other common sources of stress were performance guilt (worrying that they could have done more to help), feeling a connection with the victim and anger aroused by an incident. Junior officers reported the highest ratings for many operational stressors. It is notable that the events which were generally viewed as most stressful, for example an incident with a child injured or killed, consistently produced the most extreme ratings in junior officers. Retained fire-fighters by contrast gave lower stressfulness ratings for virtually all of the items in this list.

Compared with organizational and operational aspects of their lives, fire-fighters reported lower average levels of stress evoked by domestic and external factors, with the most stressful event being bereavement. The senior officers experienced relatively high stress from relationship difficulties. Day manning fire-fighters experienced the highest levels of external stress, with separation and divorce and housing problems being the main factors.

Taking the General Health Questionnaire (GHQ) as an indicator of general emotional well-being or global stress, it was found that day manning fire-fighters were under most overall stress, followed by senior and junior officers. Watch and retained fire-fighters experienced the lowest levels of stress as measured by the GHQ. Analysing the GHQ data from the point of view of identifying 'cases', or proportions of individuals with elevated scores, revealed that 26 per cent of senior officers, 27 per cent of junior officers, 13 per cent of watch fire-fighters, 31 per cent of day manning fire-fighters and 15 per cent of retained fire-fighters recorded serious levels of emotional or psychiatric distress.

In terms of burnout, the factor of emotional exhaustion was the only dimension to differentiate between work groups, with higher scores in senior and junior officers. There were no statistically significant differences across groups regarding other burnout factors (depersonalization, lack of personal accomplishment). The PTSD scale indicated generally low levels of post-traumatic stress symptoms, with the exception of junior officers, where almost 10 per cent had high scores.

## Do fire-fighters suffer from stress?

What does all this mean? Do fire-fighters suffer from stress? The findings of this study can be interpreted in a number of different ways. Fire-fighters appear to report slightly *lower* levels of overall stress in comparison with members of occupational groups, such as teachers or nurses (Cooper and Payne 1988). There are, however, serious problems involved in making this kind of comparison. Fire-fighters need to be physically fit and receive ongoing fitness training and medical checks. These factors are likely to attenuate levels of stress, since there is evidence that regular activity and exercise reduces anxiety. Also, the organizational culture of the Fire Service is one which can place pressure on individuals to conceal or deny emotional distress or psychological symptoms. This, presumably, would lead to lower self-reporting of stress on questionnaires such as the GHQ. It is therefore difficult to argue that fire-fighters suffer more or less stress than other occupational groups. They experience their own particular patterns of stress, and it is clear that at least some fire-fighters can be severely affected by the emotional demands of their job. There is certainly no doubt that fire-fighter stress exists.

---

*Box 9.2*    **How do fire-fighters cope with stress?**

In the research interviews, fire-fighters were asked about how they coped with stress, and what the brigade could do to help them to cope better.

Humour is there all the time, aimed at one another or at inter-station rivalry. It's like a release valve. Outsiders might think it's callous, but that's how things are, how it's always done. When the pressure is off a job that's when the humour starts. If a person is dead pressure is off or if a casualty is stable, then humour starts. If in a bad way then pressure is still on. We have running jokes that go on and on it doesn't mean anything to an outsider. You don't joke if children involved.

I talk to friends. I find myself doing that, telling them about incidents. I don't really say how I'm feeling. I don't know if people pick up I'm upset. You have to accept these things happen.

Coping? Sex makes me feel better . . . definitely. I don't go out drinking with the lads at work. I like being with the family, being alone, going out walking, burning off energy.

Don't like taking problems home. Don't talk about the job much to the wife, what happens at work. I like to protect her. I don't let everything out to her. I don't burden her with troubles and worries I might have at work. Yet she's strong enough perhaps it's just my way.

There ought to be someone in the brigade who could take care of someone suffering from stress . . . somebody who had been through the service maybe. I've noticed some people pick up hassle vibes they get so wound up over nothing. I don't think people would go to a counsellor . . . They have to preserve the image – it's like an alcoholic admitting he is an alcoholic.

---

Within the Fire Service, it seems clear that individuals in different roles experience varying patterns of stress and cope in different ways (see Box 9.2). The highest overall levels of stress were found in day manning fire-fighters, who live close to the station and were frequently on call. For these personnel, it appeared as though the job intruded significantly on their family life, and conversely that family life (for example disputes between neighbours living in the same fire service housing estate) could intrude on work life.

Sub-officers were the group of fire-fighters most likely to experience symptoms of post-traumatic stress disorder, reflecting the extent to which they were first on the scene at incidents, and were probably the ones most intensely exposed to the suffering of fire or road traffic accident victims. Those fire-fighters most centrally involved with the organizational dynamics and politics of the service (senior and junior officers) had the highest levels of organizational stress, while those least involved with these aspects of the work (retained fire-fighters) showed the lowest levels of organizational stress.

From the individual interviews and the questionnaire data it was clear that different sources of stress could have a cumulative effect. For example, experiencing marital problems or a bereavement could make a fire-fighter more vulnerable to post-traumatic stress following a serious incident.

Although not reported in any detail here, it was also apparent that the different modes of coping available to the various groups of fire-fighters made a difference to the stress that they experienced. Specifically, many watch fire-fighters (but not all) reported that they received good support from the other members of their team. By contrast, station officers (senior officers who would usually be in command of a fire station) described a greater degree of isolation and use of individual rather than group based coping strategies, such as listening to music or walking in the countryside.

## Responding to stress: what can be done?

Our role as external observers or consultants involved not only assessing the extent of stress, but also working with the brigade to evaluate the implications of our findings, and to recommend what might be done to alleviate stress. It seemed important to us to approach this stage of the project with two main goals. First, it was necessary to disseminate a better understanding of the nature of stress in the Fire Service. Second, it was important to introduce practical forms of help.

### The nature of stress in the Fire Service

The phenomenon of stress in the Fire Service illustrates the potential value of applied psychology, and also some of its limitations and frustrations. There are certainly many ways in which psychological methods and skills can be used to assist fire-fighters suffering from stress. But, at the same time, it should be apparent from what has been written that fire-fighter stress is complex and is bound up with a whole organizational culture and a way of life that cannot easily be changed. The management style of senior officers in the Fire Service is dominated by the requirement that they are able to 'command and control' on the incident ground. Effective leadership at a serious fire, for example, involves rapid appraisal of the situation, immediate decision making and the ability to direct personnel in an unambiguous manner. Another feature of the organizational culture of the Fire Service is the emphasis on *competence*, expressed through readiness for action, detailed knowledge of relevant factual material and the expectation that tasks are carried out in a specific way. These characteristics are shaped by the need to be able to perform complex tasks under severe time pressure in circumstances of danger and to be a reliable team member. Competence is culturally reinforced through high levels of interpersonal criticism. Poor performance is publicly observable and is openly criticized by higher ranks and peers. Fire-fighters are also self-critical, as indicated by widespread reports of experiences of 'performance guilt' following incidents in which people are injured. The organizational culture of the Fire Service also places value on group cohesiveness and solidarity, because of the absolute necessity of being able to rely on colleagues in situations of extreme danger. The traditions of the Fire Service, as expressed in its organizational culture, emphasize competence, high standards, rationality, obedience and reliability. Sensitivity to emotions can be counterproductive in a job which demands that the person overrides or wards off emotions such as fear or loss in order to get on with the task in hand. Anger was the one emotion that appeared to be culturally sanctioned in this setting. There is perhaps relatively little space in this culture for people who are anxious or depressed, or who are suffering intrusive flashback memories of previous incidents. Our impression was that in many cases the only option for a fire-fighter experiencing such symptoms was to sign off sick. Once off sick, it could be difficult ever to return or rejoin the group.

## Counselling as a method of reducing the effects of stress

It is essential to acknowledge that much of the stress which fire-fighters experience is intrinsic to the work. Nevertheless, there are a number of strategies that can be used to ameliorate or minimize the effects of stress. Many organizations, both in the commercial and public service sectors, have introduced counselling services or Employee Assistance Programmes (EAPs) to help their staff deal with stress problems (see Chapter 2 for a discussion of work-based counselling approaches). In Britain, most fire brigades now have some kind of counselling service available to employees. In some cases this is a specialist counselling service, sometimes shared with another organization (for example when there is a counselling service run jointly by the police and fire departments). Some brigades offer counselling in the context of welfare help or occupational health. In some cases these different kinds of counselling services are also available to fire-fighters through telephone helplines.

The main advantage of counselling lies in its flexibility. Counselling can be useful for a range of psychological difficulties, such as family and relationship problems, career planning and work functioning, and even dealing with the consequences of traumatic incidents. There are two main disadvantages of counselling in the context of the Fire Service. The first is that, for counselling to be effective, the person must participate on a wholly voluntary basis. Many fire-fighters either do not appreciate the value of counselling or do not trust that the counselling they receive will be confidential and discreet. There are significant cultural barriers to the acceptance of counselling within the Fire Service, with the result that many people who could benefit from it may be unwilling to use it. The other disadvantage is that counselling is relatively expensive. The pressure on all public spending has meant that some fire services can afford to provide only a limited number of sessions, or do not actively disseminate information on the counselling that might be on offer.

## Critical Incident Stress Debriefing

Another important stress intervention that is practised widely within emergency services agencies is Critical Incident Stress Debriefing (CISD). This is a group method of helping people who have been exposed to traumatic incidents to deal with their feelings and reactions to the event. The aim of a CISD session is to reassure fire-fighters that experiencing a psychological and emotional reaction to a traumatic incident is a normal process that can be helped through talking about it and sharing feelings. Many brigades have CISD teams which are called in to meet with fire crews who have been involved in stressful or traumatic incidents. The CISD session usually takes place within 48 hours of an incident and lasts for about 2 hours. It consists of a structured group discussion of what happened at the incident and how individuals in the group felt about what happened. The group leaders include information on the PTSD process, as well as facilitating the discussion and sharing in the group. Subsequent one to one counselling may be offered to individual fire-fighters who require it.

## Other methods of reducing stress

In many fire brigades (as well as other organizations) stress management or stress awareness training may be used to help employees identify their own stress responses and learn how to use more productive means of coping. Stress management training has a preventive function, in providing individuals with the skills and knowledge necessary for dealing with problems as they arise. Stress workshops are also used as a means of maximizing the effectiveness of counselling and critical incident debriefing, by serving as opportunities for explaining how these interventions work, and 'selling' them to sometime sceptical personnel. Finally, some brigades have explored the usefulness of fitness and diet regimes as methods of stress reduction. Usually, such exercise and healthy eating programmes are initiated by occupational health staff, but applied psychologists may play a role in suggesting procedures for maintaining compliance with this kind of organizational initiative.

# The experience of investigating fire-fighter stress

What is it like to carry out this kind of research? The role of an applied psychologist working for an organization such as the Fire Service can be fascinating, exciting and also highly challenging. Before undertaking this study, we had little previous experience of the emergency services and took some time to come to terms with the highly disciplined, hierarchical, uniform dominated and somehow very masculine way of life within the Fire Service. We were very much outsiders, and were perceived as such by members of the brigade. It became important for them to let my research colleague and I know how it felt to be a fire-fighter. Although for legal and safety reasons we were not allowed to ride on an appliance, we were supplied with pagers (the experience of being on call) and taken to a number of incidents that they believed would be instructive for us. The impact of these incidents was very powerful. As psychologists, we had entered into their world with our research 'tools': questionnaires, interview schedules and a capacity for empathic listening. What the fire-fighters did was to show us what it was like, in a much more direct way, by allowing us to *see* burnt bodies, *smell* a fire-gutted house, *feel* the complex mix of fear, anger and loss, and then finally to *imagine* 'how?' and 'what if . . . ?'

## Experience as data

Often, applied psychologists attempt to use standardized instruments, such as questionnaires and rating scales, to develop objective and detached measures of aspects of work life. As counselling psychologists, however, my research colleague and I were also interested in using our own subjective responses to the Fire Service as data. Such an approach is consistent with the emphasis in counselling and psychotherapy that is often placed on the countertransference or congruence of the therapist (see McLeod 1996). Also, in much contemporary qualitative research there is an appreciation that researchers' reflexive self-awareness of their engagement in the research is an important source of information (Smith *et al.* 1995).

Perhaps the most significant facet of our reaction to the Fire Service was a sense of admiration and liking toward many of the fire-fighters we met. These were people who were clearly doing a worthwhile job to the highest possible standard. Their humour and generosity in many situations were remarkable. We found it hard to carry out some of the group interviews because of the level of genuinely funny banter.

Looking more closely at our responses to the Fire Service, what we experienced could be interpreted as representing a sense of just how powerful the collective reality of the 'world of the fire-fighter' is, and both how necessary it is for anyone involved with the service to be accepted within that inner circle, and how isolating it is to be outside it. Our sense was that to openly admit stress would place a fire-fighter outside of the circle. Humour, and sometimes anger, served most of the time as an effective means of externalizing painful images and emotions associated with the job. But if these images were too strong or too personal to be joked about, then there was nowhere that they could readily be taken.

## Ethical considerations

Another important dimension in this kind of research arises from the moral and ethical implications of applied research. There are some straightforward ethical procedures that any researcher needs to follow. For example, any information provided by an informant must be treated in confidence and used only for research purposes. Anyone being interviewed was asked to give informed consent, by signing a consent form. But there are difficult moral issues that lie beyond these ethical considerations. When interviewing fire-fighters about stress it became apparent that it was impossible for either the researcher or the informant to know what might emerge. Some fire-fighters remembered, in the course of the interview, details of distressing traumatic events that they had 'filed away' for years. One of the recurring images that fire-fighters used was that of 'bottling up' their feelings. On some occasions, being interviewed opened the bottle. On other occasions, interviews enabled informants to talk about matters that clearly required further counselling help. Some fire-fighters wrote on their (anonymous) questionnaires about how desperate they were. The very fact that the research was taking place seemed to lead to an impression that counselling was now available. It was essential that we were sensitive to these needs.

The political context of the research raised moral issues. Who would have access to the final report? Would the recommendations of the report reinforce the demands of the unions for a more comprehensive staff care package? Would the report reflect the feelings of many fire-fighters that their main stress arose from an authoritarian management style? As in most applied work of this kind, we had to achieve a balance between the agendas of different institutional stakeholders.

## The value of the research

The ultimate question, of course, is 'Did our research make a difference?' We are pleased to report that the fire brigade which we studied now utilizes a critical incident debriefing team. This is comprised of volunteers from all sections of the workforce; it also makes external counselling available to fire-fighters through its occupational health department. Neither of these services is perhaps as well resourced, supported or used as much as it might be, but they do exist. There is probably also a greater awareness throughout the brigade of the nature of stress and its effects. However, much remains to be done and much more research is needed in order to understand the psychological effects of continual exposure to trauma and trauma in emergency services personnel such as fire-fighters. Nevertheless, it is probably fair to say that the UK Fire Service as a whole now accepts that counselling and critical incident debriefing are part of the duty of care that is owed to those who risk their lives on behalf of us all in this demanding occupation.

---

*Discussion questions*

1 How might critical incident stress in fire-fighters be prevented? Can you think of ways of detecting vulnerability to PTSD in those who apply for fire-fighter jobs?

2 What difference might it make to levels of stress and ways of coping that there are now increasing numbers of women fire-fighters?

3 What kind of research questions about fire-fighter stress suggest themselves to you, after reading this chapter? How might you carry out research that would answer these questions?

---

# Further reading

Cooper, C. L. and Payne, R. (eds) (1988) *Causes, Coping and Consequences of Stress at Work*. Chichester: Wiley. This book provides a good review of the issues for those interested in a deeper understanding of theory and research on workplace stress.

Hodgkinson, P. E. and Stewart, M. (1991) *Coping with Catastrophe*. London: Routledge; and Mitchell, J. T. and Bray, B. (1990) *Emergency Services Stress: Guidelines for Preserving the Health and Careers of Emergency Services Personnel*. Englewood Cliffs, NJ: Prentice Hall. Both these books provide highly readable guides to critical incident debriefing.

Newton, T. (1995) *'Managing' Stress: Emotion and Power at Work*. London: Sage. This book offers an alternative interpretation of the phenomenon of job stress, emphasizing the role of organizational rather than psychological factors.

(See also the recommended reading for Chapter 2.)

# References

Cooper, C. L. and Payne, R. (eds) (1988) *Causes, Coping and Consequences of Stress at Work*. Chichester: Wiley.

Duckworth, D. H. (1986) Psychological problems arising from disaster work. *Stress Medicine*, 2: 315–23.

Fullerton, C. S., McCarroll, J. E., Ursano, R. J. and Wright, K. M. (1992) Psychological responses of rescue workers: fire fighters and trauma. *American Journal of Orthopsychiatry*, 62: 371–8.

Goldberg, D. and Williams, P. (1988) *A User's Guide to the General Health Questionnaire*. Windsor, UK: NFER-Nelson.

Hodgkinson, P. E. and Stewart, M. (1991) *Coping with Catastrophe: A Handbook of Disaster Management*. London: Routledge.

Holmes, T. and Rahe, R. (1967) The social readjustment rating scale. *Journal of Psychosomatic Research*, 11: 213–18.

Horowitz, M. J., Wilner, B. A. and Alvarez, M. A. (1979) Impact of event scale: a measure of subjective distress. *Psychosomatic Medicine*, 41: 209–18.

Jones, D. R. (1985) Secondary disaster victims: the emotional effects of recovering and identifying human remains. *American Journal of Psychiatry*, 142: 303–7.

McFarlane, A. C. (1989) The aetiology of post-traumatic morbidity: predisposing, precipitating and perpetuating factors. *British Journal of Psychiatry*, 154: 221–8.

McLeod, J. (1996) The humanistic paradigm, in R. Woolfe and W. Dryden (eds) *Handbook of Counselling Psychology*. London: Sage.

Markowitz, J. S. (1989) Long-term psychological distress among chemically exposed firefighters. *Behavioral Medicine*, 15: 75–83.

Markowitz, J. S., Gutterman, E. M., Link, B. and Rivera, M. (1987) Psychological responses of firefighters to a chemical fire. *Journal of Human Stress*, 13: 84–93.

Maslach, C. and Jackson, S. E. (1981) The measurement of experienced burnout. *Journal of Occupational Behaviour*, 2: 99–113.

Mitchell, J. T. and Bray, B. (1990) *Emergency Services Stress: Guidelines for Preserving the Health and Careers of Emergency Services Personnel*. Englewood Cliffs, NJ: Prentice Hall.

Newton, T. (1995) *'Managing' Stress: Emotion and Power at Work*. London: Sage.

Smith, J., Harré, R. and van Langenhove, L. (eds) (1995) *Rethinking Methods in Psychology*. London: Sage.

Taylor, A. J. W. and Frazer, A. G. (1982) The stress of post-disaster body handling and victim identification work. *Journal of Human Stress*, 8: 4–12.

van der Kolk, B. A. (ed.) (1987) *Psychological Trauma*. Washington, DC: American Psychiatric Press.

# Chapter 10

# Investigating homework: an outsider's view

## *James Hartley*

In this chapter I want to argue that the notion of a 'psychologist as a detached investigator' can be considered in at least two ways. I then want to illustrate these two approaches with a case study.

Psychologists may be detached investigators in the sense that they are not involved in the situation they are investigating. In Chapter 9, for instance, John McLeod was called in as a neutral observer to assess the impact of stress on fire-fighters. In this chapter I shall present the results of a survey of the research literature on what we know about homework. I am detached from this analysis by the fact that I have no children, I do not serve on the governing bodies of any schools, and nor do I have any relations who are involved in school teaching (although I used to). So, unlike many others, I am not personally involved in the issue. I hope, therefore, that I can give an independent view of what is known about homework and its effectiveness.

A second way of thinking about the psychologist as a detached investigator is to consider the idea as an example of how some people believe – and many students are taught – that psychologists can take a neutral, scientific stance when approaching their investigations. In carrying out experiments, for instance, the idea is that we can create 'control' and 'experimental' groups, we can compare them on some pertinent variable(s), and that the findings of such studies can be replicated by other investigators. Put more starkly, this view takes the line that facts exist independently of their observers, and that they can be established by a scientific approach.

Such a view has many critics, and it is not appropriate to discuss the matter here in detail. (As noted in the prologue, interested readers might enjoy the exchanges about this issue between Morgan (1998), Sherrard (1998) and N. Cooper and Stevenson (1998) in *The Psychologist* 11(10) and subsequent correspondence in 11(12)). Suffice it to say here that the argument centres around how human investigators can study people in a scientific way when we all know that our perceptions and judgements are coloured by our experiences and wishes. So, when it comes to homework, even though I may be a detached investigator in the sense of being an outside observer, I am not a neutral person. I naturally have experiences of homework and opinions about it, I teach educational psychology and I live in a political world. Moreover, when it comes to writing as a psychologist, I have views about the quality of the evidence that I assess. So, in writing a review, I make value judgements about which findings I want to emphasize, and which ones I want to be more neutral about.

## Why write reviews?

Psychologists write reviews for a number of reasons (e.g. see Fink 1998; Foster and Hammersley 1998). They might want to let people know the current state of the art as far as a particular topic is concerned. They may want to redress the balance of an argument about a particular issue. They may want to put together disparate literatures to show that more is known than was thought. They may want to use a review to reveal inadequacies in the literature and to point where further research needs to be done. None of these reasons is entirely neutral. Reviewers write to persuade their readers.

In the particular case being discussed here I decided to write my review because I was annoyed by something that I had read. The opening sentence that set me off, in two versions of a Department for Education and Employment (DfEE) discussion paper on the value of homework, was 'Research over a number of years in this and other countries has shown that homework can make an important contribution to pupils' progress at school' (DfEE 1998a, 1998b). In point of fact there is nothing particularly wrong with this sentence, except that the appropriate research was not referenced in the texts where the sentence appeared. I found this particularly irritating because these documents were being distributed nationally for discussion so that they might be later revised on the basis of the comments received. In effect the documents pre-empted any discussion of the value of homework by taking this value for granted. So my questions to myself were: What research? And is the sentence correct? I decided to find out.

## How do psychologists write reviews?

There are many ways of writing research reviews (e.g. see Cone and Foster 1993; H. Cooper 1998; Fink 1998; Froese *et al.* 1998; Hart 1998). However, in this chapter, I shall describe my approach to writing the review which follows. This approach, judging from other accounts, is fairly typical.

## Gathering the evidence

The first thing to do, when writing a review, is to find out what has been already published on the topic. This can be accomplished in different ways. In my case I first used Bath University's Information and Data Services (BIDS), one of many electronic databases; I searched under 'homework', going back to 1980. (Other databases that I could have used, but did not, include PsycLit and ERIC, the Educational Resources Information Center.) BIDS alerted me to several papers and to a key book (H. Cooper 1989a). Following this, I used my university's inter-library loan service to send for a copy of the book and for those papers that seemed from their titles and abstracts to be relevant to the topic – if they were not already available in the university library. I then checked the reference lists of Cooper and of all the papers that I obtained and I repeated the inter-library loan procedure to follow up references that I had not yet obtained but which looked of interest. In addition I also wrote to the main contributors to this field in the UK and the USA to ask them for copies of their main papers, and anything else that they had published more recently on the topic.

## Classifying the evidence

Once the evidence is obtained it has to be classified and integrated in some way. In this case it seemed useful to assemble the studies, initially following H. Cooper (1989a), to answer a series of questions about homework, such as 'How much time do students spend on homework, and is this time important?' (see pp. 168–75). Interestingly enough this initial classification dominated the review process, so that the later papers were read from this point of view. Presumably, if this initial classification had been changed, then the subsequent research literature might have been used differently.

## Assessing the evidence

Judgements have to be made about the quality of the evidence. Much of the evidence that I assembled was American and thus of questionable validity for the British scene. So it is important to clarify in a review where the evidence is coming from (and many authors fail in this respect). Some of the studies relied on self-report measures – of say, children, parents and teachers – and some on more objective measures, such as exam results. Self-reports have to be treated with caution because they might exaggerate or underemphasize certain points. (For example, some pupils might claim to do more homework than they do; some teachers might claim to mark homework more assiduously than is in fact the case.) Some of the studies reviewed were small scale ones (carried out in a single school, for instance) but some much larger (like Cooper's analyses). Indeed Cooper had assembled together so many studies of homework that he was able to conduct meta-analyses of the data that he obtained. This approach enables researchers to summarize in one overall analysis the results from many studies. (Thus, for example, Cooper reported the overall result obtained from pooling the individual results of 18 studies of the effects of the amount of time spent on homework on later academic achievement.) If I had been a perfectionist I would have obtained copies of the 200 or so studies cited by Cooper in his text and assessed them myself, rather than relying on his judgements. However, I did not do this. In writing my review I took the results of Cooper's meta-analyses at face value, but I sought to find additional studies published since his book to add to the ones that he referred to. I tended to give greater weight to large-scale quantitative studies than to small-scale qualitative ones – reflecting my bias for studies with larger sample sizes and more objective measures.

## Writing the review

When writing a review all of this information has to be put together in a form that is suitable for a particular audience – in this case A level psychology students. This means that the text has to be concise and readable. Writing a review often involves writing 2–3 line summaries of scientific studies that are 20–30 pages long and replete with detail; it is here that an author's predilections may well affect the results. Different people reading the same research papers might well come up with different organizational structures, attach different values to different studies, write different accounts and reach different conclusions. Box 10.1 provides an example showing how various authors used the results from one classic study in different ways to support the specific arguments that they were making in that section of their particular literature review.

So a research review may emerge from what appears to be a detached investigation, but this does not mean that the review gives the 'right' answers to any questions posed at the outset. It gives one author's picture. It is to be hoped that the main elements of this picture will be shared by others doing the same task, but they are unlikely to be exactly the same – just as

---

### Box 10.1 Abstract from an original study plus four different accounts of the same study

This box contains an abstract from an original study (Chen and Stevenson 1989) followed by four different reports of the same study. Note how these different reviewers select from this study the information that they need to support the argument they are making. Summarizing a journal study leads to selections, distortions and amplifications. (The abstract is reproduced with permission of the authors and the Society for Research in Child Development.)

*Abstract*

Cultural differences in the amount of time spent on homework and beliefs and attitudes about homework were investigated through interviews with more than 3500 elementary school children, their mothers and their teachers. The children lived in 5 cities: Beijing, Chicago, Minneapolis, Sendai (Japan) and Taipei. Chinese children were assigned more homework and spent more time on homework than Japanese children, who in turn were assigned more and spent more time on homework than American children. Chinese children also received more help from family members with their homework than did American and Japanese children. Chinese children were found to have more positive attitudes about homework than American children; Japanese children's attitudes were between those of the Chinese and the American children. Relations between the amount of time spent on homework by children, amount of time parents spent assisting their children with homework, and children's achievement were also explored. The views of both parents and teachers about the value of homework are discussed.

*First reviewers' account*

Furthermore, work carried out in the international field tends to suggest that countries in which pupils average the most home study (8–9 hours weekly), also average the highest test scores (Chen and Stevenson 1989; Walberg 1991).

(Faulkner and Blyth 1995)

*Second reviewers' account*

A conclusion supportive of homework was also reached by some cross-cultural studies, whereby the higher academic achievement of various cultural groups (e.g. Chinese or Japanese versus North Americans) has been partly attributed to greater parental involvement in homework (Chen and Stevenson 1989; Chen and Uttal 1988).

(Levin *et al.* 1997)

*Third reviewer's account*

Box 10.3 shows the findings from studies reported by Chen and Stevenson (1989). Here it can be seen that Chinese children did more homework than Japanese and American ones. Other studies have also reported that Asian children do more homework than children in other ethnic groups (e.g. see Keith and Benson 1992; Mau 1997).

Hartley (this chapter)

*Fourth reviewers' account*

In a major cross cultural analysis of homework, Chen and Stevenson (1989) interviewed 3500 elementary school children and their mothers and teachers from China, Japan and the USA. The findings revealed that the Chinese children were assigned more homework and spent more time doing it than the Japanese who in turn did more than the USA children. The amount of homework set varied between schools. The study found no consistent relationship between time spent doing homework and the child's academic achievement. However, the comparison may be misleading. Although the Japanese children do less homework they tend to go to study classes after school. Overall the relationships between achievement and time spent on homework varied across the cities involved and at different grade levels.

(Hallam and Cowan 1998)

individual painters produce different pictures of the same object, depending on the size, perspective and media of the picture that they are painting.

Some attempts to overcome these difficulties have been made by authors not only by specifying the appropriate procedures that writers should follow in writing reviews (especially in the medical field: see Dixon *et al.* 1997) but also by using techniques of meta-analysis which identify the rules for including or excluding particular studies (Zakzanis 1998). Often it seems that the only way of coming to a more objective or impartial point of view is through 'triangulation' where the opinions of different observers of the same events are compared. In this connection readers might like to compare my review with the review by Hallam and Cowan (1998) that I obtained after I had completed mine. Essentially we reach the same conclusions but we arrive at them by rather different routes. Bearing all of these points in mind, here is my review.

## Is homework good for you? A review by James Hartley

In May 1998, David Blunkett, the then UK Secretary of State for Education, issued draft guidelines for discussion in British primary and secondary schools about homework (see DfEE 1998a; 1998b). The guidelines were based upon recommended good practice (e.g. Office for Standards in Education (Ofsted) 1998). Indeed, the opening sentence of both the guidelines for primary schools and the ones for secondary schools said, *'Research over a number of years in this and other countries has shown that homework can make an important contribution to pupils' progress at school.'* However, no details concerning this research were given.

This paper sets out to review the evidence for this assertion. Psychologists normally prefer more detailed statements than this. We like to know *what* research, by *whom*, and using what *measures*? We like to see the *references*. And, once we have found them and begin to look into the matter, we usually find that the issue is not as simple as it seems. Indeed, in the context of homework, there are a number of interrelated problems to consider. This article discusses some of them.

### Does homework actually work?

To answer a question like this properly one would have to set up studies where everything else was the same, and the pupils involved were randomly assigned to either an experimental (homework) condition or a control group (no homework). The performance of the pupils in the two groups on a later test or examination would then show whether or not homework had an effect. Of course this is difficult, if not impossible, to do in real life. So what has happened in practice is that a variety of methods have been employed. H. Cooper (1989a), for example, described 17 comparison studies conducted in the USA where, within them, 5 different methods for assigning pupils to the treatment conditions were used. These were: random assignment of students; random assignment of classes; matched students within classes; matched classes; and nonequivalent control groups. The amount of time the pupils spent doing homework in these 17 studies varied from 2 to 30 weeks, with an average time of between 9 and 10 weeks. The effects of homework were assessed in a variety of different subject matters, but Maths and English were the most common.

H. Cooper (1989a) found that the overall results did indeed suggest that doing homework was useful but that the results were affected by age levels. It appeared that doing homework had little effect with primary school pupils but that it was more effective with secondary school pupils. Four subsequent US studies have confirmed these findings (see H. Cooper *et al.* 1998).

There has been little parallel research on this question in the UK. The Ofsted (1998) report does give an impressionistic picture, gathered from HMI inspections, but few quantitative data are supplied. Other studies, similarly, give limited information. For example, Rutter *et al.* (1979: 109) in their study of effective *secondary* schools remark, 'The findings show that schools which set homework frequently and where there was some kind of check on whether staff did set it, tended to have better outcomes than schools which made little use of homework'.

So, referring back to the opening sentence of the DfEE (1998a) guidelines for *primary* schools, there is, in fact, no hard evidence to support the idea that homework makes a strong contribution here – unless, possibly, one looks at issues wider than academic achievement. Some commentators suggest, for instance, that homework might encourage other virtues, such as learning to work independently, and the development of long term study habits. But there are very few studies in this area (nonetheless see e.g. Sharpe and Thomas 1993; Wharton 1997).

## Are there any better alternatives to homework?

H. Cooper (1989a) outlined eight US studies that assessed the effects of providing other activities for the no-homework groups, so that pupils in both situations did work of some kind. Here he found mixed results. It appeared that, overall, pupils in *primary* schools did better with in-class supervised study than they did with homework, but that pupils in *secondary* schools did better with homework than they did with in-class supervised study. So here again there was an age difference, with homework being more effective for older pupils than it was for younger ones. I can find no British comparison studies in this respect, but these American findings suggest that British teachers in primary (and secondary) schools might like to think more about the wisdom of arranging for periods of supervised study (or homework clubs and study support centres) rather than just giving out homework. Some work along these lines has been reported in Scotland (MacBeath 1993) and there is currently much interest in 'study support' (e.g. see DfEE 1998c).

## Does the amount of time pupils spend on homework have an effect?

If homework has an effect – especially at secondary level – then how much time should pupils spend on homework? This was one of the issues that was picked up by David Blunkett and it received wide attention in the media. Schools in Britain vary widely in how much time they ask their pupils to spend on homework. Some require none: some require a good deal (e.g. see West *et al.* 1998). David Blunkett wanted those schools who did not provide much homework to look to their practices in this respect. He also wanted to encourage homework in primary schools. Box 10.2 shows the then recommended guidelines.

---

*Box 10.2*  **Amount of daily homework appropriate for pupils of different ages (initially suggested by DfEE: see DfEE 1998a, 1998b)**

|  | *Reading* | *Other home activities* | *Total per day* |
|---|---|---|---|
| Reception Year | 10 mins | 10 mins | 20 mins |
| Years 1 and 2 | 20 mins | 10 mins | 30 mins |
| Years 3 and 4 | 20 mins | 20 mins | 40 mins |
| Years 5 and 6 | 20 mins | 30 mins | 50 mins |
| Years 7 and 8 |  |  | 45–90 mins |
| Year 9 |  |  | 1–2 hours |
| Years 10–11 |  |  | 1.5–2.5 hours |

Note that the times suggested for homework in primary schools were reduced in a later report (DfEE 1998d). These were changed to 1 hour per *week* for Years 1 and 2, 1.5 hours per *week* for Years 3 and 4, and 30 mins per *day* for Years 5 and 6. The recommended times suggested for secondary school pupils were not altered.

---

But what does the evidence say? Again, basing my judgements on work in US schools (see H. Cooper 1989a; H. Cooper *et al.* 1998), it seems that the amount of time pupils spend on homework has little effect in primary schools, but that time spent is a more important factor in secondary schools. Cooper (1989a) examined in detail 18 studies that reported, among them, 50 separate correlations between the amount of time spent on homework and academic achievement. He concluded:

The optimum amount of homework also varies with grade level [age]. For elementary [primary school] students, no amount of home-work – large or small – affects achievement. For junior high school students [pupils aged 12 to 16yrs], achievement continues to improve with more homework until assignments last between one and two hours a night. For high school students [over 16yrs], the more homework, the better the achievement – within reason of course.
(H. Cooper 1989b: 88)

Again there is little parallel research in the UK. Nonetheless, the results of two British studies fit in with this overall picture. Holmes and Croll (1989) found – with pupils from one single-sex grammar school – a clear relationship between the time that the pupils reported that they spent on homework and achievement in school examinations, with the best achievement being recorded by pupils who spent over 75 minutes each weekday evening on their homework. Tymms and Fitz-Gibbon (1992), in a much larger study of A level pupils, found less clear-cut results, but they still concluded that 'there was a tendency for those doing more homework to obtain better grades'. Here pupils who worked more than seven hours a week 'tended to get a third of a grade better than students of the same gender and ability who worked less than two hours a week' (Tymms and Fitz-Gibbon 1992: 3, 7). However, both Holmes and Croll (1989) and Tymms and Fitz-Gibbon (1992) also found additional factors – such as verbal ability, social class, prior achievement and parental monitoring – to be important. And indeed, both studies (together with that of Rutter *et al.* (1979) mentioned earlier) found that there were large ranges in the amounts of time individual pupils spent on their homework in their various schools. Tymms and Fitz-Gibbon concluded:

It is clear that A-level students do a lot of homework and that, for the sake of their own success, they are well advised to work hard, However, it is also clear that A-level teachers who pile on the work are not necessarily the teachers associated with 'good' results. Teach-ers who do demand many hours of students' home time per week might well look at this analysis and decide to ease up on this blanket pressure and monitor the outcomes which follow. The analysis also implies that students can work hard to do themselves justice at A-level and still be left with plenty of time to enjoy life.
(Tymms and Fitz-Gibbon 1992: 9)

## Are there differences in the amount of homework that children do in different countries?

As we have seen, most of the research findings outlined above have come from US studies and there has been very little work on

> **Box 10.3  Some differences in the amount of homework done in different countries (approx. numbers of minutes per day: each row entry from a separate study)**
>
> |        | 6–7yrs | 8–9yrs | 10–11yrs |
> |--------|--------|--------|----------|
> | USA    | 25     | 40     | 50       |
> |        | 05     |        | 30       |
> | Japan  | 20     |        | 50       |
> |        | 20     |        | 30       |
> | China  | 35     | 120    | 90       |
> |        | 40     |        | 65       |
> |        | 60     |        | 100      |
>
> *Source*: data adapted from Chen and Stevenson (1989) with permission of the authors

homework in the UK. Some investigators, however, have tried to assess the approximate amount of homework that primary and secondary school children do in different countries. Box 10.3 shows the findings from studies reported by Chen and Stevenson (1989). Here it can be seen that Chinese children did more homework than Japanese and American ones. Other studies have also reported that Asian children do more homework than children in other ethnic groups (e.g. see Keith and Benson 1992; Mau 1997). In other international studies a curvilinear relationship has been found between the amount of time spent and academic achievement (in maths and science) in many countries, with the highest achievement being associated with moderate amounts of homework per day (one to three hours).

However, what is more important perhaps, is what pupils do in the time they spend on homework, rather than the amount of time itself. Keith and Benson (1992) reported that Asian pupils made better use of their time, in the sense that each hour of homework that they completed had a greater effect on their learning than it did for the other groups in their study.

Nonetheless, a word of caution is needed here. Much of these data on time and homework are dated, and things may have changed since they were reported. Carol Fitz-Gibbon (personal communication), for instance, has reported that the amount of homework that children do in secondary schools while studying for their A levels has declined (from about six hours per week in 1989 to about three hours per week in 1996) but the causes for this are obscure. Maybe A levels are easier than they were? Maybe A level pupils have different interests these days?

## What about the role of teachers in relation to homework?

It seems odd to focus purely on the time spent on homework as one of the main issues of discussion. Clearly what is done in that time – the kind of homework carried out – and how homework is incorporated into further classroom activity is more important. Yet there has been surprisingly little research into these aspects of homework. One study which is of relevance here was conducted in the USA by Murphy and Decker (1989). These investigators surveyed nearly 3000 teachers. They found teachers claimed that they used homework most often to reinforce previous class activities rather than to introduce new material. Homework was most often assigned orally at the end of class – with the result that many children might forget what they were supposed to do. Some teachers did write the requirements on the blackboard, but few issued actual written instructions. Almost 90 per cent of the teachers in this sample claimed that they regularly checked the homework they had set within one or two days.

Other investigators have suggested how teachers' marking loads can be reduced – and students' study habits improved – by introducing self-checking procedures into doing and marking homework (e.g. Miller *et al.* 1993; Sharpe and Thomas 1993). Looking to the future, we might expect developments in the computer assisted setting and evaluation of homework.

## What about the role of parents?

Homework is not done in a vacuum. Children, particularly in the primary schools, might ask for or be given help by their parents. Cooper (1989a) and his colleagues (H. Cooper *et al.* 1998) examined the contribution of American parents in assessing the effectiveness of homework. Cooper (1989a) reported the results of eight studies on whether or not parental involvement related to achievement. He concluded that the results were mixed and that, 'as yet, there is no reliable evidence on whether parental involvement affects student achievement' (Cooper 1989a: 140).

Other studies have also reported conflicting results. For example, Levin *et al.* (1997) found that maternal help with homework had no effect on academic achievement with 6–8-year-olds in Israel. In contrast, in the USA, Bowen and Bowen (1998) found a clear relationship between parental help with homework and the academic achievement of 11–18-year-olds who were at risk of school failure. Zellman and Waterman (in press) found that mothers of high IQ children aged 7 and 10 gave less help with homework than did mothers with low IQ children. In one interesting study Ginsburg and Bronstein (1993) found that the more that US parents were involved in overseeing the homework of their 9–12-year-old children in their sample, the more the children became dependent on external sources to guide their academic work, and the poorer became their grades and academic achievement. Similar results were reported by Mau (1997) for US parents of 16-year-olds.

We should also remember here that parents who come from different ethnic backgrounds might also differ in the amount of help that they give with homework (e.g. see Chen and Stevenson 1989; Mau 1997; Leung *et al.* 1998).

It would thus appear from many studies that parents vary in the amount and kind of help that they give their children, and in their attitudes to homework. Even if the parents are not actually involved in helping children with their homework, their attitudes towards it will still be important. (After all, making sure that homework is completed is often a source of friction between parents and children.) Hoover-Dempsey, *et al.* (1995) report that many US parents often feel ill prepared for helping with homework, and not sure what they should do.

The Ofsted (1998) report suggests that British parents and teachers generally have positive attitudes towards homework. Likewise, H. Cooper *et al.* (1998) found that the US parents, teachers and the pupils involved in their study had positive attitudes towards homework, but that these were more marked for the parents and the teachers than they were for the children. However, these investigators found no clear relationship between parental attitudes to homework and resulting pupil achievement at primary level and only a modest relationship at secondary level.

## What other factors might affect the effectiveness of homework?

Finally, we need to pause and think about what other factors might affect the effectiveness of homework. Box 10.4 provides some suggestions from other research studies not referenced in this review. Perhaps you can think of more.

## Conclusions

I started out with a simple question: does homework work? Analysis shows that this is an oversimple question to ask, and that the answer is not straightforward. In particular there is no strong evidence – and certainly no strong British evidence – to support David Blunkett's views about the amount of time that children of different ages should spend doing homework in primary schools. There is evidence, however, that does support the use of homework in secondary schools. Nonetheless, a number of other important issues interact

***Box 10.4*** **Factors that might affect the effectiveness of homework**

*Pupil variables*

- ability
- prior knowledge
- motivation
- gender
- good working conditions at home

*Purpose of homework*

- practice
- revision
- consolidation
- extend class work
- preparation for future class work

*Teacher/school variables*

- amount set
- subject matter
- clarity of requirements
- speedy feedback
- detailed feedback
- sanctions for non-completion
- monitoring within the school to ensure that all teachers follow the same policies and practice

*Parental variables*

- socio-economic status
- attitudes
- knowledge of the topic
- degree of involvement
- sanctions for non-completion

with doing homework – e.g. the kind it is; the quality of teacher feedback; the attitudes of parents and teachers; and the social and cultural situation in which it is embedded. The moral of this tale is that we must not always believe what it is our politicians tell us, even when they claim to cite research.

In November 1998 the UK government issued more definitive documents in the light of the discussion that had taken place (DfEE 1998d). Now one or two general references were provided.

## Conclusions

At the beginning of this chapter I suggested that there are two ways of considering the psychologist as a detached investigator. The review presented above is written by a detached investigator in the sense that I am not personally involved in issues connected with homework. But, as I tried to indicate before presenting my review, reviewers are forced to organize, judge and select from the evidence in order to put forward an argument. Standing back from the review, I now see this argument as being mainly that:

- there is not sufficient evidence to support the idea that homework helps at primary level
- to do meaningful research on homework is very difficult because of all the interacting variables (listed in Box 10.4).

In my view – speaking as an outsider – the most important thing to explore now is the value of alternatives to homework, carried out in school, in more highly controlled conditions.

---

*Discussion questions*

1 What needs to be done to make homework more effective? How can you assess this?

2 What can readers do to evaluate the quality of a literature review?

3 Take a well known study. Assemble together as many accounts of it as you can. What do the results tell you? Can psychologists be detached investigators?

---

## Further reading

Fink, A. (1998) *Conducting Research Literature Reviews: From Paper to the Internet*. Thousand Oaks, CA: Sage. A very readable account of the process of writing reviews.

Girden, E. R. (1996) *Evaluating Research Articles from Start to Finish*. London: Sage. Loads of examples of good and poor studies to help readers learn to read research critically.

Hallam, S. and Cowan, R. (1998) What do we know about homework? A literature review. Paper available from the authors, Institute of Education, University of London, London WC1H OAL. An extensive review of the research on homework.

# References

Bowen, N. K. and Bowen, G. L. (1998) The mediating role of educational meaning in the relationship between home academic culture and academic performance. *Family Relations*, 47(1): 45–51.

Chen, C. and Stevenson, H. W. (1989) Homework: a cross-cultural examination. *Child Development*, 60: 551–61.

Chen, C. and Uttal, D. (1988) Cultural values, parent's beliefs, and children's achievements in the United States and China. *Human Development*, 31: 331–9.

Cone, J. D. and Foster, S. L. (1993) *Dissertations and Theses from Start to Finish*. Washington, DC: American Psychological Association.

Cooper, H. (1989a) *Homework*. New York: Longman.

Cooper, H. (1989b) Synthesis of research on homework. *Educational Leadership*, 47(3): 85–91.

Cooper, H. (1998) *Synthesizing Research: A Guide for Literature Reviews*, 3rd edn. London: Sage.

Cooper, H., Lindsay, J. J., Nye, B. and Greathouse, S. (1998) Relationships among attitudes about homework, amount of homework assigned and completed, and student achievement. *Journal of Educational Psychology*, 90(1): 70–83.

Cooper, N. and Stevenson, C. (1998) 'New science' and psychology. *The Psychologist*, 11(10): 484–5.

DfEE (1998a) *Homework: Guidelines for Primary Schools*. London: DfEE.

DfEE (1998b) *Homework: Guidelines for Secondary Schools*. London: DfEE.

DfEE (1998c) *Extending Opportunity: A National Framework for Study Support*. London: DfEE.

DfEE (1998d) *Homework: Guidelines for Primary and Secondary Schools*. London: DfEE.

Dixon, R. A., Munro, J. F. and Silcocks, P. B. (1997) *The Evidence-Based Medicine Workbook*. London: Heinemann.

Faulkner, J. and Blyth, C. (1995) Homework: is it really worth all the bother? *Educational Studies*, 21(3): 447–54.

Fink, A. (1998) *Conducting Research Literature Reviews: From Paper to the Internet*. Thousand Oaks, CA: Sage.

Foster, P. and Hammersley, M. (1998) A review of reviews: structure and function in reviews of educational research. *British Journal of Educational Research*, 24(5): 609–28.

Froese, A. D., Gantz, B. S. and Henry, A. L. (1998) Teaching students to write literature reviews: a meta-analytic method. *Teaching of Psychology*, 25(2):102–5.

Ginsburg, G. S. and Bronstein, P. (1993) Family factors related to children's intrinsic/extrinsic motivational orientation and academic performance. *Child Development*, 64(5): 1461–74.

Hallam, S. and Cowan, R. (1998) What do we know about homework? A literature review. Paper available from the authors, Institute of Education, University of London, London WC1H OAL.

Hart, C. (1998) *Doing a Literature Review*. London: Sage.

Holmes, M. and Croll, P. (1989) Time spent on homework and academic achievement. *Educational Research*, 31(3): 36–45.

Hoover-Dempsey, K. V., Bassler, O. C. and Burow, R. (1995) Parents' reported involvement in students' homework: strategies and practices. *Elementary School Journal*, 95(5): 435–50.

Keith, T. Z. and Benson, M. J. (1992) Effects of manipulable influences on high school grades across five ethnic groups. *Journal of Educational Research*, 86(2): 85–93.

Leung, K., Lau, S. and Lam, W.-L. (1998) Parenting styles and academic achievement: a cross-cultural study. *Merrill Palmer Quarterly*, 44(2): 157–72.

Levin, I., Levy-Shiff, R., Applebaum-Peled, T. *et al.* (1997) Antecedents and consequences of maternal involvement in children's homework: a longitudinal analysis. *Journal of Applied Developmental Psychology*, 18: 207–22.

MacBeath, J. (1993). *Learning for Yourself: Supported Study in Strathclyde Schools*. Glasgow: Faculty of Education, University of Strathclyde.

Mau, W.-C. (1997) Parental influences on the high school students' academic achievement: a comparison of Asian immigrants, Asian Americans, and white Americans. *Psychology in the Schools*, 34(3): 267–77.

Miller, T. L., Duffy, S. E. and Zane, T. Z. (1993) Improving the accuracy of self-corrected mathematics homework. *Journal of Educational Research*, 86(3): 184–9.

Morgan, M. (1998) Qualitative research: science or pseudo-science? *The Psychologist*, 11(10): 481–3, 488.

Murphy, J. and Decker, K. (1989) Teachers' use of homework in high schools. *Journal of Educational Research*, 82(5): 261–9.

Office for Standards in Education (1998) *Homework in Primary and Secondary Schools*. London: Stationery Office.

Rutter, M., Maughan, B., Mortimore, P. and Ouston, J. (1979) *15,000 Hours: Secondary Schools and their Effects on Children*. West Compton House, Shepton Mallet, UK: Open Books.

Sharpe, C. and Thomas, J. W. (1993) Promoting independent learning in the middle grades – the role of instructional support practices. *Elementary School Journal*, 93(5): 575–91.

Sherrard, C. (1998) Social dimensions of research. *The Psychologist*, 11(10): 486–7.

Tymms, P. B. and Fitz-Gibbon, C. T. (1992) The relationship of homework to A-level results. *Educational Research*, 34(1): 3–10.

Walberg, H. J. (1991) Does homework help? *School Community Journal*, 1: 13–15.

West, A., Noden, P., Edge, A. and David, M. (1998) Parental involvement in education in and out of school. *British Educational Research Journal*, 24(4): 461–84.

Wharton, P. (1997) Learning about responsibility: lessons from homework. *British Journal of Educational Psychology*, 67: 213–21.

Zakzanis, K. (1998) The reliability of meta-analytic review. *Psychological Reports*, 83: 215–22.

Zellman, G. L. and Waterman, J. M. (in press) Understanding the impact of parent school involvement on children's educational outcomes. *Journal of Educational Research*.

# The psychologist as theoretician

# Chapter 11

# Autism and 'theory of mind'

## Simon Baron-Cohen

Most people carry in their heads what psychologists call a 'theory of mind'. Such a theory allows us to infer mental states (beliefs, desires, intentions, imagination, emotions, etc.) in other people. We seem to do this an enormous amount, as a natural way of thinking about why people do what they do.

For example, you might wonder why some friends have not phoned you for a while. You may speculate that maybe you have *offended* them in some way, or at least that they *think* you have. Or maybe they are *trying* to avoid you because they *feel* that the friendship is suffocating. Or maybe they just *want* more space. So you phone them up and they say that everything is fine. You then start wondering whether, when they say that, do they actually *mean* it? Perhaps they are *intending* to keep things polite but really *wish* the friendship was over?

In the above paragraph you can see that there are lots of words referring to what goes on in one's own and other people's minds. Psychologists call this using a 'theory' of mind (Astington 1994) simply because there is often little if any evidence for what the other person is actually thinking or feeling, so people speculate (theorize) in just this way. But this theorizing about what might be in someone's mind is a crucial way to help us make sense of behaviour, and predict what that person might do next. In brief, a theory of mind is the ability to be able to reflect on the contents of one's own and other's minds.

## Autism

In this chapter I shall be describing some of the evidence for the argument that the condition of autism involves difficulties in working out what is going on in someone else's mind. But first, a word about autism (Baron-Cohen and Bolton 1993). Autism is considered to be the most severe of the childhood psychiatric conditions. It is diagnosed on the basis of abnormal development of social behaviour, communication and imagination, often in the presence of marked obsessional, repetitive or ritualistic behaviour. Such children find it difficult to be part of a social group and dominate their families by insisting on their own preoccupations and bizarre routines.

Some children with autism suffer from moderate or severe degrees of mental learning difficulties, suggesting that they have autism plus more diffuse problems. The proportion of children with autism who also have learning difficulties is reported to be 65–75 per cent, with a corresponding 25–35 per cent having intelligence (an IQ) in the average or above average range.

Just as autism can co-occur with learning difficulties, so it can co-occur with mutism. However, those children with autism who do have speech are inevitably delayed in starting to speak, and when they do communicate, they do this in a very one sided way, rather than using reciprocal dialogue. They tend to talk at you, rather than to you or with you. They may frequently also misunderstand a speaker's intended meaning and provide insufficient information for their listener to understand what they mean. These communication abnormalities are thought to reflect their failure to take into account what their listener might be thinking or interested in. Instead, language is used almost exclusively in literal and factual ways, to answer questions, to collect information or to obtain things.

Finally, children with autism have unusual perception, frequently noticing small details that others miss (such as the serial numbers on the back of street lamp-posts) or recalling information with considerable precision (such as the exact time and date they last visited a theatre, three years earlier) or paying attention to textures that others may not notice (such as the feel of a wall) or becoming upset by sounds in their environment (such as the shrill tone of a telephone).

## Autism and 'theory of mind'

This chapter opened with a description of how, in the normal case, we interpret each other's actions and speech in terms of what people have in their minds. We called this using a 'theory of mind' and it is the main way in which we make sense of other people. However, not everyone seems to be able to do this quite so easily or in the same way. Abnormality in understanding other people's minds – in developing a normal theory of mind – is not the only psychological feature of autism, but it seems to be a core and possibly a universal abnormality among such individuals (Baron-Cohen *et al.* 1993b). Some people with autism lack almost all signs of a theory of mind. One might think of such extreme cases as a form of 'mindblindness' (Baron-Cohen 1995). More commonly, people with autism have some of the basics of a theory of mind, but have some difficulties in using it at a level that one would expect, given their intelligence in other areas. If you like, their social intelligence is lagging behind their non-social intelligence. In their case, one might say they have degrees of mindblindness, ranging from severe through to moderate, or even just very mild.

This chapter describes some of the manifestations of this and emphasizes how developmentally appropriate tests are needed in order to reveal it. Note that the terms 'theory of mind' and 'mindreading' can to some extent be used synonymously. The chapter is also intended to serve as an illustration of theory building in psychology, since the idea that autism might involve problems in theory of mind is a useful way of making sense of some key symptoms of the condition: their social and communication problems and, to some extent, their limited imagination. (Note, however, that this theory has little or no relevance to other symptoms in autism, such as their unusual perception.) Nonetheless the theory has helped applied psychologists working with these children to understand more about the condition and hopefully, in the long term, to find better ways of treating it.

## The mental–physical distinction

Perhaps the best place to start in illustrating the normal theory of mind, and how this develops abnormally in autism, is with the mental–physical distinction, since many consider that this distinction is a fundamental cornerstone of the theory of mind. The test for this is a good way to convey what it is. The test involves a child listening to stories in which one character is having a mental experience (e.g. thinking about a dog) while a second character is having a physical experience (e.g. holding a dog). The experimenter then asks the child to judge which of the two characters can perform different actions (e.g. which character can stroke the dog?). Normal 3–4-year-old children can easily make these judgements (e.g. they can judge that it is only the character holding the dog that can stroke it), thereby demonstrating their grasp of the distinction between mental and physical things. Children with severe autism have difficulty making such judgements despite having a mental age of at least a 4-year-old level (Baron-Cohen 1989a).

## Understanding the functions of the brain

Normally developing 3–4-year-olds also already know that the brain has a set of mental functions, such as dreaming, wanting, thinking, keeping secrets, etc. Some also know it has physical functions (such as making you move, or helping you to stay alive, etc.). In contrast, children with autism (but who have a mental age above a 4-year-old level) appear to know about the physical functions, but most fail to mention any mental function of the brain (Baron-Cohen 1989a).

## The appearance–reality distinction

Children from about the age of 4 years are normally able to distinguish between appearance and reality, that is, talk about objects that might have misleading identities. For example, they may say, when presented with a candle fashioned in the shape of an apple, that it looks like an apple but is really a candle. Children with autism, presented with the same sort of test, may not talk about objects in the same way, instead saying the object really is an apple, or really is a candle, but not capture the object's dual identity in their spontaneous descriptions (Baron-Cohen 1989a). Given that this requires being able to simultaneously keep track of how an object appears (to your mind) versus what it actually is, this is an additional clue that in autism there is a difficulty in the development of a theory of mind. Alternative interpretations of this difficulty are certainly possible however, since this task relies on quite complex language skills.

## First-order false belief tests

First-order false belief tests measure a child's understanding of the fact that different people can have different thoughts about the same situation. They are called first-order tests because they involve inferring only one person's mental state. (See pp. 189–90 for discussion of second-order tests.) Normally developing 4-year-olds can keep track of how different people might think different things about the world (Wimmer and Perner 1983). For example, when interpreting well known stories such as *Little Red Riding Hood* or *Snow White*, even 4-year-olds will say things like: 'Little Red Riding Hood *thinks* that it's her grandmother in the bed, but really it's the wicked wolf!' or 'Snow White thinks the old woman is giving her a nice juicy apple. She doesn't *know* that it's really her wicked stepmother all dressed up, and that the apple is poisoned!' A large number of studies have repeatedly demonstrated that children with autism have difficulties in shifting their perspective to judge what someone else might think, instead of simply reporting what they themselves know (Baron-Cohen *et al.* 1985).

## 'Seeing leads to knowing'

Yet another cornerstone of the normal child's theory of mind is an understanding of where knowledge comes from, so that the child can work out who knows what, and more importantly, who does not know what. This is a key development simply because it underpins appropriate communication (telling people what they do not know – informing others – rather than telling them what they already know). It also underpins an understanding of deception, since before considering changing someone's beliefs about what is true, you first have to work out what they know or do not know. Deception obviously fails if you cannot keep track of what the other person might know or not know. (We return to discuss deception on pp. 187–8.)

Normally developing 3-year-olds can understand the 'seeing leads to knowing' principle in that, when given a story about two characters, one of whom looks into a box and the other of whom touches a box, they can work out that it is only the one who looked who knows what is in the box. In contrast, children with autism perform virtually at chance on this test, and are as much likely to pick one character as the other when asked 'Which

The question: which one knows what is in the box?

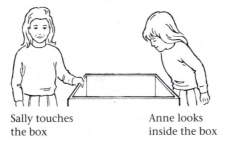

Sally touches
the box

Anne looks
inside the box

***Figure 11.1***   A schematic illustration of the seeing-leads-to-knowing test

one knows what is in the box?' (Baron-Cohen and Goodhart 1994). (See Figure 11.1 for a schematic illustration of the experiment.)

## Recognizing mental state words

It turns out that by 4 years old, normally developing children can also pick out words from a word list that refer to what goes on in the mind or what the mind can do. These words include 'think', 'know', 'dream', 'pretend', 'hope', 'wish' and 'imagine'. These are easily distinguished from other kinds of (non-mental) verbs like 'jump', 'eat' or 'move', or other kinds of (non-mental) nouns, like 'door', 'school' or 'computer'. Children with autism have much more difficulty in making this judgement (Baron-Cohen *et al.* 1994). This is really a test of their mental vocabulary, but it may well be an indicator that conceptual development in this domain is also less well developed than would be expected for the child's general mental age.

## Mental state words in spontaneous speech

The previous finding dovetails with reports that children with autism produce fewer mental state words in their spontaneous descriptions of picture stories involving action and deception, compared to their normal counterparts (Baron-Cohen *et al.* 1986; Tager-Flusberg 1992). Of course, just because they do not use these words so readily, this may not necessarily reflect a lack of competence. It may be simply a lack of interest. But when taken together with other experimental evidence summarized in this chapter, the likelihood is that this reflects delays or difficulties in comprehension of mental state concepts or, at the very least, reduced attention to such phenomena.

## Spontaneous pretend play

Many studies since the mid-1970s have reported a lower frequency of pretend play in the spontaneous play of children with autism (Wing *et al.* 1977;

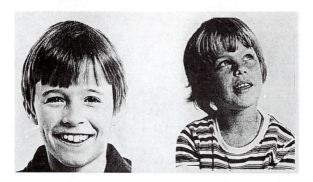

*Figure 11.2*   The test of 'Which one is thinking?'

Baron-Cohen 1987). This can be interpreted in various ways. For example, it might reflect a failure to reflect on one's own imagination – a mindreading difficulty. Or it might reflect a failure to switch attention flexibly from 'reality mode' to 'pretend mode', as a result of some aspect of what is called executive function (Jarrold *et al.* 1994). Or it could mean both.

## Understanding causes of emotion

Emotions can be caused by physical events (e.g. falling over causes you to cry, or being given a present makes you feel happy). But emotions can also be caused by mental states such as desires and beliefs. For example, you can be happy because you get what you *want*, or because you *think* you are getting what you want. Normally developing 4–6-year-olds understand both types of emotional causes. In contrast, studies show that children with autism at this mental age have difficulty with the more complex mental states as causes of emotion (Baron-Cohen 1991; Baron-Cohen *et al.* 1993a).

## Inferring from gaze direction

Why do we spend so much time looking at people's eyes? In the 1980s, it was not clear what the information around someone's eyes conveyed to another person. We now know that even young normal children (age 4 years) can work out from gaze direction when someone is thinking about something (e.g. a gaze directed upwards and away, at nothing in particular, strongly signifies the person is thinking: see Figure 11.2). Gaze direction also allows young normal children of the same age to work out which of several objects a person wants (see Figure 11.3). Children with autism in contrast are relatively blind to such information from gaze direction, even though they can answer the explicit question, 'What is Charlie looking at?' Mentalistic interpretation of the eyes of another person does not seem to come naturally to them (Baron-Cohen and Cross 1992; Baron-Cohen *et al.* 1995).

***Figure 11.3*** The test of 'Which one does Charlie want?'

## Monitoring one's own intentions

We have covered a number of tests of understanding other people's thoughts, but another important class of mental states is intentions. Working out why people behave as they do is all about keeping track of people's intentions, since tracking actions alone gives you a description of what people do, but not why they do it. In a novel test of this, 4-year-old normal children were asked to shoot a toy gun at one of six targets, stating their intended target. Then, unbeknownst to the children, the outcome was manipulated by the experimenter such that sometimes the children hit their chosen target, and sometimes they did not. Normally developing 4-year-olds could correctly answer the question, 'Which one did you mean to hit?', even when they did not get what they intended, but children with autism more usually referred to the one that they actually hit (Phillips *et al.* 1998).

## Deception

Deception is relevant to understanding other people's minds simply because it involves trying to make someone else *believe* that something is true when in fact it is false. In other words, it is all about trying to change someone else's mind. By the age of 4 years the normally developing child is showing both an interest in deception, and beginning to be more adept at it. Leaving moral aspects aside, such signs of deception can be taken as a yardstick that the child is understanding other minds. Of course, the child's early attempts at deception may be clumsy and ineffective, such as the young child claiming that he did not take the chocolate cookie, while the telltale evidence is all over his face, or the young child in a game of hide and seek, calling out from her hiding place behind the curtains to 'come and find me!' In these instances, the child is arguably trying to deceive, but is not keeping track of the clues that would lead the other person to know the truth.

Children with autism have been shown to have difficulties both in production of deception, and in understanding when someone else is deceiving them. An example of one test is the 'penny hiding game' (Baron-Cohen 1992), where the aim of the game is not to reveal in which hand you have hidden a penny. Young children with autism, despite having a mental age above that of a 4-year-old, often make errors in this game, which suggests that they do not understand how to deceive very well. Examples of their errors include hiding the penny in one hand, but leaving the other hand open; or between trials, transferring the penny from one closed fist to the other; or putting the penny out of sight, and then telling the other person 'it's in here!', and so on.

## Understanding metaphor, sarcasm and irony

Happé (1994) has tested if children with autism understand figurative speech through story comprehension. Figurative speech also requires an understanding of the speaker's intentions, in order to move beyond the literal level of simply mapping words on to their referents. Examples of figurative language include sarcasm ('How clean your room looks today!', uttered by an exasperated parent to a child) and metaphor ('You've got a sharp tongue!'). Results suggest that this more advanced mindreading test (pitched at the level of a normal 8-year-old) reveals more subtle mindreading difficulties in higher functioning individuals with autism spectrum conditions. A similar finding using a simpler test comes from a study of normal preschoolers based on testing to see if they can understand someone's intention to joke. Children as young as 3 years old heard utterances like 'This is a shoe', spoken by the experimenter while pointing at a cup, and were asked why the experimenter said that. Whereas normal children referred in their explanations to 'joking' and 'pretending', children with autism tended to refer to the speaker having got it wrong ('It's not a shoe, it's a cup') (Baron-Cohen 1997).

## Pragmatics

Understanding figurative speech and humour is a subset of pragmatics, or the use of language appropriate to the social context (Baron-Cohen 1988). Pragmatics includes at least the following:

- tailoring your speech to a particular listener
- adapting the content of your speech to what your listener already knows or needs to know
- respecting conversational principles such as being truthful, relevant, concise, and polite
- turn taking appropriately so that there is space for both participants in the dialogue
- being sensitive to the other person's contribution to the conversation
- recognizing what is the wrong or right thing to say in a particular context
- staying on topic
- appropriately helping your listener to follow when a topic change is occurring.

Almost every aspect of pragmatics involves sensitivity to speaker and listener mental states and hence mindreading, although it is important to note that pragmatics also involves using context. This means that a difficulty in pragmatics could occur for at least two different reasons: some degree of mindblindness, or some degree of what Frith (1989) calls 'weak central coherence' (use of context). Two experimental studies of pragmatics in children with autism have included a test of whether the principles of conversational relevance can be recognized, and a test of recognizing when someone said the wrong thing (faux pas). Both studies suggest that children with autism have difficulties in this area (Surian *et al.* 1996; Baron-Cohen *et al.* in press).

## Imagination

We discussed the relevance of pretend play earlier, but this is only one possible way that imagination can be expressed. More broadly, imagination is relevant to theory of mind since it involves building an unreal world that exists purely in your own mind, and being able to reflect on this virtual world. In one study Scott and Baron-Cohen (1996) investigated the ability of children with autism to draw pictures of unreal or impossible objects (such as two-headed people) and found that children with autism were either more reluctant or less able to produce such drawings than normal children.

These results may be due to the so-called 'executive function' (the need to suppress routine approaches to drawing, and override these with novel approaches). However, there is experimental evidence for persisting imagination impairments in both children with autism and Asperger Syndrome on a range of tasks not restricted to drawing (such as story telling, and standard creativity measures). (Asperger Syndrome is a milder form of autism, without the delay in cognitive development, but with the abnormalities of social interaction and repetitive or stereotyped activities.) This evidence is clearly in line with the clinical descriptions of impaired imagination in people with an autism spectrum condition, and as specified in most diagnostic classification systems.

## Correlation with real life social skills

One might raise here the concern that theory of mind tasks simply measure aspects of social understanding under laboratory conditions and, as such, have no relevance to social impairment in the real world. For this reason, Frith and her colleagues have examined the correlation of theory of mind skills in children with autism in relation to real world behaviour. Using a questionnaire with teachers, asking about real life skills such as keeping secrets, comforting others and understanding others' intentions, they report that the laboratory tests are indeed significantly correlated with these relevant behaviours, thus providing some measure of validity of the tests (Frith, Happé and Siddons 1994).

## Second-order false belief tests

The universality of theory of mind difficulties in autism has been questioned simply because a proportion of children with autism pass first-order tests.

First-order tests, including most of those reviewed above, involve simply inferring one person's mental state. Happé (1996) points out that this could still mean that these abnormalities are universal, since there are no reported cases of autistic children who pass first-order theory of mind tests at the right mental age. Thus, a high functioning individual with an autism spectrum condition (e.g. with Asperger Syndrome) who has normal intelligence, should be able to pass such tests at 3–4 years of age. Typically, however, they are older than this when they pass such tests. Equally, Happé (1996) finds that on average a mental age of 9 years is needed for children with autism to pass such tests, and that the youngest mental age of an individual with autism passing such tests is 5 and a half years.

As one might expect, as a result of a delay in acquiring first-order theory of mind competence, these individuals often fail second-order false belief tests (Baron-Cohen 1989b). Second-order tests involve considering embedded mental states (e.g. one person's thoughts about another person's thoughts). Whereas first-order tests correspond to a normal 4-year-old mental age level, second-order tests correspond to a 6-year-old mental age level. This may be another way of revealing if there is a specific developmental delay in theory of mind at a point later in development. Some individuals with autism or Asperger Syndrome who are high functioning (in terms of IQ and language level), and who are usually adults, may pass even second-order false belief tests. Those who can pass such second-order tests however may have difficulties in more advanced theory of mind tests such as inferring complex mental states such as bluff and double bluff in story characters – an 8 year mental age level test (Happé 1994) – or in decoding complex mental states from an expression in the eye-region of the face (Baron-Cohen *et al.* 1997).

## Applications of the theory to the classroom

It is one thing to build theories about a condition like autism, but as Marx said, the point is not just to describe the world: the point is to change it. Do such theories have any practical application to the world of these children, such that we could improve their situation? Here I shall briefly mention a practical application of the theory of mind approach to autism.

There have been attempts to try to teach children with autism to mindread. This is the most logical practical application. If the tests described above highlight specific difficulties in what these children understand, then focused teaching methods might make a difference. A particular example of this involved the teacher (a psychologist) explaining to children with autism that thoughts are like photos inside people's heads (Swettenham *et al.* 1996). This gives children with autism a concrete analogy to help them grasp what thoughts are. Since children with autism have no difficulty understanding what cameras and photos are, you can go quite a long way using this analogy.

Specifically, you tell the child that the mind is like a camera, and the camera lens is like the eye. The teacher then explains that just as when you point a camera at something and click the button, this produces a picture of that thing inside the camera, so when a person faces something and looks at it (blinks an eye), this produces a picture of that thing inside the person's head.

The teacher then illustrates this using a polaroid camera, since the child can then practise using this to see the instant picture being produced. The next step of the teaching involved telling the child that sometimes pictures are out of date, because things change in the world without changing in the picture. (For example, you might move house but the picture of your house is still of your old one.) In the same way, people might have out of date pictures in their minds (beliefs which are no longer true) because they were not present when things changed. Teaching them this step allows children with autism to work out why someone might act in the way that they do, on the basis of an outdated picture in their minds. The last step involves teaching the child that if people are looking for something, they will go to find it in the place shown in the picture in their head.

With this somewhat elaborate teaching method, psychologists have shown that children with autism can learn to work out where someone will look if something is moved when the person was not present – they can work out that that person will go to where he or she *thinks* the object is, rather than to where it actually is. That is, autistic children can be taught to pass first-order false belief tests. This is just the beginning of helping children with autism to get an idea of how to mindread.

## Conclusions

Difficulties in mindreading in autism spectrum conditions appear early on (from at least the end of the first year of life, if you include joint attention abnormalities, such as not following what others are interested in). They also appear to be universal (if you test for these either at the right point in development or, in the case of high-functioning older individuals, by using sensitive, age-appropriate tests).

Some clues relating to the brain basis of theory of mind difficulties in autism are being gathered from both functional neuro-imaging (Baron-Cohen and Ring 1994; Happé *et al.* 1996), and studies of acquired brain damage (Stone *et al.* 1998a; 1998b). It is hoped that future research in this area will refine both the techniques for studying this skill, and make further headway in understanding the underlying mechanisms essential for mindreading. Finally, most importantly, much of the basic research in this field may have clinical applications in the areas of both intervention/teaching, or diagnosis (Baron-Cohen *et al.* 1996). This is an area which needs systematic exploration.

### Acknowledgements

Dr Baron-Cohen was supported by the Medical Research Council during the period of this work.

---

*Discussion questions*

1 How do we know that other people have minds?

2 Can you try to imagine what the world would be like if you did not realize that other people had minds?

3 Why is it so important to our survival to be social?

---

## Further reading

Baron-Cohen, S. (1995) *Mindblindness: An Essay on Autism and Theory of Mind*. Cambridge, MA: MIT Press/Bradford Books. This provides an overview of the field of autism and theory of mind.

Baron-Cohen, S. and Bolton, P. (1993) *Autism: The Facts*. Oxford: Oxford University Press. This is a book on autism written in a user-friendly style for parents and general readers.

Frith, U. (1989) *Autism: Explaining the Enigma*. Oxford: Basil Blackwell; Happé, F. (1996) *Autism*. London: UCL Press. These are two good introductory books on autism for students of psychology.

## References

Astington, J. (1994) *The Child's Discovery of the Mind*. Cambridge, MA: Harvard University Press.

Baron-Cohen, S. (1987) Autism and symbolic play. *British Journal of Developmental Psychology*, 5: 139–48.

Baron-Cohen, S. (1988) Social and pragmatic deficits in autism: cognitive or affective? *Journal of Autism and Developmental Disorders*, 18: 379–402.

Baron-Cohen, S. (1989a) Are autistic children behaviourists? An examination of their mental–physical and appearance–reality distinctions. *Journal of Autism and Developmental Disorders*, 19: 579–600.

Baron-Cohen, S. (1989b) The autistic child's theory of mind: a case of specific developmental delay. *Journal of Child Psychology and Psychiatry*, 30: 285–98.

Baron-Cohen, S. (1991) Do people with autism understand what causes emotion? *Child Development*, 62: 385–95.

Baron-Cohen, S. (1992) Out of sight or out of mind: another look at deception in autism. *Journal of Child Psychology and Psychiatry*, 33: 1141–55.

Baron-Cohen, S. (1995) *Mindblindness: An Essay on Autism and Theory of Mind*. Cambridge, MA: MIT Press/Bradford Books.

Baron-Cohen, S. (1997) Hey! It was just a joke! Understanding propositions and propositional attitudes by normally developing children and children with autism. *Israel Journal of Psychiatry*, 34: 174–8.

Baron-Cohen, S. and Bolton, P. (1993) *Autism: The Facts*. Oxford: Oxford University Press.

Baron-Cohen, S. and Cross, P. (1992) Reading the eyes: evidence for the role of perception in the development of a theory of mind. *Mind and Language*, 6: 173–86.

Baron-Cohen, S. and Goodhart, F. (1994) The 'seeing leads to knowing' deficit in autism: the Pratt and Bryant probe. *British Journal of Developmental Psychology*, 12: 397–402.

Baron-Cohen, S. and Ring, H. (1994) A model of the mindreading system: neuro-psychological and neurobiological perspectives, in P. Mitchell and C. Lewis (eds) *Origins of an Understanding of Mind*. Hillsdale, NJ: Erlbaum.

Baron-Cohen, S., Leslie, A. M. and Frith, U. (1985) Does the autistic child have a 'theory of mind'? *Cognition*, 21: 37–46.

Baron-Cohen, S., Leslie, A. M. and Frith, U. (1986) Mechanical, behavioural and intentional understanding of picture stories in autistic children. *British Journal of Developmental Psychology*, 4: 113–25.

Baron-Cohen, S., Spitz, A. and Cross, P. (1993a) Can children with autism recognize surprise? *Cognition and Emotion*, 7: 507–16.

Baron-Cohen, S., Tager-Flusberg, H. and Cohen, D. (eds) (1993b) *Understanding Other Minds: Perspectives from Autism*. Oxford: Oxford University Press.

Baron-Cohen, S., Ring, H., Moriarty, J., Shmitz, P., Costa, D. and Ell, P. (1994) Recognition of mental state terms: a clinical study of autism, and a functional neuroimaging study of normal adults. *British Journal of Psychiatry*, 165: 640–9.

Baron-Cohen, S., Campbell, R., Karmiloff-Smith, A., Grant, J. and Walker, J. (1995) Are children with autism blind to the mentalistic significance of the eyes? *British Journal of Developmental Psychology*, 13: 379–98.

Baron-Cohen, S., Cox, A., Baird, G., Swettenham, J., Drew, A., Nightingale, N., Morgan, K. and Charman, T. (1996) Psychological markers of autism at 18 months of age in a large population. *British Journal of Psychiatry*, 168: 158–63.

Baron-Cohen, S., Wheelwright, S. and Jolliffe, T. (1997) Is there a 'language of the eyes'? Evidence from normal adults and adults with autism or Asperger syndrome. *Visual Cognition*, 4: 311–31.

Baron-Cohen, S., O'Riordan, M., Jones, R., Stone, V. and Plaistead, K. (in press). Can children with Asperger Syndrome detect faux pas? *Journal of Autism and Developmental Disorders*.

Frith, U. (1989) *Autism: Explaining the Enigma*. Oxford: Basil Blackwell.

Frith, U., Happé, F. and Siddons, F. (1994). Autism and theory of mind in everyday life. *Social Development*, 3: 108–24.

Happe, F. (1994) An advanced test of theory of mind: understanding of story characters' thoughts and feelings by able autistic, mentally handicapped, and normal children and adults. *Journal of Autism and Development Disorders*, 24: 129–54.

Happe, F. (1996) *Autism*. London: UCL Press.

Happe, F., Ehlers, S., Fletcher, P., Frith, U., Johansson, M., Gillberg, C., Dolan, R., Frackowiak, R. and Frith, C. (1996) 'Theory of mind' in the brain. Evidence from a PET scan study of Asperger Syndrome. *NeuroReport*, 8: 197–201.

Jarrold, C., Boucher, J. and Smith, P. (1994) Executive function deficits and the pretend play of children with autism: a research note. *Journal of Child Psychology and Psychiatry*, 35: 1473–82.

Phillips, W., Baron-Cohen, S. and Rutter, M. (1998). Can children with autism understand intentions?

Scott, F. and Baron-Cohen, S. (1996) Imagining real and unreal objects: an investigation of imagination in autism. *Journal of Cognitive Neuroscience*, 8: 400–11.

Stone, V., Baron-Cohen, S., Young, A. and Calder, A. (1998a) *Patients with Amygdalectomy Show Impairments in Theory of Mind*. Cambridge: Cambridge University Press.

Stone, V., Baron-Cohen, S. and Knight, K. (1998b). Frontal lobe contributions to theory of mind. *Journal of Cognitive Neuroscience*, 10: 640–56.

Surian, L., Baron-Cohen, S. and Van der Lely, H. (1996) Are children with autism deaf to Gricean Maxims? *Cognitive Neuropsychiatry*, 1: 55–72.

Swettenham, J., Baron-Cohen, S., Gomez, J-C. and Walsh, S. (1996) What's inside a person's head? Conceiving of the mind as a camera helps children with autism develop an alternative theory of mind. *Cognitive Neuropsychiatry*, 1: 73–88.

Tager-Flusberg, H. (1992) Autistic children's talk about psychological states: deficits in the early acquisition of a theory of mind. *Child Development*, 63: 161–72.

Wimmer, H. and Perner, J. (1983) Beliefs about beliefs: representation and constraining function of wrong beliefs in young children's understanding of deception. *Cognition*, 13: 103–28.

Wing, L., Gould, J., Yeates, S. R. and Brierley, L. M. (1977) Symbolic play in severely mentally retarded and in autistic children. *Journal of Child Psychology and Psychiatry*, 18: 167–78.

# Chapter **12**

# What is a 'good' theory? The case for a pragmatic approach

## *J. Fredrik Brown and Chris Cullen*

**What is a 'good' theory? A pragmatic approach**

When Lewin (1951) wrote 'there is nothing as practical as a good theory', he succinctly summarized the position that today is known as the scientist-practitioner model (cf. Dallos and Cullen 1990). However, some 50 years on there is still continuing debate on the nature of the scientist-practitioner model. At issue is how we define theory, and more fundamentally, what we understand to be the objective of psychological science. It is easy to dismiss the question of how we define theory as a distant philosophical debate, but in fact it is central to the development of our profession.

For many in contemporary psychology, a 'good' theory is one that both corresponds with our observations and accurately predicts new data patterns. As such, the objective of science is to produce theories with predictive power. However, predictive theories are not always practically useful; they do not always tell us how the observed events might be changed. For example, although personality theories enable accurate predictions to be made about how people are likely to behave, they throw little light on how to change those behaviours. Clearly, theories with little or no practical utility beyond their predictive function offer little guidance to clinicians interested in helping their clients to change. A pragmatic alternative is to define a 'good' theory by its practical utility. That is, 'good' theories are those that tell us how to bring about change. Such a conceptualization extends the objective of science to prediction *and* the identification of those variables that directly affect the observations under scrutiny (Dallos and Cullen 1990). A pragmatic conceptualization of theory is clearly relevant to applied psychologists and their clients.

Although clinical psychologists stress the importance of the theory–practice relationship, it is not always clear how the profession links the two. Some have even argued that this may be nothing more than a political stance aimed at securing status and value in society (Pilgrim and Treacher 1992). Much depends on what is meant by the term 'theory'. This chapter will outline one approach to clinical psychology's relationship with theory and lead on to a discussion of what constitutes a pragmatic theory and how it can be used clinically.

## Theory in clinical psychology

In the late 1980s, a group called the Management Advisory Service (MAS) was commissioned in the UK by the Department of Health to review the role, activity and staffing levels of clinical psychology within the National Health Service (NHS). Of the many observations and conclusions made in the MAS (1989) report, perhaps the most important was the assertion that clinical psychologists 'have a particular skill level, as a product of their scientific training, unmatched by others in the NHS' (Pilgrim and Treacher 1992: 164).

The MAS report differentiated between three levels of psychological proficiency operating in the NHS:

- Level one related to general listening, rapport and 'bedside manner' abilities that all competent staff should possess.
- Level two related to the application of predetermined sets of therapeutic interventions, 'cookbook fashion', to address specific problems.
- Level three related to the complex integration of theory and practice.

The report concluded that, as a result of their academic training, clinical psychologists were alone in underpinning their work with theoretical models and as such offered something unique to the NHS. Indeed, the final recommendation of the MAS report was that the number of clinical psychologists working in the NHS should effectively double by the year 2000.

It initially seemed, following the break-up of the NHS regions into smaller NHS Trusts, that this bold recommendation might be avoided. However, according to Gray (1997), the number of clinical psychology training places has steadily risen in the UK from 181 in 1994–5 to approximately 300 in 1997–8. This suggests that the MAS report conclusions did not go unnoticed.

The singling out of clinical psychology as the only discipline in the NHS to apply psychological theory systematically to clinical practice and organizational questions predated the current vogue for evidence-based practice. The MAS conclusions were also consistent with the adopted model of the scientist-practitioner. This model, developed initially by US applied psychologists seeking a framework for what they could offer clients, 'laid down that clinical psychologists were to be trained as scientific psychologists first and as professional service providers second' (Leahey 1991: 386). The aim is to provide a thoroughly evidence-based approach to psychological problems.

## What is theory?

At first glance psychology appears to have a well developed theoretical base. As Page (1996: 105) has pointed out, however, the discipline is fragmented into several competing philosophical positions with 'an abundance of theories and minimal consensual knowledge'.

Chiesa (1992) has outlined three common uses of the term *theory* in psychology today:

- The first type of theory involves guesses or presumptions. These can be predictive (i.e. something will happen) or explanatory (i.e. an event was caused by something), but either way they involve speculation and require additional data for confirmation.
- The second usage of the term theory relates to models that employ hypothetical constructs to explain observed data. For example, many psychological theories invoke hypothetical variables to account for observed data (e.g. the concept of 'memory' was developed to explain how past experiences change current and future behaviour – it is hypothetical because it is not directly accessible, but must be inferred from observations). Theories that include such hypothetical factors (referred to here as hypothetical models) are also speculative and, like guesses, require further experimentation to validate them.
- The third use of the term theory is as an explanatory system that summarizes regularities in recorded data. This definition of theory is different from both hypothetical models and guesses because it is not speculative and hence does not require further experimentation to validate it. By this definition, a theory is the description of *existing* data patterns: that is, it is the summary of functional relationships between data (cf. Skinner 1950). As such, theoretical limitations are not due to a paucity of 'explanatory' conceptual constructs, but instead reflect an insufficient database from which to identify consistent patterns. For example, Skinner (1974) argues that behaviourism is incomplete not because of a lack of theory, but because of a lack of data from or understanding by, other disciplines such as physiology. Therefore, when faced with gaps in a theoretical account, the solution is not to introduce more hypothetical constructs, but to undertake further research to identify the data regularities (science starts with the premise that there is order in the world).

The method of theory construction that involves moving from observations of specific instances to the description of general laws or principles is usually referred to as induction. A simple example of an inductive theory is provided by the relationship between temperature, volume and pressure. Some 300 years ago in laboratories of Oxford University, experiments with different gases showed that temperature was directly proportional to pressure and volume (i.e. as temperature increases, so does pressure and volume) and that volume and pressure were inversely proportional to one another (i.e. at a constant temperature, as volume increases, pressure decreases, and vice versa). These regularities were eventually summarized as the ideal gas equation, $T = PV$ (temperature is a function of pressure and volume). This statement is a description of consistent relations between the data. It is not speculative and one expects all future measurements to fit the pattern.

Many psychological approaches, however, are not content to define theory as the summary description of data patterns and instead prefer to use hypothetical models to explain observed data. The nub of the issue here is what constitutes an explanation. For the first and second definitions of theory, explanation refers to determining the assumed underlying causes, whereas for inductive theories, explanation is the description of functional relations. But does it make any difference if we use hypothetical constructs in our theories?

## Tautologies and pragmatism

The central limitation of hypothetical models is that – because they do not describe functional relationships between data – their explanatory power is illusory. This is because inferring the existence of a hypothetical construct from an observation and then using that same construct to explain the original observation is clearly tautological (or circular) and adds nothing to the analysis. For example, even though the construct 'intelligence' can be inferred only from observed behaviours, it is regularly used to explain similar behaviours. It is common to hear the explanation that 'intelligent' children do well at school but doing well at school may be one of the defining characteristics of 'intelligence'! To say that people are 'intelligent' is simply to re-describe their actions and is not an explanation (Howe 1997).

But what do we mean by explanation? Dougher (1995) has suggested that the continued use of hypothetical models reflects the view that the primary objective of scientific theory is to facilitate accurate prediction. Therefore, theories that allow accurate prediction of events are acceptable to a psychological science, whether they include tautologies or not. For example, it is usually the case that if someone does well in an exam, they are likely to do well in future exams and thus the term 'intelligence' is accepted as explanatory because it fulfils a predictive function. So, if the objective of science is solely to produce theories with predictive accuracy, a 'good' theory is one that *corresponds* with the collected data. Consequently, as 'prediction is the most stringent form of correspondence' (Dougher 1995: 216), the best test for a theory is to see whether observed data are consistent with derived predictions (hypotheses). This process of testing hypotheses is commonly referred to as the hypothetico-deductive method of theory construction. Hypothetico-deduction can be thought of as the opposite of induction, as instead of moving from specific events to general laws, it predicts specific events from general premises.

However, hypothetical models may be less than useful because they do not specify the variables that will facilitate change. A pragmatic alternative would insist that theories should be practically useful as well as predictive. A clear example of pragmatism in modern psychology is behaviour analysis. For behaviour analysts, the basic datum in a psychological science is the relationship between behaviour and the environment. This technical usage of 'behaviour' is often misunderstood to refer solely to skeletal movements. This is not the case. Behaviour refers to anything the human organism does in relation to the environment context (both historical and current). Clearly, a small part of the environment is inside every person and therefore inner or private events (i.e. thoughts, emotions and physiological processes) play an important role in behaviour analysis. Thus, in order to understand individuals' behaviour we need to understand how they are affected by events occurring both inside and outside their bodies, and by their history.

In behaviour analysis, the objective of science is not solely to produce theories with predictive power: theories should also help us to change events. This is, they should point to how we can manipulate the data. By this view, the role of theory is prediction *and* control.

The basic premise is that there is a reason for everything (to take another view is to render science impossible) and it is those reasons that are the 'controlling variables' that science seeks to identify. Therefore, for behaviour analysis, theoretical variables must be accessible in principle and this therefore rules out hypothetical constructs in preference to environmental phenomena. It is important to remember that there are real events occurring inside every organism (e.g. thoughts and emotions) and these need to be included if the account is not to be incomplete. To return to the above example, as it is not possible in principle to manipulate 'intelligence' directly, it is not pragmatic to include such a construct within a theory. Although some claim (e.g. Bandura 1995) that hypothetical entities can be directly manipulated, as Dougher (1995) states:

> that literally cannot be true. What are varied are those factors thought to affect [the hypothetical construct] and what is measured are verbal reports, which are assumed to reflect [the construct]. It would be quite impossible to vary [the construct] directly, and that is the primary objection of behaviour analysis to [their use]. However, it is important to remember that this objection stems from the pragmatic nature of behaviour analysis, not some fundamental objection to talking about inferred concepts per se.
>
> (Dougher 1995: 217)

Hence, if prediction is the sole objective of science, hypothetical models are as good as environmental explanations. If we are interested in influencing events, a theory that includes directly manipulable variables will be of more use. Clearly, for the applied psychologist, pragmatic theories offer a distinct advantage.

## The diversionary nature of hypothetical constructs

Chiesa (1992) traced the modern origin of the debate on 'theory' to the German philosopher Ernst Mach and his reservations at the end of the nineteenth century about the appeal to atomic models as explanations for experimental data. Mach did not argue against the *reality* of atoms. Instead he cautioned against the use of hypothetical constructs in theories as he suspected that they tended to become the focus of research and thus they diverted attention away from the phenomenon that originally attracted the interest.

Within psychology a good example of this is the hypothetical construct, memory. What has to be explained is that, following one experience, a person will behave in the future in a way that seems to be influenced by the earlier experience. In the course of the last 100 years, memory has been the focus of a prodigious amount of research and the invention of ever more complex theories invoking an increasing number of hypothetical constructs (e.g. long term and short term memory, working memory, articulatory loops, etc.). In the process, the original problem of how experience changes future behaviour has been relegated to one of secondary interest. Theories of memory that do not invoke hypothetical constructs would simply describe how events affect the occurrence of future behaviour, and research would identify the data regularities in ever more diverse and complex circumstances. In this way, how events influence future behaviour can be charted without the tautology of explaining observed data by reference to hypothetical constructs inferred from those same events. In recent years some psychologists and other biological scientists have realized that research in memory may have identified many interesting phenomena without coming to a real understanding (cf. Rosenfield 1988).

The diversionary nature of hypothetical constructs can be illustrated in the history of the discovery of the role of oxygen in combustion by the French accountant and chemist Antoine Lavoisier (1743–94). The generally accepted understanding of combustion at the time was that substances gave off an element called phlogiston when they burned. The phlogiston theory was a classic hypothetical model because the existence of phlogiston could not be directly observed, but was inferred from observations. However, Lavoisier found that the ash of a burned substance was heavier than the substance before it was burned. These data suggested that far from giving off phlogiston, something was added during combustion. Further experiments showed that the increase in substance mass following combustion was equal to the decrease in the amount of oxygen in the surrounding air. This discovery of oxidizing combustion led to much of what we now know as modern chemistry, but it was not due to the phlogiston theory. In fact, Lavoisier was not looking for phlogiston, but for the most efficient gunpowder compound for use by the French military. Had he been concerned with phlogiston he may well have never carried out the experiments he did, as the hypothetical construct may have distracted him (as it had his colleagues) from the real task of science, the description of functional relations between sets of data.

The concept of 'schizophrenia' provides a psychological example of the diversionary effect of hypothetical constructs. Schizophrenia is a hypothetical construct that is inferred from the presence of particular symptoms and is then taken to underlie and explain them. Bentall *et al.* (1988) have pointed out that the search for the entity known as 'schizophrenia' has not proved fruitful and all we are left with following years of research is a concept of dubious reliability, validity and aetiology. They suggest that it is now time to abandon the concept of schizophrenia and instead study the individual symptoms that are said to instantiate it.

We believe that researchers should stay much closer to the observed data and be less distracted by the search for entities that do not exist beyond the observations from which they were inferred. The practice of transforming inferred entities into apparent realities has a long history in psychology:

> Instead of 'memory' we should say 'remembering'; instead of 'thought' we should say 'thinking'; instead of 'sensation' we should say 'seeing', 'hearing' etc. But . . . psychology is prone to transform its verbs into nouns. Then what happens? We forget that our nouns are merely substitutes for verbs and go hunting for the things denoted 'by the nouns'; but there are no such things, there are only the activities that we started with, seeing, remembering and so on . . . It is a safe rule, then, on encountering any menacing psychological noun, to strip off its linguistic mask and see what manner of activity lies behind!
>
> (Woodworth 1921: 5–6)

## Return to the laboratory

The everyday world is often too complex for the efficient description of the effects that variables have upon each other. To gain the necessary level of systematic control we require, psychologists usually head for the laboratory. The laboratory is an artificial environment where variables are isolated and in this form we can more easily separate and describe their effects and interactions (i.e. functional relations). Without the level of control that a laboratory provides, meaningful investigation would often be impossible, or at least far slower.

In psychology, much laboratory work in the past was carried out with non-human animals. To many, the data from these studies had little relevance to humans, but this view may be premature. As Hayes and Hayes (1992) pointed out, the evolutionary continuity of species means that there are great similarities between the different phyla. Chimpanzees are 98.4% genetically identical to humans, for example. However, it is also recognized that there are great differences too and, therefore, researchers have not taken continuity to be a fundamental principle, but rather to use it as a research strategy. That is to say, researchers 'bet that the same basic processes would prevail across species and that they would be revealed more readily by studying simple non-human behaviour in relatively simple environments than by studying human complexity directly' (Hayes and Hayes 1992: 1383). As a research strategy, continuity has proved to be extremely useful. Human and non-humans often react similarly to environmental variables, and many now taken for granted clinical tools come directly from basic research carried out in laboratories with non-humans (McDowell 1988).

However, it is now becoming increasingly evident that the primary difference between humans and other animals resides in what we broadly call language. For example, pre-verbal children show behaviour patterns similar to those of non-humans, and in the case of young children, their performances become more adult like as they develop language (Bentall *et al.* 1985). How language affects other human behaviour (and vice versa) is the current focus of intense research activity in behaviour analysis and looks like being a key area for psychological science, both inside and outside the laboratory. The laboratory therefore represents an important, if not essential, aspect of psychology's attempts to understand more about the human condition.

## Choices and the matching law

A good example of how basic laboratory research can lead to the formulation of a theory that has far reaching clinical applications is the study of 'the matching law' (Herrnstein 1961). The matching law relates to how the probability of behaviour is *matched* to the probability of its consequences. It is essentially a quantified model of choice. The matching law offers an explanation of why we do one thing rather than another. For example, why, when we are at a party, do we spend more time talking to some people than to others; or why do we choose to go shopping rather than weed the lawn; or why do we play tennis rather than watch television? In everyday life, when we make a choice, we usually say we 'like' that choice more than the alternatives. Put technically, we choose the more *reinforcing* option, and logically it makes sense that we should do the things that we like (find reinforcing) more frequently than the things that we do not like. The matching law is a quantified theory of how we distribute our time and energy across the available alternatives.

Choices are ever present in our lives and as such they represent what we might broadly describe as our lifestyle. Taken together, life's choices are extremely complex and, therefore, it is not surprising that researchers first tackled this problem in the laboratory. The primary simplification that took place was to work with pigeons rather than humans. This decision was a research strategy with the aim of throwing light on similar processes taking place in humans. (The matching law was shown later to account for many instances of the distribution of human behaviour across alternative options: see McDowell (1988) for a review.) Another step was to study only the positive reasons for choices, thereby excluding actions that were motivated by the avoidance of negative consequences (e.g. in humans, buying a parking ticket to avoid a fine). The final step was initially to limit the number of choices to two alternatives.

In 1961, Richard Herrnstein reported data from a series of experiments in which food-deprived pigeons were exposed to an environment in which pecking on two keys concurrently produced food (positive reinforcement) according to variable interval (VI) schedules. A VI schedule is a system of reinforcer delivery where the first key press after a variable time interval produces reinforcement. For example, a VI ten-second schedule varies the period of time between one and, say, sixty seconds after which a key press will produce reinforcement, with the average time being ten seconds. Two concurrently available VI schedules allow the pigeon to receive reinforcers from both keys at the same time.

Herrnstein (1961) found that if the overall reinforcer rate was kept steady, the pigeon distributed its responses across the two keys in direct proportion to their relative VI schedule values. In effect, the pigeons 'matched' their efforts according to the probability of reinforcement, such that when one key was twice as likely to produce reinforcement as the other, it received twice as many presses. It should be stressed that the matching law describes the relative distribution of choice behaviour and not the overall level of behaviour.

> It is important to recognise that organisms respond on concurrent schedules far more often than is necessary to obtain all the scheduled reinforcers. For example, pigeons may peck thousands of times to obtain a hundred or fewer reinforcers . . . [but] notice that the question of interest in the laboratory is the same as the question of interest in the natural human environment, namely, what governs the distribution of behaviour across concurrently available response alternatives.
>
> (McDowell 1988: 98)

Herrnstein (1961) summarized the distribution of responses across two concurrently available choices in the following way:

$$\frac{\text{Choices on Key 1}}{\text{Choices on Key 1 + Key 2}} = \frac{\text{Reinforcements on Key 1}}{\text{Reinforcement on Key 1 + Key 2}}$$

The above general equation represents the probability of choosing one key relative to another. Although the overall level at which one key is chosen is independent of choices on the other key, the probability of choosing one key depends on how often the other key is chosen. Therefore, the probability of choosing either key is calculated by dividing the number of times it is chosen by the total number of responses, (e.g. if Key 1 = 5 and Key 2 = 5, then the probability of choosing Key 1 is 50 per cent but if Key 2 = 45, although the absolute level of Key 1 responses is the same, the probability of choosing Key 1 is reduced to 10 per cent). The notation of the above summary equation can be simplified to:

$$\frac{C1}{C1+C2} = \frac{R1}{R1+R2} \tag{1}$$

C1 and C2 are the response rates on the two keys and R1 and R2 are the reinforcement rates for the two keys. Herrnstein (1961) proposed that the total choice rate (i.e. presses on Keys 1 and 2) could be represented by the constant $k$ $(k = C1 + C2)$. Putting this into equation (1) gives:

$$C1 = \frac{kR1}{R1+R2} \tag{2}$$

Equation (2) represents a two choice situation, but life rarely offers only two discrete choices and, although our linguistic convention tends to reduce questions to either/or scenarios, there are usually many other alternatives.

For example, asking the question 'Should I visit a friend or play tennis this afternoon?' hides the fact that there are other options available. To take into account a multiple choice situation, Herrnstein (1970) extended equation (2) to account for the selection of one choice from a potentially infinite selection by representing the reinforcers available from all other possible sources (i.e. R2 + R3 + R4 . . . ) as R*e* (*e* stands for *extraneous* reinforcers) giving equation (3):

$$C = \frac{kR}{R + Re} \tag{3}$$

Equation (3) became known as the 'single alternative matching equation' and it represents the culmination of a series of tightly controlled laboratory experiments. As such, it is the briefest summary of the proportional distribution of behaviour across alternative choices. As a theory, the matching law describes functional regularities between observed data and it represents an example of the inductive method of theory construction. That is, repeated experimentation uncovered regularities between functionally dependent events that were eventually summarized by the matching law. In line with the pragmatic ethos of behaviour analysis, the matching law describes the relationship between directly observable and manipulable variables without invoking hypothetical constructs as after-the-event explanations.

## The matching law and human behaviour

Extending this equation beyond the laboratory to the outside world of human behaviour is not an easy task. In the laboratory, for example, we can control precisely the maximum level of reinforcement, but at our current level of methodology, this is simply not possible or desirable in the everyday world.

Nonetheless, we can use some of the general principles of the matching law to interpret new phenomena and to make predictions about what we would expect in some contexts. Martens *et al.* (1992), for example, showed how the matching law described the work patterns of children in school environments. Social reinforcers were delivered on a variable interval schedule to two children contingent on academic engagement. Academic engagement was defined as the child remaining task orientated over a ten second interval. Reinforcement consisted of experimenter approval. The results showed that the children increased their average academic effort in direct proportion to the amount of social reinforcement given. As the level of social reinforcement increased so did the children's academic engagement. Indeed, the matching equation accounted for 88–99 per cent of the variance in the data scores.

McDowell (1988) similarly reported the case of a developmentally normal 10-year-old boy with severe self-injurious face scratching behaviour that was unwittingly maintained by contingent social reinforcement from his family. Baseline assessments showed that as the face scratching increased, so did the social reinforcement. The matching law accounted for 99.7 per cent of the data variance.

The matching law highlights the importance of the broader context in which behaviour occurs. Early research showed that behaviour is functionally related to its consequences and this led to the basic reinforcement paradigm that behaviour is controlled by its consequences. The matching law extends this model to show how the environment also affects the overall emission level of a behaviour. Referring to equation (3), if extraneous reinforcement is increased (i.e. the denominator) the target behaviour (i.e. the product) will decrease.

Introducing reinforcers for non-target behaviour is usually called non-contingent reinforcement and has a long history of being an effective treatment strategy. For example, Horner (1980) showed that increasing the 'richness' (i.e. density of reinforcement) of an environment decreased the level of problem behaviour emitted by institutionalized children. In another example, McDowell (1982) reported the case of a man who emitted high levels of aggressive and defiant negative behaviour. Assessment suggested that the man's behaviour was reinforced by social consequences but that placing the behaviour on an extinction schedule (i.e. ignoring it) was not acceptable because of the risk of increased aggression during that period. Instead, equation (3) was used to inform the treatment strategy by recognizing that increasing the level of extraneous reinforcement would decrease the overall level of the problem behaviour. Therefore, tokens were made contingent on behaviours that were not aggressive or defiant. The treatment immediately reduced the incidence of the target behaviour by 80 per cent. What is interesting is that the original contingency between the aggressive behaviour and social reinforcement was not altered, and yet changing the context in which it occurred reduced the frequency of behaviour. This point underlines the importance of identifying all, or as many as possible, of the sources of reinforcement that are available in an environment. Understanding the ecology of an individual's total repertoire has long been recognized as important in behaviour analysis (cf. Goldiamond 1974) and the matching law allows for a quantified analysis.

# Summary

Psychology's relationship with theory is uncertain. This is in part because different psychologists have different understandings of what is a theory. Most of psychology's currently popular paradigms continue to view prediction as the sole objective of science and thus a theory's validity is judged in terms of its correspondence with predicted data patterns. As a consequence, hypothetical constructs are regularly included in theoretical frameworks in spite of the fact that their inaccessibility and diversionary nature limit the theory's practical utility.

The pragmatic emphasis of behaviour analysis has led to a different objective for science that includes both the prediction of new data *and* the control of the variables responsible for those data. By its insistence on prediction and control, behaviour analysis represents the foremost advocate of pragmatism in contemporary psychology. Pragmatism favours the use of directly accessible variables and defines theory as the description of functional relations between data. Thus, hypothetical constructs (that is, those entities inferred from observations) are avoided as they cannot be directly manipulated and therefore reduce a theory's practical utility. This is not to say that hypothetical variables can never be included in theory, but when present, they should not be given explanatory status, but rather should be seen as a deficiency of research data.

If psychological science is to fulfil its promise, it will need to increase the practical utility of its theories. This will be facilitated if theories relate to directly manipulable variables, rather than hypothetical constructs that can never be verified.

---

### Discussion questions

1 How would behaviour analysts explain choice?

2 What is a hypothetical construct?

3 How does the theory described in this chapter differ from the one described in Chapter 11?

---

## Further reading

Catania, A. C. (1992) *Learning*. Englewood Cliffs, NJ: Prentice Hall. This book gives a thorough review of behavioural research. It shows how the science has developed since Watson – the founder of behaviourism in the 1920s – and introduces readers to contemporary issues within behaviour analysis.

Chiesa, M. (1992) *Radical Behaviourism: The Philosophy and the Science*. Boston, MA: Authors Cooperative. This book gives readers insight into some of the philosophical issues related to behaviourism. It addresses some of the misconceptions about behaviour analysis and brings together the philosophy and science of behaviour.

Skinner, B. F. (1974) *About Behaviourism*. New York: Knopf. This easy to read book gives readers a brief introduction to Skinner's writing and the issues pertinent within behaviour analysis.

## References

Bandura, A. (1995) Comments on the crusade against the causal efficacy of human thought. *Journal of Behavioural Therapy and Experimental Psychiatry*, 26: 179–90.

Bentall, R. P., Lowe, C. F. and Beasty, A. (1985) The role of verbal behaviour in human learning II: developmental differences. *Journal of the Experimental Analysis of Behavior*, 43: 165–81.

Bentall, R. P., Jackson, H. F. and Pilgrim, D. (1988) Abandoning the concept of 'schizophrenia': some implications of validity arguments for psychological research into psychotic phenomena. *British Journal of Clinical Psychology*, 27: 303–24.

Chiesa, M. (1992) *Radical Behaviourism: The Philosophy and the Science*. Boston, MA: Authors Cooperative.

Dallos, R. and Cullen, C. (1990) Applications to problems, in I. Roth (ed.) *Introduction to Psychology*. Milton Keynes: Open University.

Dougher, M. J. (1995) A bigger picture: cause and cognition in relation to differing scientific frameworks. *Journal of Behaviour Therapy and Experimental Psychiatry*, 26: 215–19.

Goldiamond, I. (1974) Toward a constructional approach to social problems: ethical and constitutional issues raised by applied behavior analysis. *Behaviourism*, 2: 1–84.

Gray, I. (1997) A follow up survey of clinical psychology training resources carried out by the Group of Trainers in Clinical Psychology. *Clinical Psychology Forum*, 108: 36–40.

Hayes, S. C. and Hayes, L. J. (1992) Verbal relations and the evolution of Behaviour Analysis. *American Psychologist* 47: 1383–95.

Herrnstein, R. J. (1961) Relative and absolute strength of response as a function of frequency of reinforcement. *Journal of the Experimental Analysis of Behavior*, 4: 123–32.

Herrnstein, R. J. (1970) The Law of Effect. *Journal of the Experimental Analysis of Behavior*, 13: 243–66.

Horner, R. D. (1980) The effects of an environmental 'enrichment' program on the behaviour of institutionalised profoundly retarded children. *Journal of Applied Behaviour Analysis*, 24: 473–91.

Howe, M. J. A. (1997) *IQ in Question: The Truth about Intelligence*. London: Sage.

Leahey, T. H. (1991) *A History of Modern Psychology*. Englewood Cliffs, NJ: Prentice Hall.

Lewin, K. (1951) *Field Theory in Social Science*. Chicago: University of Chicago Press.

McDowell, J. J. (1982) The importance of Herrnstein's mathematical statement on the law of effect for behaviour therapy. *American Psychologist*, 37: 771–9.

McDowell, J. J. (1988) Matching Theory in natural human environments. *Behaviour Analyst*, 11: 95–109.

Management Advisory Service (MAS) (1989) *Review of Clinical Psychology Services*. London: Department of Health.

Martens, B. K., Lochner, D. G. and Kelly, S. Q. (1992) The effects of variable-interval reinforcement on academic engagement: a demonstration of matching theory. *Journal of Applied Behaviour Analysis*, 25: 143–51.

Page, A. C. (1996) The scientist-practitioner model: more faces than Eve. *Australian Psychologist*, 31: 103–8.

Pilgrim, A. and Treacher, D. (1992) *Clinical Psychology Observed*. London: Tavistock.

Rosenfield, I. (1988) *The Invention of Memory: A New View of the Brain*. New York: Basic Books.

Skinner, B. F. (1950) Are theories of learning necessary? *Psychological Review*, 57: 193–216.

Skinner, B. F. (1974) *About Behaviourism*. New York: Knopf.

Woodworth, R. S. (1921) *Psychology*, rev. edn. New York: Holt.

*Section* **G**

# The psychologist as change agent

*Chapter* **13**

# Bullying in schools: changing attitudes and behaviour

## *Michael Boulton*

As the chapters in this volume indicate, applied psychologists concern them-selves with a vast array of different issues. However, at the core of all their endeavours is a 'problem' of one sort or another that requires attention. In this chapter, I shall consider a problem that has attracted increasing atten-tion from applied psychologists since the 1980s – that of childhood bullying. Applied psychologists have, in a relatively short space of time, made signifi-cant progress in tackling this problem. How they have gone about doing so will be described in this chapter. However, it would be wrong to give the impression that we have solved the problem of childhood bullying since, as children themselves still attest, it remains a commonplace occurrence. Thus, in writing the chapter, I also raise some of the more fundamental issues that lie at the heart of a psychological approach to anti-bullying work and some of the limitations of the work carried out by applied psychologists in this field.

## Bullying as a problem

### How many children are involved?

School bullying counts as a 'problem' because it affects so many pupils. Since the early 1980s numerous surveys have been carried out. Figures have varied enormously, depending on such matters as how bullying was defined and how the data were collected (e.g. interviews versus questionnaires, self-reports versus other reports). The earliest studies were small scale affairs, involving only one or a few schools. For example, Boulton and Underwood (1992) found that out of a sample of 296 middle school pupils in England, some 22 per cent reported that they were bullied 'sometimes' or more often. Psychologists are aware that extrapolating from relatively small data sets should be done with the utmost caution. Consequently, larger scale surveys were carried out. These have confirmed the scope of the problem. For example, in a well-cited survey of 2623 primary school children carried out by Whitney and Smith (1993), some 27 per cent indicated that they had been regularly bullied.

It is not just British pupils that bully their peers. Similar surveys have indicated that bullying is a pervasive problem in many different countries, including Australia (Rigby and Slee 1991), Ireland (O'Moore and Hillery 1989), Norway and Sweden (Olweus 1993), and the USA (Perry *et al.* 1988).

## How are victims affected?

Just because bullying involves so many children does not make it a problem. Rather, it also needs to be demonstrated that being bullied (and for that matter, bullying others) has negative consequences. Many studies have found strong associations between the extent to which children are bullied and psychological maladjustment. For example, Boulton and Smith (1994) reported that victims tended to have lower self-esteem than their non-bullied peers. Results from studies such as these that examined the correlation between levels of being bullied and levels of maladjustment are generally taken as supporting the commonsense notion that bullying causes psychological distress. However, as students of psychology are taught from their earliest classes, a correlation between variables does not necessarily indicate cause and effect. Stronger evidence for such a conclusion has come from more recent studies that have followed the same children over a period of time. For example, David Hawker and I found that earlier experiences of bullying contributed towards *increasing* depression (Hawker and Boulton, unpublished). Taken together, the available evidence provides strong support for the view that school bullying damages the psychological well-being of young people. Tragically, there are well documented cases of children committing suicide because their lives were made so miserable by the bullying actions of their peers (see Ross 1996).

Further research suggests that the harmful effects of bullying can extend well beyond the school years and into adulthood. In one investigation, Amber Arazi and I asked a sample of around 300 adults if they could recall being bullied during their school years, and more than 95 per cent were able to do so (Boulton and Arazi, in preparation). About three-quarters of these indicated that they could still remember the negative feeling and emotions associated with such experiences, and about the same proportion said that the bullying had had a long-lasting effect on them. For example, it was common for respondents to indicate that they were less trusting of other people because they had been bullied at school. A problem with these data is that they are reliant on participants' self-reports about their feelings and childhood experiences. It is quite possible that studies of this type produce data that are biased because of limitations of memory and participant effects. The optimum design would be to study a group of participants over time as they progress from childhood to adulthood, but to date no such investigation has been carried out.

## So what needs to be changed?

The previous section implies that many children are bullied by their peers at school, and that such experiences can have damaging consequences over the short and long term. Given that bullying represents such an important problem, how can applied psychologists use their skills to help? One way that they can do so is as agents for change. In considering this role, we need to ask 'what is it exactly that we want to change?' To many people, this may seem an unnecessary thing to do. Surely, they would argue, it is obvious that we want to stop children beating each other up. This is true, but only partially. The applied psychologist would suggest that this idea takes for granted some fundamental issues – such as 'what actually is bullying?' – and focuses on children's behaviour at the expense of their underlying attitudes and beliefs.

Consider first the basic issue of what behaviours count as bullying and, as such, should be changed. Researchers no longer accept the stereotypical view of bullying as consisting of 'just' physical assaults that involve hitting, kicking and the like. Rather, they believe that some non-physical interactions also have features that suggest they too should be viewed as forms of bullying. For example, Olweus (1993) pointed out that some (many!) instances of teasing, leaving people out of games and activities, and making faces and rude gestures are carried out with malicious intent by pupils. Studies by David Hawker and myself which we are preparing for publication, leave little room for doubt that these 'psychological' forms of bullying can damage children's mental well-being at least to the same extent as, and in some cases more than, physical assaults.

However, not everyone shares researchers' views. I asked a group of junior and secondary school pupils and teachers to indicate whether or not they thought that a range of specific behaviours counted as bullying. Among all of these groups, far fewer individuals accepted that name calling was bullying compared with hitting, kicking and pushing. How people conceptualize bullying is not a trivial issue. It would not be unreasonable to suggest that people – adults or children – would be more likely to act in a certain way, and would be more resistant to external pressure to refrain from doing so, if they did not regard that behaviour as bullying. Thus, before applied psychologists can begin the work of reducing the incidence of bullying, they must solicit, and if necessary challenge and clarify, people's definitions of it.

## Bringing about change

### No 'quick fix' solution

It would be wonderful if applied psychologists could offer schools a quick, simple solution to the problem of bullying. After all, people working and studying in schools face many demands and pressures. Teachers now point to heavy and increasing administration loads on top of their already considerable teaching responsibilities. Pupils from a relatively early age work towards National Curriculum assessments that have far reaching consequences for them, their teachers and their schools. It is not surprising that a common reason why schools do not take up the anti-bullying interventions suggested by applied psychologists is because they would take up too much time. Indeed, alternative approaches are often selected because they can be put into immediate action (Whitney *et al.* 1994).

However, while these concerns must be taken into account by applied psychologists, they should not disguise the truth of the matter that bullying is resistant to change in many cases. I believe that all too often in the past, those concerned with tackling bullying in schools have looked for a 'quick fix'. My point is not that these sorts of interventions are worthless but rather that, on their own, they will be of limited value.

Ian Flemington and I carried out a study in which we set out to demonstrate the effects of such a 'quick fix' solution (Boulton and Flemington 1996). While we kept an open mind about what sort of results we would obtain, prior anti-bullying research suggested that little would be achieved. For this study, we chose to examine the impact of showing secondary school pupils an anti-bullying video. Such an approach is likely to be popular with schools due to low cost and minimal effort required. Within the study, classes of pupils from the first four years (ages 11–15) were selected. At each year, one class was randomly assigned to the 'experimental' condition and another to the 'control' condition. Both classes completed a questionnaire on two occasions separated by two weeks concerning their involvement in, and beliefs about, bullying. In the intervening period, pupils in the experimental classes, but not those in the control classes, were shown the anti-bullying video. Statistical analysis indicated that those pupils who had watched the video did *not* report less bullying of other pupils than those who had not watched it. Nor was there evidence that the video led to more negative attitudes towards bullying in general. In contrast, one encouraging result was that more of the participants who had watched the video extended their definition of bullying to include non-physical actions such as name calling. Armed with such findings, the clear message that applied psychologists can take back to schools is that bullying is unlikely to yield to simple, single interventions. So (as we shall see in the next section) applied psychologists believe that such a pervasive problem as bullying requires a variety of actions to be taken over a prolonged period of time.

## Reducing the incidence of bullying

While teachers and staff may recognize that certain individuals require focused help and attention because they occupy well known bully or victim roles, they are more often concerned with reducing the general incidence of bullying within their institution. Since the mid-1980s there has been a rapid increase in the number and nature of anti-bullying interventions of this type offered by psychologists (for examples, see Smith and Sharp 1994). Rather than attempting to review them all in this section, I shall use the government funded Sheffield Anti-Bullying Project (henceforward shortened to the 'Sheffield Project') to illustrate the broad range of actions that psychologists have employed to combat bullying in schools. These interventions were taken up by 16 primary schools and 7 secondary schools.

The psychologists decided that the 'core' intervention in each school would be a whole-school anti-bullying policy, since this would help establish an overarching framework that would involve all members of the school community and provide the background for all other interventions. All 23 participating schools were helped to create a statement of intent that could be used to guide actions and organizations within them. In each case, the statement was designed to ensure that pupils, staff and parents had a chance to agree on what bullying was, why it was unacceptable and what actions should and would be taken to prevent and respond to bullying behaviour. In actual practice, policy development tends to be a protracted procedure. Moreover, there is no one 'best' way of devising a policy and, since it is designed to be 'owned' by the school community, it is not appropriate for 'outsiders' such as psychologists to impose one. Sharp and Thompson (1994), who were primarily responsible for this aspect of the Sheffield Project, identified five distinct stages. At each of these stages they presented a number of issues that schools were invited to consider as they created their own unique document (see Box 13.1). Box 13.2 shows an actual example of a whole-school anti-bullying policy.

Sharp and Thompson (1994) cautioned that successful implementation of a whole-school anti-bullying policy is far from easy. They were right to do so. In addition to the considerable time and effort required to establish a policy in the first place, it has to be recognized that this is just the start. Even though it may have very important beneficial effects in its own right (e.g. consciousness raising, setting implicit social norms, etc.), how the policy works on an ongoing basis has to be considered. Studies, such as that of Roland (1993), have demonstrated that the effects of anti-bullying initiatives can be shortlived if they are not continually monitored and if necessary modified. However, where these things do take place, positive results can be maintained (Foster *et al.* 1990).

In addition to the core development of a whole-school anti-bullying policy, schools in the Sheffield Project were also offered a broad range of optional interventions by the psychologists involved. These were grouped under three headings: 'curriculum-based strategies', 'working directly with bullies and victims' and 'making changes to playgrounds and breaktimes'. Box 13.3 contains an outline of some of these interventions.

## Widening pupils' conceptions of bullying

This aspect of the applied psychologist's role as agent for change starts with the premise that it would be easier to dissuade pupils from behaving in certain ways if they accept that these actions count as bullying. However (as we saw on pp. 213–14), a substantial proportion of pupils (and adults) do not accept that many common behaviours that have negative consequences for recipients actually involve bullying. Various techniques have be employed in an attempt to widen pupils' conceptions of bullying. Gobey (1991), for

---

*Box 13.1*  **Five stages in developing a whole-school anti-bullying policy**

1 *Awareness raising to make people confront the problem of bullying*

- provide people with up-to-date information about bullying
- dispel some of the myths about bullying (e.g. 'it's character building')
- begin the process of agreeing what bullying is

2 *Consultation*

- ask the different groups in the school for their ideas about the policy
- involve all groups from the school including senior managers, teaching staff, non-teaching staff, parents, governors as well as pupils

3 *Preparation of draft and transmission to final policy*

- pull together ideas from previous stage
- circulate draft policy to all groups
- provide opportunity for discussion and written comments
- specify aims of policy, definition of bullying, strategies for prevention of bullying, mechanisms for reporting bullying, mechanisms for responding to bullying
- clarify roles and responsibilities of all groups
- specify how policy will be monitored and evaluated

4 *Communication and implementation*

- launch the policy
- monitor closely bullying incidents

5 *Maintenance and review*

- regularly remind groups about the policy
- identify how well it is working
- identify the need for modifications

*Source:* based on Sharp and Thompson (1994)

---

example, used drama by having pupils watch scenes that involved various forms of social interaction. Some actions were 'obviously' bullying, for instance when a bigger, more powerful individual physically assaulted a smaller, less powerful peer. Others were more 'ambiguous', such as one person being left out of the group. The aim was to lead the audience to accept that if the intention of the bully and the suffering of the victim are similar, then it does not matter if one act involves a blow to the head and the other a refusal of a request to join in – they both should count as bullying.

*Box 13.2*   **Acland Burghley School anti-bullying policy (reproduced with permission)**

Acland Burghley is a happy, positive and friendly community. Students and their families are attracted to the school because they welcome and enjoy the atmosphere. We are a hard working school and expect high standards from our students in their work and behaviour. We are strongly committed to equal opportunities and every member of our community has the right to be able to reach his or her full potential in a safe and happy environment. No member of our community should be made to feel unhappy or unsafe. They have the right to expect support and action when their happiness and safety are threatened. Bullying is one of the main types of behaviour which cause distress. This is our policy to tackle the problem of bullying. It has been written by the students for our school community.

*What is a bully?*

'A bully is someone who physically or verbally hurts someone'.
'A bully is someone who likes to be in control of other people'.
'A bully can be a girl, a boy, a man, or a woman'.
'A bully usually picks on people who cannot defend themselves'.

There is no clear cut definition of what is a bully as bullying happens in so many different forms but a clear definition of bullying is: 'It is the wilful, conscious desire to hurt, threaten or frighten someone'.

*What kinds of things are bullying behaviour?*

'Verbal abuse, stealing, physical abuse, threatening and blackmail are all forms of a bully's behaviour'
'Being racist and sexist can be called bullying'
'The bully usually sees the hurt she/he has caused as a joke'
'Making someone feel inferior'

The term 'bullying' covers a very wide range of possible situations. Name calling, teasing, stealing, abuse of any kind are all forms of bullying. A bully uses *threat and fear* as weapons.

*What steps should you take if you are bullied or see someone else being bullied?*

'Tell someone you trust'
'Tell your parents, don't be scared'
'You should tell someone so that the bully can be stopped, the bully can be helped, as well as the victim'
'Only by telling someone can a bully be stopped'

If a bully is found quickly maybe she/he can be stopped from hurting anyone else. Bullies can only be stopped effectively if parents, teachers and students are aware of the problems and willing to stop them.

*What should happen to bullies?*

'Bullying is wrong and if anyone is bullying they should be punished'

There are different levels of bullying, this should be taken into account when deciding on a punishment. A possible 'plan' of punishment is:

1 Interview with teacher
2 Letter home
3 Suspension/exclusion
4 Expulsion/permanent exclusion

Acland Burghley School does not want to have to resort to step 4 but a bully's victim(s) must be protected and if this protection can only come from the removal of the bully, then so be it. Some bullies need the type of help that Acland Burghley cannot provide. Bullying must be identified and steps taken to prevent it. After all prevention is better than cure.

*What should you do if you are bullied?*

If you are bullied *tell someone*. Tell a teacher and your parent/carer straight away. Telling someone will make a big difference.

*What should you do if you see someone being bullied?*

You should *tell someone*. You may feel able to confront the bully yourself. You may be able to persuade the victim to tell a teacher themselves. But you must still *tell someone*.

*What should happen to the bully?*

The bully should be interviewed by the tutor/Head of Year/Deputy Head/Headteacher and asked why they are doing this. It should be explained to the bully what they are doing to the victim, how the victim feels and if possible the bully could be given a chance to *stop*. The bully's parents should be informed immediately, and a discussion should take place with the parents of the bully. The parents of the victim should be informed. If the bullying continues then the bully should be excluded and their future at the school should be carefully considered. They could be given help to change such as counselling. Although we care for each student at Acland Burghley, if the bully does not change then we have to protect the rest of the school community and therefore the bully should be asked to leave or be permanently excluded.

*What should happen to the victim?*

The victim will need to talk to someone about how they feel once the bullying has stopped. An organized discussion between the bully and the victim could help the bully to know how the victim feels.

*Box 13.3* **Some optional interventions in the Sheffield Anti-Bullying Project**

*Curriculum-based strategies*

Drama, role play and video were used to help pupils understand their experiences as bullies, victims and onlookers. Through watching live or filmed models taking on these different roles, or role playing them themselves, the pupils were encouraged to consider how other people think and feel in bullying situations, and to face up to disturbing emotions such as anger, fear and hate. They were given the opportunity to share their own insights gained from these exercises in group discussions.

Literature was used to raise pupils' awareness of bullying, and to foster feelings of empathy for victims. For example, *The Heartstone Odyssey* (Kumar 1985) was written explicitly to combat racist bullying. By listening to the narrative, the pupils were given opportunities to think about and challenge some of their own misconceptions about bullying and racism. These opportunities arose out of particular scenes of prejudice and discrimination involving characters within the story. After each reading, pupils were encouraged by their teachers to share their feelings with the class.

*Working directly with bullies and victims*

Assertiveness training for victims was designed to equip them with the skills of responding in ways that discouraged further bullying. An assertive response is one that allows individuals to stand up for their own rights without violating those of the bully. Recipients of this intervention were given opportunities to practise specific techniques in safe role play sessions before being encouraged to use them when faced with actual bullying. One such technique is 'fogging' in which the victim responds to hostile name calling or taunts with a neutral statement designed to de-escalate the situation. Statements such as 'You might think so' and 'Possibly' are illustrations.

The *Method of Shared Concern* was used to challenge pupils who were persistent bullies. It was devised by the Swedish psychologist Anatol Pikas. The technique involves regular meetings between the offending pupil and an adult. The latter does not set out to discover what went on in the bullying episodes nor even to 'extract a confession'. Instead, the aim is to get the pupil to agree that the peer being bullied is 'having a bad time' without the need for confrontation. Once this has been established, the adult gets the pupil to consider how she/he can contribute to solving this problem.

*Making changes to playgrounds and breaktimes*

Training courses were offered to lunchtime supervisors. These considered a range of issues, including how lunchtime supervisors could raise their often low status in the eyes of both teaching staff and pupils, how actual bullying incidents could be identified, how actual bullying incidents could be responded to, and how pupils could be encouraged to engage in positive behaviour. For example, lunchtime supervisors were presented with arguments in favour of having a hierarchy of sanctions to apply to perpetrators of bullying, and invited to discuss the merits of such a system.

Ways in which schools could improve their grounds were presented. The rationale for this approach came from environmental psychology. Research in this branch of psychology supports the view that people are more likely to behave in an antisocial manner if their physical environment is impoverished. Many, though by no means all, school grounds are dull concrete, brick and tarmac affairs with little to stimulate pupils. Allied to this, many are also characterized by overcrowding and unequal use of space. All in all, such physical settings do little to help create an anti-bullying ethos. Cath Higgins worked with several of the schools in the Sheffield Project to improve their grounds. However, it was not just the physical changes that were important. Involving pupils themselves in the process of change should foster a sense of ownership, reduce levels of aggression and squabbling on the playground, and provide opportunities for a greater variety of play.

*Source:* based on Smith and Sharp (1994)

## Evaluating our efforts

Applied psychologists recognize the need to determine the relative effectiveness of their interventions. Wherever possible they try to build evaluation of their actions into the design of the project from the outset. It is a pity that many anti-bullying projects have failed to do this. Without a formal evaluation of change it is simply not possible to determine whether or not things have actually improved. It is hardly convincing to gather and present a few comments along the lines of 'I think there is much less bullying now than there was before'. If the aim of the intervention is to reduce the general incidence of bullying in a school, then it is essential that levels are measured at least before and after the intervention, if not at intervals in between. Psychologists can bring their expertise as 'toolmakers' to this exercise, either by providing an instrument that has already been used successfully to measure bullying or by helping clients to devise their own. Either way, the instrument should be suitable for those who will provide the data.

The Sheffield Project (see Box 13.3) provides a real life example of how an evaluation was carried out. As part of this study, the research team wanted to determine if levels of bullying were reduced following a package of measures that focused on enhancing playground supervision and improving the way in which actual bullying incidents were monitored and responded to. This optional intervention was taken up by thirteen of the participating schools. In order to do this, pupils at the schools were asked to complete a record of their experiences of bullying prior to and following the interventions, and during each intervening half-term. The questionnaire used for this purpose was kept deliberately brief and simple since the pupils were required to complete one every day for a week (in some cases a fortnight) during afternoon registration. They simply did not have the time to respond to a lengthy questionnaire. The efficacy of the intervention was assessed on the basis of these pupil responses.

## So how effective are anti-bullying initiatives?

Literally hundreds of anti-bullying projects have been carried out since the mid-1980s. In many cases, these were of small scale and duration, and the results were not disseminated beyond the schools involved. Nevertheless, a growing number of well documented, large scale investigations exist. In this section, I shall summarize the overall results from some influential studies.

The earliest large scale anti-bullying project was directed by Dan Olweus. It was carried out in all 3500 Norwegian schools, prompted by media concerns about a number of suicides attributed to bullying. In May 1983, a nationwide survey to measure the extent of bullying was conducted. Following this, the research team provided each school with a package of materials, including a video to stimulate classroom discussion, and a folder of advice for parents. Together, these materials were designed to reduce as far as possible existing bully/victim problems and to prevent the development of new problems.

Two evaluations of this project have been reported. Olweus (1993) did so by focusing on 2500 11–14-year-old pupils from 42 primary and secondary/junior high schools in the Bergen area. The initial survey, which consisted mainly of pupils' self-reports of involvement in bullying, was repeated in May 1984 and then again in May 1985.

Note that in trying to determine the effects of the interventions it is not appropriate to look at changes in levels of bullying within the same group of children. The reason for this is that levels of bullying tend to decrease with age. Thus, for example, a decrease in frequency from 11 to 12 to 13 years could be due to age effects rather than the interventions themselves.

To overcome this problem, Olweus employed a 'selection-cohorts' design. That is, he compared age-equivalent groups. For example, he compared 11-year-olds in 1983 who had no experience of the intervention, with those pupils who were 11 years old in 1984 who had one year's experience of the interventions, and with those pupils who were 11 years old in 1985 that had two years' experience of the interventions. The main findings of this project were encouraging. Over the two year period of the study, overall rates of reported levels of bullying fell from about 9 per cent to about 5 per cent. The number of new victims was also reduced. In addition, Olweus also found evidence for a 'dosage–response' effect. That is, those classes that showed the largest reductions in levels of bullying had put more effort into their anti-bullying interventions.

A separate evaluation of the Norwegian campaign was conducted by Erling Roland in the Stavanger district (Roland 1993). He worked with 37 schools over a three year period from 1983 to 1986. His results were far less encouraging than those of Olweus. Most notably, Roland did not find clear reductions in levels of bullying; in some schools there was actually an increase in the number of children reporting that they were victims. One consistency between the two evaluations was that, like Olweus, Roland also found that the schools that did more found the greatest decreases in bullying levels, though these were still modest.

Smith and Sharp (1994) considered how the two sets of results could be reconciled. They pointed out that on closer examination, the nature of the intervention was not the same in the two cases. Olweus (1993) tended to provide continuing and intensive support to the schools over the period of his study, whereas Roland (1993) did not. Smith and Sharp (1994: 11) concluded that 'Olweus' more spectacular results may reflect what can be achieved with intensive input, while Roland's may reflect the result of simply providing a modest package without any further back-up'.

Two large scale evaluations of anti-bullying actions have also been carried out in the UK. One involved the Sheffield Project. A survey of bullying was carried out in November–December 1990 and then again two years later. The interventions were implemented in the intervening period. The researchers calculated change scores for a number of key indicators in order to evaluate the effects of the anti-bullying work. Positive results were obtained on a number of these indicators, but in all cases, the effects were more in evidence in the primary schools than in the secondary schools. For example, there was a 17 per cent increase in the proportion of younger pupils that indicated that they had not been bullied, but a 2 per cent decrease among the older pupils. Similarly, there was a 15 per cent decrease in the proportion of younger pupils, and a 7 per cent decrease in the proportion of older pupils, that indicated they had been bullied frequently.

The other evaluation in the UK was of the 'Safer Schools – Safer Cities' Anti-Bullying Project, led by Graham Smith (1997). This project set out to establish the extent and nature of bullying in a representative sample of schools in Wolverhampton, to put in place a package of anti-bullying interventions, and to conduct a follow-up survey to investigate the efficacy of this action. As in the other large scale projects, a variety of anti-bullying measures were offered by the psychologists and their colleagues. These included developing a whole-school anti-bullying policy, the Method of Shared Concern (see Box 13.3), setting up Bully Courts, and developing play activities and playtimes. I would describe the results of this evaluation as 'mixed', and most changes were small. For example, the overall proportion of secondary school boys (aged 11–16) who were bullied rose from 12 to 15 per cent, whereas the corresponding values for girls dropped from 10 to 8 per cent. Similarly, among infant/primary school pupils (aged 5–11), the proportion of boys who were bullied fell from 27 to 26 per cent whereas it rose from 21 to 22 per cent among girls.

The results of these evaluation studies suggest:

• anti-bullying interventions can have a positive effect
• the more conscientiously schools adopt interventions the greater the reduction will be

- it is harder and/or takes longer to reduce bullying in secondary schools than in junior and infant schools
- even among the most successful schools, levels of bullying remain at unacceptable levels.

## Conducting pure research to guide applied interventions

The preceding section indicates that the work of applied psychologists can help reduce the problem of school bullying in significant ways. Nevertheless, it remains the case that bullying resists our attempts to eliminate it completely. Even after reducing by half the number of children victimized on a regular basis, we are still faced with the reality that many thousands continue to be abused by their peers in this way. In recognition of this fact, my research programme since 1990 has been trying to identify some of the ways in which the lives of those pupils who, through no fault of their own, habitually serve as victims, can be made less miserable. Put simply, while I do not condone the continued existence of bullying in schools, I realize that it is likely to remain the case for some considerable period of time. As such, I have set out to investigate those variables that can lessen the harmful effects that so often accompany bullying.

To give a flavour of this work, I shall describe a study I carried out with Cam Chau in 1998 (Boulton and Chau unpublished) This study set out to test the hypothesis that victims of bullying that have good quality friendships, and separately, have many friends, will show fewer signs of psychological maladjustment than other victims who lack these supportive peer relationships. Our project followed up a group of just over 400 children for six months. Measures of the extent to which the participants were bullied, showed signs of maladjustment, and the number and quality of their friendships were taken at the start and end of this period. Statistical analysis of the data obtained led us to conclude that one key friendship variable can help reduce the distress being bullied brings. That friendship variable is having a very close friendship that is strongly reciprocated (child A likes child B best and vice versa). Further investigation suggests that the positive effects of belonging to such a relationship stem from having an ally that can help fend off the bully, summon help where this is not possible, and enable the victim to realize that the bully was to blame.

In carrying out this study, we were not acting as 'applied psychologists' in the true sense of the term. Rather, this may be described more accurately as a piece of 'pure' research not directed at solving a real life problem. Nevertheless, the project was motivated by a desire to obtain information that could, in turn, be used by applied psychologists concerned with tackling the problem of bullying. We would argue that our results suggest that school authorities should pay more attention to what might be termed children's 'positive peer relationships'. By encouraging children to form friendships within school and by creating the right conditions to enable them to do so, schools could go a long way to reducing the negative consequences for victims. However, I do not want to imply that schools need not try to tackle the problem of bullying. Rather, I would like to suggest that fostering positive peer relationships is another valuable line of attack alongside these efforts.

## Summary

Bullying represents a considerable problem for many school pupils. In tackling it, applied psychologists have used a wide range of skills and knowledge. Rather than assuming that everyone agrees about the nature of the problem, they have sought to build a consensus about what bullying is and how it could be tackled. They have also recognized that the phenomenon of bullying is as much about underlying attitudes as it is about actual aggressive behaviour. Consequently, they have set about changing both. However, they recognize that persuading people to change their beliefs and behaviour is a complex process. Thus, they have drawn on a wide range of interventions, some that operate at the whole-school level while others involve working with individuals and small groups. An integral part of much of the work of applied psychologists has been the design and implementation of formal evaluations of the effects of the intervention. These have produced mixed results. Nevertheless, it seems that concerted effort over a sustained period can help reduce the number of pupils involved. Finally, while we await the development of much more effective anti-bullying interventions than exist currently, applied psychologists use information gathered in 'pure' research projects to help alleviate the distress that often accompanies bullying.

---

### Discussion questions

1 Consider some of the problems faced by psychologists seeking to reduce the level of bullying. How might they be overcome?

2 How would you go about evaluating the effects of an anti-bullying intervention project?

3 Why do you think it is necessary to use such a wide range of different interventions to reduce the level of bullying?

---

## Further reading

Ross, D. M. (1996) *Childhood Bullying and Teasing*. Alexandria, VA: American Counseling Association. With a very readable style, this useful book provides a detailed overview of research on bullying as well as an account of intervention programmes.

Smith, P. K. and Sharp, S. (eds) (1994) *School Bullying: Insights and Perspectives*. London: Routledge. An excellent text that provides a theoretical background to a range of anti-bullying interventions. It also contains the most detailed account of the evaluation of the Sheffield Anti-Bullying Project.

Tattum, D. and Herbert, G. (1997) *Bullying: Home, School and Community*. London: David Fulton. This book does justice to the complex nature of bullying by considering it in a range of contexts both within and outside school. It contains chapters by a range of professionals in addition to psychologists.

# References

Boulton, M. J. and Chau, C. (unpublished) 'Does friendship moderate the harmful effects of peer victimization and if so how?' Manuscript submitted for publication.

Boulton, M. J. and Flemington, I. (1996) The effects of a short video intervention on secondary school pupils' involvement in, definitions of, and attitudes towards, bullying. *School Psychology International*, 17: 343–57.

Boulton, M. J. and Smith, P. K. (1994) Bully/victim problems in middle school children. *British Journal of Developmental Psychology*, 12: 315–29.

Boulton, M. J. and Underwood, K. (1992) Bully/victim problems among middle school children. *British Journal of Educational Psychology*, 62: 73–87.

Foster, P., Arora, T. and Thompson, D. (1990) A whole-school approach to bullying. *Pastoral Care in Education*, 8: 13–17.

Gobey, F. (1991) A practical approach through drama and workshops, in P. K. Smith and D. Thompson (eds) *Practical Approaches to Bullying*. London: David Fulton.

Hawker D. and Boulton, M. (unpublished) 'Peer victimization: cause and consequence of psychosocial maladjustment.' Manuscript submitted for publication.

Kumar, A. (1985) *The Heartstone Odyssey*. Allied Mouse Ltd, Longgen Court, Spring Gardens, Buxton SK17 6BZ, UK.

Olweus, D. (1993) *Bullying in Schools: What We Know and What We Can Do*. Oxford: Blackwell.

O'Moore, A. and Hillery, B. (1989) Bullying in Dublin schools. *Irish Journal of Psychology*, 10: 426–41.

Perry, D. G., Kusel, S. J. and Perry, L. (1988) Victims of peer aggression. *Developmental Psychology*, 24: 801–14.

Rigby, K. and Slee, P. (1991) Bullying among Australian school children: reported behaviour and attitudes towards victims. *Journal of Social Psychology*, 131: 615–27.

Roland, E. (1993) Bullying: a developing tradition of research and management, in D. Tattum (ed.) *Understanding and Managing Bullying*. Oxford: Heinemann Educational.

Ross, D. M. (1996) *Childhood Bullying and Teasing*. Alexandria, VA: American Counseling Association.

Sharp, S. and Thompson, D. (1994) The role of whole-school policies in tackling bullying behaviour in schools, in P. K. Smith and S. Sharp (eds) *School Bullying: Insights and Perspectives*. London: Routledge.

Smith, G. (1997) The 'Safer Schools – Safer Cities' Bullying Project, in D. Tattum and G. Herbert (eds) *Bullying: Home, School and Community*. London: David Fulton.

Smith, P. K. and Sharp, S. (eds) (1994) *School Bullying: Insights and Perspectives*. London: Routledge.

Whitney, I. and Smith, P. K. (1993) A survey of the nature and extent of bully/victim problems in junior/middle and secondary schools. *Educational Research*, 35: 3–25.

Whitney, I., Rivers, I., Smith, P. K. and Sharp, S. (1994) The Sheffield Project: methodology and findings, in P. K. Smith and S. Sharp (eds) *School Bullying: Insights and Perspectives*. London: Routledge.

# Chapter **14**

# Psychology and humanitarian assistance

## *Alastair Ager*

Since the 1940s there has been a dramatic increase in the scale of international humanitarian assistance. Agencies such as Oxfam, founded during the Second World War to assist famine victims in Nazi-occupied Europe, have grown into complex organizations engaged in relief and development work throughout the world. Such work is now undertaken by a wide range of non-governmental organizations (NGOs), including Save the Children Fund (and sister agencies within the International Save the Children Alliance), Christian Aid, the Catholic Fund for Overseas Development, and Actionaid. Within the UK alone there are now over 200 NGOs working in the field of international development, with an increasing number having established a specific focus on a particular geographical region or development issue (e.g. family planning or appropriate technology). Internationally, NGOs such as World Vision and Médecins Sans Frontières have taken an increasingly prominent role in responding to humanitarian needs within the developing world.

The postwar rise of NGOs defines only one component of the contemporary humanitarian regime. So-called 'intergovernmental' agencies, such as the World Food Programme and the United Nations High Commissioner for Refugees, often play important coordinating roles during humanitarian crises. Others, such as the World Bank, may seek to play a similar role in longer term development assistance to a given country. Both short term emergency aid following flood, earthquake or war, and longer term development assistance targeting economic or social development, take place within a complex world of global politics. Whether channelled through intergovernmental or non-governmental organizations, the majority of the funding for international humanitarian assistance comes from the governments of the most economically developed nations, and its focus is generally in line with the perceived interests of these countries.

## The role and relevance of psychology

Within this world of humanitarian assistance a wide range of disciplines are called upon to guide the planning, delivery and evaluation of interventions. Medical and health sciences are clearly fundamental to planning health programmes, as is engineering and logistics to the development of infrastructure for water supply, transport, etc. Economic appraisal is a key component of much development planning, and sociology and social anthropology are widely seen as providing an important foundation for the analysis of appropriate means of working with communities to develop effective programmes. Generally speaking, however, psychology has not been perceived as a discipline relevant to the tasks of emergency assistance and development (Carr 1996).

I first became acutely aware of this situation when, having taken up a post at the University of Malawi in the late 1980s, I learned that, although the UK government supported a number of posts at the university, they would not do so for psychology – as the subject was not considered 'developmentally relevant'. When I subsequently examined the curriculum previously delivered to students in Malawi I could see the grounds for this judgement. What insight did the 'classic' introductory texts in psychology and lab experiments in such topics as social attraction and visual illusions really provide of relevance to a society where one in four of the children were not surviving until their fifth birthday and where the average wage was less than £50 a year?

Debate about the relevance of a psychology grounded in the western scientific tradition to developing societies with widely differing cultural values periodically surfaces within the discipline of psychology. Unfortunately, the structure of such debate has tended to follow a rather too familiar routine. Assertions are made about the potential contribution of psychology in addressing some aspect of international development or humanitarian assistance within the developing world, focusing perhaps on potential applications in fostering economic and social development, or health belief and behaviour, or in resolving conflict. Respondents react by noting the racist and 'classist' history of psychology, the 'culture-bound' framework of 'positivist' science, and the imperialism assumed in valuing 'western' psychology above local, indigenous 'psychologies' (see e.g. Carr and MacLachlan 1993 and the subsequent critique by Owusu-Bempah and Howitt 1995).

Such debates have tended to generate more heat than light. The work of Berry *et al.* (1992), however, has indicated a potential route away from such sterile contentions. In terms of the phenomena addressed by psychologists, Berry *et al.* reject both *absolutism* (assuming fundamental similarity across cultures) and *relativism* (assuming fundamental difference across cultures). In their place they propose what they term *universalism*, which 'adopts the working assumption that basic psychological processes are likely to be common features of human life everywhere, but that their manifestations are ... influenced by culture' (Berry *et al.* 1992: 258). The challenge then is to determine what aspects of our psychological analysis are tapping, potentially at least, universal processes and what aspects simply reflect their 'manifestation' within western culture.

The 'sifting' of psychological analysis to determine the general insight from the cultural artefact is a fascinating challenge. The 'bystander intervention effect', the Muller-Lyer illusion, the effect of different schedules of reinforcement on behaviour, the delayed cognitive processing of emotional material – these are the sorts of finding that form the 'bedrock' of contemporary general psychology. However, to what extent do they represent insights into common psychological processes in humankind? Or do they tell us rather more about the concerns and characteristics of western culture? These are crucially empirical questions, which an increasing number of psychologists – from a range of cultural backgrounds – are now addressing within a resurgent field of cross-cultural psychology.

For the applied psychologist working across cultural boundaries there are three major consequences of adopting a 'universalist' position. First, they can acknowledge the potential relevance of their disciplinary knowledge to understanding behaviour in non-western contexts. Second, however, they must demonstrate considerable sensitivity to the local meanings and cultural mores shaping belief and behaviour in such settings. Third, they need to demonstrate humility in fostering integration between these two sources of knowledge, particularly in the interrogation and amendment of the former in the light of the latter. The involvement of psychologists from non-western cultures – socialized into both the approaches and assumptions of 'scientific' psychology and the meanings and structures of a non-western culture – is particularly crucial for fostering such integration.

Within this context, this chapter considers the contribution which psychological analysis can make in the furtherance of appropriate humanitarian assistance. It examines three illustrative areas of work in which the applied psychologist – generally working alongside professionals in other disciplines – may make a distinctive contribution. The areas considered are the planning of assistance programmes and their sustainability, assistance for refugee populations and working with humanitarian assistance agencies.

## Planning of assistance programmes and their sustainability

In recent years concepts such as 'community participation' and 'needs led planning' have been increasingly seen as a means of ensuring greater coherence between assistance programmes and the needs and capacities of local communities. Despite some successes, there is a tendency for these terms to be poorly defined. As they have taken on the status of 'slogans', they may even be used with respect to projects involving high levels of central planning and direction. There is a need for some rigorous bases for assessing the coherence between programmes and local context.

The concept of sustainability offers some promise in this respect. Sustainability has come to be a key concern in conceptualizing development programmes. In the past, many such programmes in the developing world have proved unsustainable, in that they have either ultimately collapsed or required continued external support to remain viable. Whether it is in the area of Information, Education and Communication (IEC) targeting health behaviour change, the development of new local industries such as fish farming or soap manufacture or collaborative programmes for bridge building and road maintenance in remote rural settings, ways of ensuring the sustainability of programmes are now seen as key issues in the development process.

There is danger here, too, that 'sustainability' will take on the status of a mere slogan. The term, however, lends itself to rather clearer definition than many other concepts. Sustainability focuses attention on the environment in which an innovation is planned and poses the question 'What exists here that will encourage the planned changes?' If mechanisms and resources cannot be identified that will act plausibly to foster and maintain innovation, that innovation may be considered 'unsustainable' in that setting.

Identifying mechanisms and resources within a community that may serve to support a development programme remains no easy task. However, the behaviour analytic literature provides useful guidance on how this might be accomplished. Behaviour analysis is a tradition within applied psychology which focuses on the way the environment exerts influence over human behaviour (see Chapter 12). The comprehensive study of the relationship between environmental conditions and behaviour has suggested a number of principles which predict the frequency of subsequent behaviours. This is of clear relevance here, where the concern is with whether there are suitable environmental resources to sustain the behaviours required for a successful programme.

In behaviour analytic theory a distinction is made between what are termed antecedent and consequent events. Antecedent events are those which precede some action, acting either to signal its appropriateness or prompt its occurrence. Consequent events are those which follow an action, serving to either encourage or discourage its repetition. In terms of programme planning, antecedent events are essentially the prerequisites for the functioning of the programme. They are the conditions that are necessary before tasks can be carried out. Consequent events are, straightforwardly, the consequences of the operation of the programme.

For a programme to be sustainable, appropriate antecedent and consequent conditions must be met. But it is insufficient for these conditions merely to exist. They must also be arranged and sequenced (in behavioural analytic terms, scheduled) in an effective manner. Using a behaviour analytic framework to examine the concept of sustainability thus suggests certain required conditions for a 'sustainable programme' in a given setting. Such conditions (summarized in Table 14.1) are considered in turn below.

*Table 14.1* Conditions supporting programme sustainability

| *Antecedent conditions* | *Consequent conditions* |
| --- | --- |
| Consistency | Valued outcomes |
| Control | Reliable outcomes |
|  | Prompt outcomes |
|  | Natural outcomes |

## Antecedent conditions

### *Consistency*

For a programme to function, a large number of environmental conditions must be established. A programme may require buildings, certain equipment may be vital, some form of staffing (often with a certain level of education and training) will be necessary, and so on. The requirement for *consistency* simply asserts that for a programme to be sustainable these conditions will have to be met continually. To ensure this, either appropriate mechanisms within the community must be identified or else a reliable contract with some 'sponsor' outside the community must be established.

It may initially appear to be unwarranted to draw attention to such an obvious requirement. Nevertheless, a lack of consistency in the availability of resources prerequisite for the functioning of a programme is probably one of the most common causes of failure in humanitarian development and assistance work (Harrell-Bond 1986). Problems in the recruitment of adequately trained staff are widespread across many programmes. Transport difficulties plague many rural-based schemes, especially in nations where motor transport – through a combination of lack of spare parts and inadequate road maintenance – is often functionally unsustainable. Where the use of specialized equipment is a key part of an engineering or health project, problems in securing adequate maintenance can have dire consequences. In all of these cases, the lack of consistency in the provision of essentially prerequisite antecedent conditions renders a programme unsustainable.

### *Control*

In behavioural terms, the antecedent conditions of greatest importance are those which exert functional *control* over the programme. That is, some things are functionally vital for the effective running of the programme, while others may be thought of value but are, in practice, of less crucial significance in determining success. The problem is that it is not always easy to distinguish between the two (Harrell-Bond 1986).

Behavioural research has long shown that the things which exert functional control over behaviour are not always the most obvious. In the context of humanitarian assistance, we may think that a certain aspect of a programme is vital for its success, only to discover that its presence still fails to deliver targeted results. For instance, agencies had supplied 'safe delivery kits' of equipment and supplies to auxiliary midwives in a region where I was examining low rates of access to government health services. The kits had been supplied on the presumption that such equipment would be a key factor in fostering greater uptake of services. Kits shelved unopened at local clinics vividly illustrated that other conditions (notably staff training and community acceptance of government health workers) needed to be met before utilization was likely to increase.

For a programme to be sustainable it is important that the key sources of functional control are determined. Where such control is associated with impermanent features of the programme, means must be sought to transfer functional control to more permanent features. The clearest example of this is the frequent difficulty experienced in transfer of responsibility from short term, innovating 'consultants' to indigenous community personnel. While there is an extensive literature on means of encouraging transfer of functional control, certain shifts appear to be considerably easier to engineer than others. For instance, programmes which initially foster a high level of control by transitory 'innovators' are likely to prove less sustainable than those which, from the outset, invest responsibility in local personnel. Returning to Malawi in 1998, for instance, after an absence of six years I was struck by the contrast between programme initiatives which had withered and those that had become firmly rooted – with the extent of initial local control a significant predictor of these alternative outcomes.

## Consequent conditions

### Valued outcomes

Programmes clearly aim to provide *valued outcomes* for their users (generally referred to in humanitarian assistance work as 'beneficiaries'). They do not always succeed in this, however. Programmes may simply fail to produce targeted outcomes. Even if they succeed, however, it may be that the outcome is not of value to intended beneficiaries, a common risk if there has not been adequate consultation before framing programme goals. It should also be acknowledged that what beneficiaries want of a programme will change over time. What may be of value today may be irrelevant tomorrow, a frequent concern in agricultural projects where alterations in the market value of produce and climatic variation may significantly influence village farmers' perceptions of needs.

### Reliable outcomes

A good deal of behavioural research has shown that the *reliability* of the rewarding outcome(s) can have significant effects on the durability of behaviour change. Research has generally confirmed what may appear common sense. People can tolerate a certain degree of unreliability in receiving anticipated benefits. With prolonged absence of reward, however, people return to behaving as they did previously. I have frequently found non-availability of medicines – or personnel – following long and difficult journeys to health posts cited as a reason for reluctance to access government health facilities. Local pharmacies or traditional healers often prove far more reliable sources of health assistance in rural areas within the developing world.

### Prompt outcomes

Research has clearly demonstrated that the longer it takes for a course of action to produce a positive outcome for an individual, the less likely it is that they will persevere with that action. In other words, outcomes need to be *prompt*. A programme that requires considerable investment of time and other resources by beneficiaries before any benefit is found is clearly likely to be less sustainable than one which produces immediate benefits. This is not to say that all programmes must achieve immediate results. Rather it is to acknowledge that programmes will be best served if they produce some tangible outcomes for beneficiaries from the outset, as a form of 'first fruits' of a hoped-for harvest. Witnessing the growing display within a refugee camp of the woollen articles prepared by refugee women as part of an income generating programme indicated greater sensitivity to the value of the programme's profile with visiting agencies than the women's receipt of valuable income contingent upon deployment of their new skills.

### Natural outcomes

Natural outcomes generally prove more successful in maintaining changes in behaviour than do contrived ones. It is thus preferable for the outcome to flow as a *natural consequence* of participation in a programme, rather than being in some way contrived or artificial. There are likely to be two factors favouring reliance on natural outcomes.

The first, reinforcing an earlier point, is that a natural outcome is plausibly a reliable outcome. This is not always the case, obviously, but contrived outcomes will often prove the more problematic to maintain. Participation in an under-5s clinic will be encouraged more by giving mothers advice and support that they perceive as helpful rather than by fostering attendance with provision of potentially short-lived food supplies.

This example also illustrates the second benefit of reliance on natural outcomes: they are less likely to encourage inappropriate behaviour. Contrived outcomes can encourage contrived behaviour, that is behaviour motivated solely by the availability of this artificial reward. With food supplies to reward attendance at an under-5s clinic one can find an increasing number of parents of older children attending, deflecting the programme from its central purpose and objectives.

## Appraisal of development programmes

The above framework may prove a valuable tool for appraising development programmes. I was once involved, for instance, in an evaluation of an assistance programme for Mozambican refugees in Malawi. Here vocational training was a major component in targeting income generation (and thus poverty alleviation). The programme involved manipulating a number of antecedent conditions (including the provision of training in such skills as tinsmithing and knitting, and the supply of raw materials). Evaluation suggested that while this frequently resulted in increased competence in the targeted skills, the impact on income generation was negligible. Indeed, Table 14.2 indicates

*Table 14.2* Comparison between income generating activity (IGA) projects and 'indigenous' economic activity as a source of income for Mozambican refugees

|  | *Mean estimated daily adult income (tambala)* |
| --- | --- |
| All refugees | 29 t |
| All 'income earners' | 67 t |
| Those engaged in IGA projects | 14 t |

Source: Ager *et al.* (1991)

that income from households not engaged in such activities was, in fact, higher than those recruited to such programmes. With little prior analysis of the markets for the goods produced, sales (and thus generated income) was not a reliable, prompt or natural outcome of the refugees' programmed work. Analysis suggested that a more profitable strategy would have been to build upon the existing local demands and skills (e.g. cultivation) and social structures (e.g. women's networks). The conclusions from this evaluation were that the sustainability of these programmes would have been considerably improved by a closer examination of the conditions under which several entrepreneurs within the Mozambican community were producing sustained income.

While the above analysis has a clear practical application, it is nonetheless principally a psychological critique of humanitarian assistance programmes. With regard to the next issue addressed – assistance to refugee populations – psychologists in the last ten years or so have had a much more explicit involvement, utilizing concepts and analysis from such areas as social, clinical and organizational psychology.

## Assistance for refugee populations

The displacement of over 1 million Rwandans into neighbouring Zaire within the space of 72 hours in July 1994 was – in terms of its magnitude and suddenness – undoubtedly one of the most dramatic refugee crises of the last 20 years. Yet with approximately 5 million other refugees within sub-Saharan Africa, 2 million displaced by conflict in the Balkans, and an estimated 7 million Asian refugees (predominantly within Iran and Pakistan), the Rwandan crisis needs to be seen in the context of evolving global trends in forced migration (see Ager 1999). The world refugee population is now estimated at approaching 20 million, with significant growth during the 1980s and 1990s.

Refugees from the former Yugoslavia, because of their geographical and cultural proximity, appear to have brought the psychological dimensions of the refugee experience to European consciousness in a manner that previous refugee crises within Africa and Asia failed to achieve. It now seems self-evident that to be a refugee involves not only a threat to food supply and health, but also a fundamental assault on one's self-esteem and identity. People not only lose their home but, commonly, experience the fragmentation of their whole community. While addressing the physical threats and privations brought about through forced migration rightly remains at the forefront of refugee assistance programmes, assistance agencies are, however, increasingly acknowledging the salience of the psychosocial needs of refugees and tentatively exploring appropriate means of addressing them.

### Phases of the refugee experience

In terms of identifying the multiple stressors which impact on refugees, discrete phases in the refugee experience are generally acknowledged (see Table 14.3). The *pre-flight* phase can be seen as that period leading up to a

*Table 14.3* Examples of potential threats at each phase of
the refugee experience

| Phase | Potential threats include |
|---|---|
| Pre-flight | economic hardship<br>social disruption<br>political oppression and violence |
| Flight | separation<br>loss<br>hazardous passage |
| Asylum or temporary settlement | life in refugee camp<br>living with uncertainty<br>restricted incomes/employment |
| Resettlement or repatriation | culture conflict<br>loss of social status through work<br>intergenerational stresses |

final decision to flee one's national borders. In some instances the events
precipitating flight can be unexpected. More commonly, the decision to
flee is made when events – coming on top of a sustained period of exposure
to economic hardship, political oppression and physical violence – finally
lead individuals to view the uncertainty and material loss associated with
refugeehood as preferable to the prevailing circumstances.

*Flight* itself commonly brings additional stressors of loss and separation as
well as the extreme dangers of physical passage. The dangers of flight faced
by the Vietnamese 'boat people' are widely known. Flight across land borders
as reported by Mozambican refugees was frequently no less harrowing (Ager
*et al.* 1995) involving avoidance of both mines and armed personnel. The
sexual abuse of women refugees during flight is also commonly reported.

The period of *asylum or temporary settlement* may take a variety of forms.
These can range from informal settlement among the indigenous population
(the most common pattern for Croatian and Bosnian refugees who fled to
Slovenia, for example) to residence within formal refugee camps (frequently
the option preferred by host governments and the only viable solution with
mass influxes such as in Central Africa). In terms of psychological stressors,
however, the most consistent features include uncertainty (regarding
application for asylum and/or impending return to home country) and the
impact of restricted employment opportunities on economic resources and
self-esteem.

The final phase of the refugee experience essentially involves either *resettlement or repatriation*. Resettlement involves adjustment to long term relocation within a new country, which may be widely distant in cultural terms
from a refugee's country of origin. Repatriation is increasingly the option
favoured by most host societies and, in general terms, by the aid community itself. However, this involves the psychological adjustment of a return
to what is frequently a significantly changed society. Returning refugees
frequently find their home country transformed through both time and
political development.

## Psychological core of the refugee experience

Clearly the routes by which refugees pass through the above phases of experience are many and varied. Yet, in psychological terms, there are really only two issues commonly at the core of the refugee experience. One of these is the social adjustment required of refugees moving across widely varied cultures, each with distinctive social mores and expectations. The extensive literature on culture shock documents the psychological tensions created by acculturative processes (see Furnham and Bochner 1986). As with all migrants, refugees face the task of resocialization within a new culture, learning new behaviours and new meanings. Typically, refugees will, in fact, be exposed to an indeterminate stream of cultural settings – each with their own codes and meanings – as they progress through their refugee 'career'.

The second issue – superimposed upon the first for many refugees – is the personal challenge of reconstructing their worldview that has been shattered by the experience of violence, pain and humiliation. Within contemporary refugee movements, reported exposure to murder, mutilation and rape is extremely high. The developing literature on post-traumatic stress disorder indicates the ready potential for such events to disrupt one's fundamental psychological appraisals of the nature and predictability of the world. Like the victims of catastrophic disaster, refugees potentially face the world with their accustomed means of understanding and interpreting human behaviour and events incapable of navigating them through the realm of experience into which they have entered.

For many refugees their internal representations of the world – with respect to which identity has been formed – are thus consistently challenged by the pervasive instability of the external environment. Simultaneous challenges to one's fundamental assumptions about the world and their appropriate expression in social behaviour leave little stable ground for (re)constructing a coherent self-image.

## Psychological impact of displacement

Given the common events of the refugee experience – and their plausible effect on an individual's capacity to interpret the world – what actual evidence is there of increased risk of mental ill-health and of more general difficulties in psychological functioning among refugees?

The earliest studies addressing such questions were completed in the period following the Second World War, with refugees from Central and Eastern Europe resettling in such countries as Norway, Australia and the UK (see Ager 1999 for a review). These early studies demonstrated significantly higher rates of major psychiatric disorder in refugees than among the indigenous populations over periods extending to ten years beyond initial relocation. Furthermore, these studies demonstrated a clear link between the severity of an individual's war experiences prior to flight and the likelihood of the person developing such disorders.

Studies in the context of more recent population movements – notably from Vietnam and, later, Cambodia – have suggested increased risk for a broad range of psychological difficulties. Mollica *et al.* (1987), for example, found that 92 per cent of Hmong/Laotian patients attending their Indo-Chinese Psychiatry Clinic met diagnostic criteria for post-traumatic stress disorder (PTSD), while 50 per cent of a non-clinical high school sample of Cambodian refugees met similar criteria in a study by Kinzie and Sack (1991). Notwithstanding debates regarding the validity – and utility – of the specific PTSD diagnosis, these studies clearly assert the widespread occurrence of psychological difficulties with adjustment among resettled refugees. Conditions and experiences within the pre-flight environment are consistently found to be significant predictors of psychological distress on resettlement.

## Treatment approaches

In developed nations with significant refugee populations a number of specialized treatment centres have evolved as a means of facilitating intensive and culturally appropriate forms of intervention. Kinzie and Sack (1991), Mollica (1989) and Westermeyer (1991) each describe specialist provision within the US context. There are now a number of similar centres in Europe, including the highly acclaimed Medical Foundation for the Care of Victims of Torture in London, which provides a service for a significant number of refugees.

Such centres typically adopt a range of therapeutic approaches, with cultural sensitivity enforcing a broadly flexible approach. Nonetheless, the use of psychotherapeutic techniques developed in a western context with predominantly non-western refugees clearly raises a number of cross-cultural questions. While the notion of ventilation (i.e. expressing thoughts and feelings) is central to most established approaches, it is an alien procedure within many cultures. As a result, Mollica (1989) has called its presumptive use into question. Kinzie *et al.* (1984) claimed that ventilation served to significantly intensify rather than reduce the existing symptoms in Cambodians who had experienced atrocities under the Pol Pot regime.

While these findings query the applicability of many existing models of intervention on the grounds of clinical effectiveness, for myself the viability of individually focused treatment methods has also to be questioned on the grounds of realistically available resources. While much may be learned from the experience of working with refugees resettled into western, developed nations, a global perspective on the psychosocial needs of refugees must acknowledge that such individuals are atypical. Less than 17 per cent of the world refugee population resides in the industrialized countries of western Europe, the USA, Canada and Australia. The experience of being a refugee is typically borne in amongst the poorest countries of the world. Within such societies individually focused intervention is functionally unsustainable as a plausible response to the magnitude of need.

Questions of both clinical effectiveness and resource viability therefore encourage the conceptualization of responses to refugees' psychological needs in more preventive terms. Such approaches naturally prompt an awareness of the social and cultural factors that shape the perception of psychological need, and encourage interventions that facilitate the operation of indigenous coping mechanisms. Three factors which have an established impact on ameliorating the impact of stressors within refugee situations are family integration, kinship support and personal ideology. Each of these has clear implications for appropriate preventive action.

## Family integration

The value of family integration (nuclear or extended) in fostering adaptation to refugee situations has been firmly established from the early study of Freud and Burlingham (1943) comparing the adjustment of children evacuated from, and remaining in, London during the Second World War, through the analysis of the impact of war and displacement on the children of Biafra (Ressler *et al.* 1988) to the experience of Palestinian refugees under Israeli occupation (Punamäki and Suleiman 1989). Whether it is the sustained relationships and emotional bonds that are influential, the increased potential for positive modelling of coping behaviour within intact families, or the maintenance of day-to-day routine, or the provision for children of some explanatory narrative regarding experienced trauma, integration within a family serves as a major protective factor for refugee children.

In this context the family reunification programmes organized by a number of assistance agencies have a clear value in psychological as well as humanitarian terms. Where such reunification requires the immigration of a family member (particularly an extended family member) to developed nations of the north, the desirable outcome in psychological terms can be in direct conflict with immigration policy and/or practice. British policy towards Bosnian asylum seekers in the mid-1990s, for example, did not generally encourage re-establishing family integration, and it proved to be a source of much stress and isolation.

## Kinship support

Social support, in general, can serve as a factor bolstering the refugee's coping resources as with individuals facing any other form of life stress. However, for refugees who face clear threats to their social and cultural identity through many of the phases of displacement and relocation, support from one's own kin appears to be particularly important. The rise of Mutual Assistance Agencies amongst Indo-Chinese refugees in the USA, for example, appears to serve a valuable health promotive function (Abhay 1992). Studies in Zambia have also found that the perception of family members as a source of support significantly predicted psychological adjustment amongst Mozambican refugees (McCallin 1996).

Resettlement policy within refugee-receiving countries can again commonly work against the psychological ideal. Many nations have sought to distribute refugees over a broad geographical area in an attempt to lessen the perceived 'burden' on host societies, but this can put refugees at significant risk of cultural and social isolation. Secondary migration of refugees to established co-ethnic communities is a common pattern globally and there are clear grounds – noting the necessary political sensitivities – for facilitating rather than obstructing such settlement patterns.

## Personal ideology

The role of ideological commitment in preserving psychological adaptation through extreme trauma and distress was noted in accounts of life in the Nazi concentration camps. Similar observations have been made with regard to refugee adjustment. Punamäki's (1987) finding that 'psychological processes of healing . . . drew strength from political and ideological commitment' amongst Palestinian refugee women has subsequently been echoed in a number of other studies, including her own work with other population groups (Punamäki 1996). Kanaaneh and Netland's (1992) finding of a negative correlation between anxiety and withdrawal and degree of nationalistic identity amongst Palestinian youth provides perhaps the clearest illustration of the protective function which ideology may exert.

As with family integration and kinship support, the facilitation of personal ideology may promote psychological adjustment, but it is at odds with much existing policy and practice regarding refugee assistance. In refugee camps and resettlement zones alike, governments and agencies tend to fear ideological zeal – whether it be religious or political. Nonetheless, from a psychological perspective, refugee adjustment must involve the successful renegotiation of personal identity, and will inevitably involve addressing (if not necessarily reasserting) the ideological commitments held prior to displacement.

## European perspectives

The analyses described above have drawn an increasing number of applied psychologists to work with refugees. The European Federation of Professional Psychologists Associations (EFPPA) formed a Task Force on Refugees and Forced Migration, which undertook a review of work by psychologists in this field across Europe (EFPPA 1996). The largest number of psychologists are working in clinical and counselling situations with refugees, though many are also involved in consultancy with refugee assistance agencies and training work. These findings prompted EFPPA to support the development of 'Guidance Notes on Assistance to Displaced Persons, Asylum Seekers and Refugees'. These notes seek to indicate the psychological principles that underpin good practice in refugee assistance work. They identify a prominent role for preventive, community-based work – based upon innovative work in Scandinavia – including anti-racist work within refugee-receiving communities.

## Working with humanitarian assistance agencies

I noted earlier how there has been a rapid increase in the number of agencies – both non-governmental and intergovernmental – working in the field of humanitarian assistance and development. The former organizations (NGOs) have often been started by a committed individual or small group responding to a particular concern or issue, and the 'volunteer ethic' (particularly

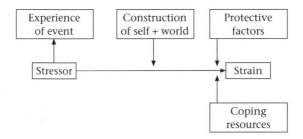

***Figure 14.1*** Factors influencing impact of stressors

regarding service to beneficiaries coming before personal gain) frequently remains a strong value for such organizations. Unfortunately, such a 'volunteer ethic' can be associated with an insensitivity by organizations to the needs of their workers, with an assumption that such people 'knew what the job involved when they signed up'.

The 1990s, however, saw a steady move towards the professionalization of humanitarian assistance agencies and, with that, a clearer commitment to support and care for their staff. In 1995, for instance, the British Red Cross and Save the Children Fund, together with other agencies, commissioned a study to examine the experience of field staff in a number of agencies working in the contexts of emergency relief and longer term development assistance. The findings indicated poor levels of preparation and support for many workers. Approaching 50 per cent of workers considered that they had not received appropriate security briefing before they were deployed overseas, for instance. Many reported high levels of stress at some stage during their work overseas, with the most frequently cited stressors being overwork, organizational difficulties and security.

Such studies have placed stress management and, more broadly, good human resource management practice on the agenda of many agencies. Applied psychologists clearly have relevant skills in this area and are making a contribution at various levels (including selection and recruitment and organizational development). I have been involved in training with agencies such as Médecins Sans Frontières and Oxfam. The focus of such training was not just consideration of the range of stressors that workers are likely to experience when deployed in the field, but also the organizational context of such stressors. That is, working as a humanitarian assistance worker for a particular agency puts the experience of an event or series of difficult circumstances in a very particular context. It is a context that may make such events more likely and predictable (humanitarian workers are particularly vulnerable to kidnapping in some conflict zones, for instance). It is also a context in which the expectations and culture of the organization shape responses to such events (some organizations are decidedly 'macho' in their response to danger situations).

Figure 14.1 shows a diagram that I have used in such training sessions to place the humanitarian worker's capacity to cope with stressful events in an appropriate context. In the course of deployment overseas humanitarian workers are likely to experience a range of stressors. These can range from extreme examples of violence (e.g. physical or sexual assault) through work-related issues (e.g. difficulties with bureaucracy) to personal or social circumstances (e.g. relationship problems with other workers). While the former events do occur, for many humanitarian assistance workers it is the latter category of circumstances which produce the greatest strain. The link between stressors and strain is, indeed, complex. Individual coping styles and other protective factors (including the social and physical environment in which people are working) may act to mitigate the effects of stressors, and limit the experience of personal strain. Conversely, inappropriate coping strategies and an unsupportive work environment can result in individuals experiencing considerable strain as a result of even quite minor stressors.

Such an analysis clearly encourages work to identify appropriate coping skills and stress management techniques for use by workers and their managers. However, the model of Figure 14.1 seeks to move away from a simple 'balance sheet' of stressors and coping resources in determining experience. The model acknowledges that stressors are not just objective events: they are interpreted or (to use the more precise term) constructed with respect to the individual values and beliefs of the individual. Understanding the vulnerability or resilience of assistance workers requires insight into the sort of person they see themselves to be and, crucially, why they have chosen – through their humanitarian work – to put themselves at risk from many stressors (e.g. physical discomfort or danger and insecurity).

Humanitarian assistance agencies themselves have increasingly come to appreciate the role they have in shaping their workers' understandings of themselves and their work. The 'culture' of organizations – whether it be 'macho' and risk taking, cool and bureaucratic, or explicitly informal and 'cosy' – influences critically the manner in which its workers approach their work, their difficulties and the manner in which they relate to others. Such a 'culture', of course, is very often implicit within organizations, rather than formally stated. In training events with NGOs, humanitarian assistance workers have often found it helpful to make such implicit values explicit and, by so doing, note not only the filters through which the organization understands the world, but also the expectations it has of its staff's behaviour and attitudes.

While NGOs – and, indeed, intergovernmental agencies – vary with respect to their organizational cultures, Walkup (1997) has suggested a common sequence of strategies adopted by their workers in coping with the complexities and difficulties of relief and development work. In the first stage a humanitarian assistance worker responds to the mismatch between their (frequently) high expectations and limited achievements by simply *working harder*. For many agencies overwork is, indeed, a severe problem, with clear risks of 'burnout' for those working perhaps 16-hour days. Short term postings (a matter of just a few weeks in some emergency situations) clearly lead to problems of continuity in programmes, but reflect the demands of such work.

However, Walkup (1997) notes that when long hours do not lead to the resolution of goals and achievements, the next stage can be *detachment* from the situations where such mismatch causes greatest discomfort. In such circumstances, workers may particularly withdraw from contacts with intended beneficiaries, with pressures more readily resolved within the office than in the reality of the field. Where such distancing fails to protect workers from work-related strain, Walkup identifies *blaming* or *displacement* as a third potential stage for the humanitarian assistance worker. The complexities and frustrations of the situation may be displaced on to 'headquarters', 'politics', 'the United Nations' or even, perhaps, 'the locals', in an effort to explain the lack of intended progress.

Walkup's (1997) analysis – even into a fourth stage where he suggests that agencies foster *'myths'* which preserve a sense of purpose and achievement against potential evidence to the contrary – is in no way unsympathetic to the work of humanitarian agencies. Rather, he is acknowledging the considerable pressures and frustrations that commonly accompany such work. Greater awareness of the coping mechanisms that may be adopted in the face of such difficulties can usefully alert agencies to the unintended side-effects of such strategies. For instance, acknowledging that direct contact with beneficiaries can prove threatening at certain stages of a programme may lead an agency to identify other mechanisms for gaining vital feedback on community needs and perceptions. Recognition that a common will to succeed may foster an uncritical acceptance of organizational 'myths' may encourage a clear commitment to independent evaluation of project outcomes.

## Concluding comments: roles for psychology within humanitarian assistance?

In this chapter I have attempted to demonstrate the potential contribution of psychology within the field of humanitarian assistance – both in terms of conceptualization and practical application. The analysis has sought to be illustrative rather than comprehensive, and there are a number of areas beyond the three examined where a contribution may be made. Within the broad area of health, for example, work by psychologists in such areas as health beliefs and health behaviour change is clearly relevant, and is increasingly in evidence. Recent advances in the psychology of economic behaviour have major implications for development planning. As a discipline seeking a rigorous understanding of behaviour and mental processes, psychology has clear potential for a broad range of such contributions. Yet the critics of the potential role of 'scientific' psychology within the developing world are correct when they note that such science has over the past 100 years tended to support conservatism rather than the empowerment of the disadvantaged, marginalized and oppressed of our societies. To break with this trend will not simply require humility in the valuing of non-western knowledge and insight. To establish a truly global discipline will require sustained commitment to empower a more ethnically and culturally diverse discourse in its development. For me, this is the most compelling aspect of work in this field: working with psychologists from a range of backgrounds and cultures to shape a psychology increasingly capable of informing the effective, efficient and equitable delivery of global humanitarian assistance.

### Discussion questions

1 The most common participants in studies within the literature of psychology are US college students. What implications does this have for our understanding of the applicability of psychology within the developing world?

2 From a psychological perspective, what are the key issues likely to face unaccompanied children within a refugee camp who have fled from war in their home country?

3 What are the potential motivations for someone to work in the field of humanitarian assistance? To what extent may these help or hinder when facing major operational difficulties in the field?

## Further reading

Aboud, F. E. (1998) *Health Psychology in Global Perspective*. Thousand Oaks, CA: Sage. This book analyses the findings and concepts of health psychology relevant to health issues facing developing countries.

Ager, A. (ed.) (1999) *Refugees: Perspectives on the Experience of Forced Migration*. London: Cassell. An analysis from the perspectives of psychology, psychotherapy, social work, sociology and political science of factors shaping refugees' experience of flight, separation, resettlement and repatriation.

Harrell-Bond, B. E. (1986) *Imposing Aid: Emergency Assistance to Refugees*. Oxford: Oxford University Press. A classic and highly readable critique of the philosophy, politics and practice of humanitarian assistance.

## References

Abhay, K. (1992) Leadership and management: a comparative study of MAAs. *Refugee Participation Network*, 13: 9–11.

Ager, A. (ed.) (1999) *Refugees: Perspectives on the Experience of Forced Migration*. London: Cassell.

Ager, A., Ager, W. and Long, L. (1995) The differential experience of Mozambican refugee women and men. *Journal of Refugee Studies*, 8(3): 1–23.

Berry, J. W., Poortinga, Y. H., Segall, M. H. and Dasen, P. R. (1992) *Cross-Cultural Psychology: Research and Applications*. Cambridge: Cambridge University Press.

Carr, S. (1996) Social psychology and the management of aid, in S. C. Carr and J. F. Schumaker (eds) *Psychology and the Developing World*. Westport, CT: Praeger.

Carr, S. and MacLachlan, M. (1993) Asserting psychology in Malawi. *The Psychologist*, 6(9): 408–13.

European Federation of Professional Psychologists Associations (EFPPA) (1996) Special issue on Refugees and Forced Migration. *News from EFPPA* December.

Freud, A. and Burlingham, D. T. (1943) *War and Children*. New York: Ernst Willard.

Furnham, A. and Bochner, S. (1986) *Culture Shock*. London: Methuen.

Harrell-Bond, B. E. (1986) *Imposing Aid: Emergency Assistance to Refugees.* Oxford: Oxford University Press.

Kanaaneh, M. and Netland, M. (1992) *Children and Political Violence.* Jerusalem: Early Childhood Resource Centre.

Kinzie, J. D. and Sack, W. (1991) Severely traumatised Cambodian children: research findings and clinical implications, in F. L. Ahearn and J. L. Athey (eds) *Refugee Children: Theory, Research, and Services.* Baltimore, MD: Johns Hopkins University Press.

Kinzie, J. D., Fredrickson, R. B., Ben, R., Fleck, J. and Earls, W. (1984) Post-traumatic stress disorder among survivors of Cambodian concentration camps. *American Journal of Psychiatry,* 141: 645–50.

McCallin, M. (1996) *The Psychological Well-Being of Refugee Children: Research, Practice and Policy Issues,* 2nd edn. Geneva: International Catholic Child Bureau.

Mollica, R. F. (1989) Developing effective mental health policies and services for traumatised refugee patients, in D. R. Koslow and E. P. Salett (eds) *Crossing Cultures in Mental Health.* Washington, DC: International Counselling Centre.

Mollica, R. F., Wyshak, G. and Lavelle, J. (1987) The psychosocial impact of war trauma and torture on Southeast Asian refugees. *American Journal of Psychiatry,* 144: 1567–72.

Owusu-Bempah, J. and Howitt, D. (1995) How Eurocentric psychology damages Africa. *The Psychologist,* 8(10): 462–5.

Punamäki, R-L. (1987) Psychological stress of Palestinian mothers and their children in conditions of political violence. *Quarterly Newsletter of the Laboratory of Comparative Human Cognition,* 9: 116–19.

Punamäki, R-L. (1996) Can ideological commitment protect children's psychosocial well-being in situations of political violence? *Child Development,* 67: 55–69.

Punamäki, R-L. and Suleiman, R. (1989) Predictors and effectiveness of coping with political violence among Palestinian children. *British Journal of Social Psychology,* 29: 67–77.

Ressler, E. M., Boothby, N. and Steinbeck, D. J. (1988) *Unaccompanied Children.* New York: Oxford University Press.

Walkup, M. (1997) Policy dysfunction in humanitarian organisations: the role of coping strategies, institutions and organizational culture. *Journal of Refugee Studies,* 10(1): 37–60.

Westermeyer, J. (1991) Psychiatric services for refugee children, in F. L. Ahearn and J. L. Athey (eds) *Refugee Children: Theory, Research, and Services.* Baltimore, MD: Johns Hopkins University Press.

*Epilogue*

# Becoming an applied psychologist

## *James Hartley and Alan Branthwaite*

We said in the Prologue that we had asked the authors of this book to illustrate in each chapter one particular aspect of what it was like to work as an applied psychologist. We recognized from the start that our seven roles would overlap, but it soon became apparent in the writing and editing of this text just how much they interlocked. Separating the roles highlighted the implications of taking one role or another, and it served to convey the richness and the variety of the work done by applied psychologists.

Nonetheless, the roles are not distinct and applied psychologists are able to adopt and integrate different roles according to the demands of the work in hand. A psychologist working in industry, for example, might need to be a colleague in order to appreciate the practical problems presented for investigation, a toolmaker to adapt or develop appropriate measures, a detached investigator to take a less subjective view of the findings and an expert in order to convey these findings to others. Other patterns of interlocking roles are illustrated indirectly in other chapters in this textbook.

This integration of the roles, and the expertise in practising them, begins with the training of psychologists. It has its roots in the basic skills that are taught in undergraduate psychology courses. Psychology, as an undergraduate discipline, provides its students with a variety of skills. These have a wide range of uses and are prized by employers. Box E.1 lists some of them.

Approximately 8000 students (about 75 per cent of them women) graduate each year in the UK with a first degree in psychology; approximately 400,000 students (again about 75 per cent of them women) graduate each year in psychology in the USA. Most psychology undergraduates go on to jobs that

*Box E.1* **Skills acquired by psychologists in their first degree courses**

*Information gathering skills*

literature searching (paper and electronic)
critical reading, detecting biases
skills in interviewing
designing measuring instruments – tests, surveys, questionnaires

*Project planning skills*

designing appropriate investigations
organizing their implementation
identifying potential problems ahead of time
identifying the resources needed (e.g. material, people, time)
organizing team members
ability to make the best out of non-ideal situations

*Statistical and inferential skills*

computer literacy/familiarity with appropriate software
skills in statistical analysis
skills in statistical reasoning
ability to draw appropriate inferences from quantitative and qualitative
    data
appreciating that there might not be one right answer

*Writing and reporting skills*

skills in wordprocessing
ability to structure and evaluate arguments
effective use of tables and graphs
clear writing

*Presentation skills*

skills in speaking and listening
ability to present data and findings to non-technical audiences

*Awareness of the human dimension*

appreciation of individual differences and alternative points of view
recognition of selectivity in perception and interpretation
awareness of emotional biases in reasoning and evaluating information
skills in responding to individual differences in motivation, ability
    personality and social skills

*Source*: Material adapted from the APA's WWW page:
http://www.apa.org/science/skills.html

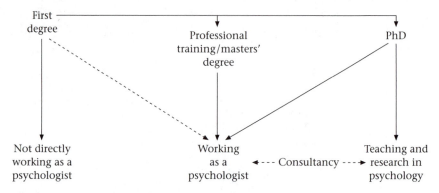

***Figure E.1*** Career paths taken by psychology graduates

are not directly related to psychology (see Figure E.1). Nonetheless, the numbers mean that there is a large pool of psychology graduates moving each year into employment in a wide variety of areas. These people are aware of the contribution that psychology can make, and have the fundamental skills that come from studying the subject.

We estimate that about 12–15 per cent of the annual cohort of undergraduates in psychology in both the UK and the USA continue on to professional training, and this requires postgraduate degree work in psychology. The four main areas of professional training are:

- clinical psychology
- educational or school psychology
- occupational or work psychology
- government and Civil Service.

In addition there are many other areas of psychology with postgraduate training, as described on pp. 250–2.

To take up a professional career in psychology in the UK it is now almost mandatory to become a 'chartered' psychologist, which is a status equivalent to that of a chartered surveyor or accountant, etc. Chartered people are licensed or accredited as competent to practise their profession. Similarly, in the USA, professional psychologists have to be 'licensed' and to have studied at an 'accredited' university.

To achieve chartered status in the UK you must not only have taken a first degree course in psychology that provides 'the graduate basis for registration (GBR)' of the British Psychological Society (BPS), but also undertaken at least three years' further full-time study or practice in psychology. Departments that provide the GBR have their courses recognized by the BPS (see contact addresses on p. 255). So, if you are thinking of applying for an undergraduate course in psychology in the UK, make sure that the department you apply to provides the GBR.

If you are a second or third year British psychology undergraduate on such a course interested in applying for further training in applied psychology, you should first, discuss the matter with the most appropriate member of staff in your psychology department, and second, obtain copies of various publications of the BPS. These include pamphlets on careers, including

*Careers in Psychology* and the *List of Approved Professional Training Courses in Psychology*, and two useful books, the *Professional Psychology Handbook* and the *Compendium of Postgraduate Studies in Psychology in the UK and Ireland*. This latter text describes most psychology departments in detail and lists departments with facilities for students with special needs, approved professional training courses and taught postgraduate courses. In the USA the equivalent volume, published annually by the American Psychological Association (APA), is called *Graduate Study in Psychology*.

For people in the UK wanting to consider applied psychology as a career but who do not have any undergraduate qualifications in psychology, there are appropriate 'conversion courses'; the BPS has a list of these. People living outside the UK wanting to work in areas of psychology in the UK are also advised to consult the BPS. UK and US students wanting to pursue careers in applied psychology in the USA should make enquiries to the APA and consult the *Graduate Study in Psychology* text. Readers interested in careers in Europe might start with *Psychology in Europe: Facts, Figures, Realities* (Schorr and Saari 1995) and keep an eye on the journal *European Psychologist*.

## Main areas of professional training

There are four main areas of professional training for students wishing to become applied psychologists. Most general textbooks in applied psychology describe these four areas in detail and, in addition, there are several more detailed textbooks that cover each topic separately.

### Clinical psychology

Clinical psychologists spend most of their time working as part of a team dealing with individual patients either within local hospitals or attending outpatient clinics. The range of possible work is varied: as we have seen in earlier chapters it can include working with post-traumatic stress, autism and with people suffering from cancer. It can also involve work with elderly, suicidal and depressed people, and with different forms of psychological therapy (e.g. see Marzillier and Hall 1992; Napier 1995; Nolen-Hoeksema 1997).

The most popular form of clinical training in the UK and in the USA is to study at a university for an MSc or MPhil in clinical psychology, although PhD courses are now appearing. Nonetheless, clinical psychology is one of the most difficult professions to enter (see Roth 1998 for details). Training places on UK clinical psychology postgraduate courses are oversubscribed, and in the USA clinical programmes are able to accept only about 10 per cent of their applicants (APA 1997). Applicants in the UK are expected, therefore, to have carried out relevant practical work (for example, by working as a psychology technician in a local hospital) or to have done postgraduate research *before* applying for clinical training. A clearing house scheme operates for all UK university applications: candidates make one application to the Clearing House for Postgraduate Courses in Clinical Psychology, and this is sent to selected institutions. This is not the case in the USA where applications have to be made to specific institutions.

An alternative method of qualifying in clinical psychology in the UK is to attend a course of in-service training as a probationer psychologist employed by the NHS. These courses prepare candidates for the Diploma in Clinical Psychology, which is awarded by the BPS. Both kinds of course usually last two to three years, and combine theoretical and practical work. For example, trainee clinical psychologists might spend periods of three to six months each working in three required areas – e.g. learning disabilities, adult psychiatry and child problems – and then at least one more period studying, for example, neuropsychology, drug/alcohol abuse or psychosexual problems. The courses are normally assessed by examinations, written assignments, case reports and a dissertation based upon an empirical project.

## Educational or school psychology

Educational psychologists are trained as specialists in education and psychology, and use their experience and knowledge from both disciplines. At one time their work mainly involved assessing individual children but, as in clinical psychology, the range of their activities has expanded. The work typically includes assessing individual children and recommending programmes of treatment and education; working with learning-disabled children and planning – with their teachers – curricula for them; advising parents, teachers and social workers on a child's learning difficulties; giving advice on school organization and management; carrying out in-service work with teachers, parents and other professionals on topics like bullying and effective teaching; and trying to do research (e.g. see Fontana 1995; Sheppard 1995; Cavill 1998; Gage and Berliner 1998).

Educational or school psychologists are typically employed (in the UK) by educational authorities, and they also need to have some experience of teaching (except in Scotland). Thus it takes a considerable amount of time to become an educational psychologist, involving as it does a first degree, training as a teacher, teaching experience and then training as an educational psychologist. The actual training as an educational psychologist normally lasts one year (in the UK) but, in the future, this time may increase. The BPS is currently thinking of requiring the training for educational psychology to be expanded from one to three years; it is likely that three-year accredited courses will start in 2001. And again, because places on educational psychology training courses are in short supply in the UK, applications are made through a clearing house.

## Occupational or work psychology

Occupational psychology is known as work psychology in continental Europe, and as industrial or organizational psychology in the USA. In this chapter we shall keep mainly to the British term – occupational psychology.

Occupational psychologists often work for large companies in both the private and the public sectors. They work with other colleagues, such as managers, personnel officers, union representatives and workers from the businesses or industries concerned. Occupational psychologists typically work in the following areas (e.g. see McCormick and Ilgen 1987; Arnold *et al.* 1995; Crawshaw 1995; Cavill 1997a):

- personnel selection and assessment
- training (needs, methods, evaluation)
- employee relations and motivation
- performance appraisal and career development
- personal development and counselling
- design of work environments, health and safety
- organizational development
- human–machine interaction.

While it is essential to be qualified as a teacher to become an educational psychologist, the expectations about prior experience are less rigorous for occupational psychology. Although most training courses in the UK require some knowledge of the world of work, not all of them do so, and it is possible to train in occupational psychology directly after the first degree. Currently there are no clearing house procedures for occupational psychology, and applicants apply directly to the courses concerned. Most of the courses run for one year only; this is then usually followed by at least two years of supervised practice.

There are typically three kinds of masters' courses. Some focus on occupational (or work) psychology, some on organizational (or management) psychology, and some on human factors (or ergonomics). In the UK such courses may accept students without qualifications in psychology, so it is likely that the course members will have more varied background experiences.

Students following courses in work psychology are likely to find themselves concerned, for example, with vocational guidance and selection (including the construction and evaluation of tests), and developing assessment and training methods. Students pursuing courses in management psychology might find themselves involved, for example, in improving communications within a company, in improving welfare and staff development, and in helping individuals increase their job satisfaction. Students pursuing courses in ergonomics are likely to find themselves concerned, for example, with the interaction between people and technology in areas such as office and instrument design, computerized banking/telephone/financial/mail systems, communication on the Internet, electronic security systems, and possibly air traffic control systems (see e.g. Shackel 1996; Nickerson 1998).

## Government and Civil Service

Many psychologists employed in government services in the UK work in areas of employment and training – for example at the Department of Employment, or in centres that provide retraining, rehabilitation and vocational guidance for disabled people. A large number of civil servants also work in the area of personnel research and selection. The Civil Service Commission, for example, is responsible for the recruitment and selection of most civil servants, and psychologists serve as members of the recruitment team. Psychologists are also employed by the Ministry of Defence, in the Army, Navy and Air Force. Such psychologists are mainly involved in problems of selection, training, leadership, management skills, human factors, and in research and development in all of these fields (see e.g. Gal and

Mangelsdorff 1991). Finally, the Prison Service employs psychologists in over 1000 establishments in England and Wales. Work may take place in prisons, special establishments or psychiatric prisons. This may involve diagnostic assessment, improving communications, evaluating change, individual and group counselling, and educational and social skills training. The work may be with prisoners and/or prison staff (see e.g. Cooke *et al.* 1993).

There are no postgraduate training courses as such provided for people who want to work as psychologists in the Civil Service in the UK. People who have a first degree or a postgraduate qualification in psychology may apply for particular posts (usually advertised in the national press or the BPS *Appointments Memorandum*), and the first one or two years are normally considered as a training programme. During this time there are courses to attend and training is 'on the job', tailored to requirements.

# Other areas of applied psychology

In addition to the four main areas of applied psychology described above, there are many other opportunities for psychologists. Students considering careers in applied psychology might do well to consider these alternatives because the competition for positions is likely to be less fierce here and the chances for career development might be greater. We list here, in alphabetical order, some of these additional career opportunities (see also the APA's web site http://www.apa.org). The BPS's *Compendium of Postgraduate Studies* and the APA's *Graduate Study in Psychology* give details of which universities offer appropriate training. There are masters' courses (and, more rarely, PhD courses) in most of the following areas.

## Community psychology

Community psychologists are involved in assisting people in the community. Thus they are concerned with local and national issues, such as making better use of school buildings for the whole community, empowering people of less status, and environmental or 'green' issues generally (see e.g. Levine and Perkins 1997). At the time of writing we know of no specific accredited postgraduate courses in this field in the UK (apart from one on clinical and community psychology) although there are over 60 such accredited courses in the USA. So one way of becoming a community psychologist in the UK is to do postgraduate research under the supervison of an expert in the field (see Research opportunities, p. 252).

## Consumer psychology (and marketing)

Consumer psychologists are concerned with the effectiveness of marketing and advertising (see Chapter 5) and why people buy what they buy. Fundamentally consumer psychologists are interested in many of the questions that intrigue psychologists in general, but here they are applied to buying and selling. Thus there is interest in how attitudes influence behaviour (and vice versa), how groups influence individuals as in the spread of fashions, and how information can be presented and processed effectively (e.g. see Foxhall and Goldsmith 1994; Beall and Allen 1997). At the time of writing we do not know of any accredited postgraduate degree courses in consumer psychology in the UK and very few in the United States which might suggest that consumer psychology is studied under a different name, or as a sub-unit in other disciplines (e.g. business studies).

## Counselling psychology

As described in Chapters 1 and 2, counselling psychologists help people to solve problems and make decisions for themselves. Counselling psychologists work in diverse settings with individuals, couples, families and groups (see e.g. Watts and Bor 1995; Parrott 1997; McLeod 1998). To become an accredited counselling psychologist in the UK, people with first degrees in psychology either follow a postgraduate training course or undertake three years' postgraduate training leading to the BPS's Diploma in Counselling Psychology. This is one of the most rapidly expanding areas of applied psychology at the time of writing: 6 masters' and 1 PhD course are available in the UK and there are over 300 accredited courses in the USA.

## Environmental psychology

Environmental psychologists look at ways in which people use the environment (both urban and rural) and assess the impact of these environments on how we live and work. Like community psychologists, environmental psychologists are also interested in problems of conservation and environmental management, and they can be involved in assessing the effects of energy savings, air and water pollution, and global and regional environmental problems (e.g. see Bonnes and Secchiaroli 1995; Nickerson and Moray 1995). In addition they might be concerned with the effects of the environment on individuals, such as assessing reactions to crowding, temperature, lighting and noise on work performance. Indeed, the design of buildings, such as university halls of residence, offices and lecture theatres could come under their ambit, but this would be unusual. At the time of writing we know of no accredited postgraduate course in environmental psychology in the UK and twelve accredited ones listed by the APA (four of which come under the heading 'ecological' psychology).

## Forensic psychology

Forensic psychologists (or criminological and legal psychologists) deal with the interface between psychology and the law – and all its ramifications (see Chapter 4). Such people may be concerned with court procedures or problems of testimony, especially that of children, juror decision making, and being an expert witness for either the defence or the prosecution in relation to a wide variety of behavioural or psychological problems (e.g. see Colman 1995; McMurran 1995; Gudjonsson and Haward 1998; Memon *et al.* 1998). There is also overlap with the work of clinical and prison psychologists (see e.g. Cavill 1997b). To become an accredited forensic psychologist in the UK, applicants normally take a masters' course in forensic/criminological psychology followed by two years of supervised practice. Currently there are six such accredited courses in the UK and fourteen listed by the APA.

## Health psychology

Health psychologists deal with social, environmental and psychological factors that affect people's health, and their attitudes, habits and values in relation to health. Health psychologists may be involved in doctor–patient communication, influencing public behaviour in relation to preventive medicine, the effects of stress and exercise, and coping with illness, disability or chronic pain (see e.g. Johnston and Weinman 1995; Baum *et al.* 1997; Pitts and Phillips 1998). This area of psychology is yet another area of rapid expansion at the time of writing. Several masters' courses are available in the UK – not all accredited – and over 50 accredited postgraduate courses listed by the APA.

## Sport psychology

Sport psychologists increasingly act as coaches to national and Olympic teams in a wide variety of sports, from football to Formula 1 racing driving. As we saw in Chapter 6 the work involves helping sports people with motivation, self-esteem, mental imagery, goal setting, anxiety and aggression (see also Butler 1997; Cox 1997). Masters' courses, sometimes coupled with leisure sciences, are beginning to appear in the UK but, surprisingly, there seem to be very few listed in America.

## Research opportunities

A final route to virtually any area of applied psychology is to conduct research, and to become well known for one's investigations and writing in a particular field. Indeed, most of the authors in this book have taken this route. One way of doing this is to become a postgraduate student and to study for a postgraduate research degree on a topic of one's choosing, directed by a supervisor. Another possibility is to conduct research with colleagues and/or employers, for example as a research assistant or research technician, or as a data analyst or technical writer. Indeed, it might be possible to move from working outside a university to working inside one, or vice versa. Whatever the case, conducting research is usually a path available only to students with good undergraduate degrees who can find a research vacancy or studentship.

# New directions in applied psychology

As noted earlier, the skills acquired for the first degree can be applied across a wide range of employment (see Box E.1). There are now more courses available than ever before as the specific uses of psychology expand. Box E.2 indicates the range of possibilities available in the USA.

We currently see the following as the growth areas in applied psychology: health planning and management; ageing; occupational safety and health; marketing, leisure and sports; economic psychology; organizational behaviour; human–computer interaction; information access and usability; traffic/transport psychology; energy and resource use; and legal and criminological issues. Nickerson (1995) has chapters on most of these topics, and some additional ones, e.g. cognitive performance under stress, and employment and disabilities.

This increase in the number of available courses reflects the need for greater expertise, understanding and intervention in all areas in modern society – from health to business, leisure to work, education to politics, and media communication to urban planning.

---

*Box E.2*  **Titles of postgraduate courses available in the USA**

- adolescence and youth
- adult development
- aging/geropsychology
- AIDS
- applied developmental
- applied social
- art therapy
- behavior therapy
- behavioral analysis
- behavioral genetics
- behavioral medicine
- behavioral neuroscience
- child development
- clinical assessment
- clinical neuropsychology
- clinical psychology
- clinical psychopathology
- cognitive psychology
- college teaching
- community psychology
- comparative psychology
- computer applications
- consumer psychology
- counseling psychology
- developmental psychology
- early childhood education

- educational/school psychology
- engineering psychology
- environmental psychology
- experimental psychology
- forensic/legal psychology
- health psychology
- human–machine interaction/human factors
- humanistic psychology
- industrial/organizational psychology
- marriage and family
- mathematical psychology
- mental health
- neuropsychology
- personality
- phenomenological psychology
- physiological psychology
- psychobiological psychology
- psycholinguistics
- psychology of women
- psychopharmacology
- reading
- social
- sports psychology
- substance abuse
- supervision and leadership

---

# References

American Psychological Association (APA) (1997) *Graduate Study in Psychology.* Washington, DC: APA.

Arnold, J., Cooper, C. L. and Robertson, I. T. (1995) *Work Psychology: Understanding Work Behaviour in the Workplace*, 2nd edn. London: Pitman.

Baum, A., Gatchel, R. and Krantz, D. (1997) *Introduction to Health Psychology*, 3rd edn. New York: McGraw-Hill.

Beall, A. E. and Allen, E. W. (1997) Why we buy what we buy: consulting in consumer psychology, in R. J. Sternberg (ed.) *Career Paths in Psychology: Where Your Degree Can Take You.* Washington, DC: American Psychological Association.

Bonnes, M. and Secchiaroli, G. (1995) *Environmental Psychology: A Psycho-Social Introduction.* London: Sage.

British Psychological Society (BPS) (1995a) *Professional Psychology Handbook.* Leicester: BPS.

British Psychological Society (1995b) *Compendium of Postgraduate Studies in the UK and Ireland*, 2nd edn. Leicester: BPS.

British Psychological Society (regularly updated) *Careers in Psychology.* Leicester: BPS.

British Psychological Society (regularly updated) *List of Approved Professional Training Courses in Psychology.* Leicester: BPS.

Butler, R. J. (ed.) (1997) *Sports Psychology in Performance.* London: Butterworth Heinemann.

Cavill, S. (1997a) Working with the London Fire Brigade. *The Psychologist*, 10(1): 27–9.

Cavill, S. (1997b) Forensic psychology in a regional secure unit. *The Psychologist*, 10(7): 313–15.

Cavill, S. (1998) Helping to make a difference. *The Psychologist*, 11(12): 597–9.

Colman, A. M. (1995) Testifying in court as an expert witness, in BPS, *Professional Psychology Handbook.* Leicester: BPS.

Cooke, D., Baldwin, P. J. and Howison, J. (1993) *Psychology in Prisons.* London: Routledge.

Cox, R. (1997) *Sport Psychology: Concepts and Applications*, 4th edn. New York: McGraw-Hill.

Crawshaw, M. (1995) Occupational psychology, in BPS, *Professional Psychology Handbook.* Leicester: BPS.

Fontana, D. (1995) *Psychology for Teachers*, 3rd edn. London: Macmillan.

Foxhall, G. R. and Goldsmith, R. E. (1994) *Consumer Psychology for Marketing.* London: Routledge.

Gage, N. L. and Berliner, D. (1998) *Educational Psychology*, 6th edn. Boston, MA: Houghton Mifflin.

Gal, R. and Mangelsdorff, A. D. (eds) (1991) *Handbook of Military Psychology.* Chichester: Wiley.

Gudjonsson, G. and Haward, L. (1998) *Forensic Psychology: A Practitioner's Guide.* London: Routledge.

Johnston, M. and Weinman, J. (1995) Health psychology, in BPS, *Professional Psychology Handbook.* Leicester: BPS.

Levine, M. and Perkins, D. V. (1997) *Principles of Community Psychology: Perspectives and Applications*, 2nd edn. New York: Oxford University Press.

McCormick, E. J. and Ilgen, D. R. (1987) *Industrial and Organizational Psychology*, 8th edn. London: Routledge.

McLeod, J. (1998) *An Introduction to Counselling*, 2nd edn. Buckingham: Open University Press.

McMurran, M. (1995) Criminological and legal psychology, in BPS, *Professional Psychology Handbook.* Leicester: BPS.

Marzillier, J. and Hall, J. (1992) *What is Clinical Psychology?* Oxford: Oxford University Press.

Memon, A., Bull, R. and Vrj, A. (1998) *Psychology and Law: Truthfulness, Accuracy and Credibility*. New York: McGraw-Hill.

Napier, B. (1995) Clinical psychology, in BPS, *Professional Psychology Handbook*. Leicester: BPS.

Nickerson, R. S. (ed.) (1995) *Emerging Needs and Opportunities for Human Factors Research*. Washington, DC: National Academy Press.

Nickerson, R. S. (1998) Applied experimental psychology. *Applied Psychology: An International Review*, 48(2): 155–73.

Nickerson, R. S. and Moray, N. P. (1995) Environmental change, in R. S. Nickerson (ed.) *Emerging Needs and Opportunities for Human Factors Research*. Washington, DC: National Academy Press.

Nolen-Hoeksema, S. (1997) *Abnormal Psychology*. New York: McGraw-Hill.

Parrott, L. (1997) *Counseling and Psychotherapy*. New York: McGraw-Hill.

Pitts, M. and Phillips, K. (1998) *The Psychology of Health*, 2nd edn. London: Routledge.

Roth, T. (1998) Getting on clinical training courses. *The Psychologist*, 11(12): 589–92.

Schorr, A. and Saari, S. (eds) (1995) *Psychology in Europe: Facts, Figures, Realities*. Gottingden: Hogrefe and Huber.

Shackel, B. (1996) Ergonomics: scope, contribution and future possibilities. *The Psychologist*, 9(7): 304–8.

Sheppard, J. (1995) Educational psychology, in BPS, *Professional Psychology Handbook*. Leicester: BPS.

Watts, M. and Bor, R. (1995) Counselling psychology, in BPS, *Professional Psychology Handbook*. Leicester: BPS.

# Useful web sites

British Psychological Society
http://www.bps.org.uk

American Psychological Association
http://www.apa.org

Non-academic careers in psychology
http://www.apa.org/science/nonacad.html

*European Psychologist* online
http://www.hhpub.com

# Useful addresses

British Psychological Society
St Andrews House
48 Princess Road East
Leicester LE1 7DR
UK
Tel: +44(0)116 254 9568

American Psychological Association
1200 17th Street, NW
Washington, DC 20036
USA

# Index

**RELATING TO OTHERS**
SECOND EDITION

**Steve Duck**

Reviews of the first edition:

> Concise, readable, up-to-date, this volume is an excellent introduction to a new and expanding field.
>
> *Counseling Psychology Quarterly*

> . . . a wonderful book.
>
> *Newsletter of the American Association for Counseling and Development*

> . . . very exciting.
>
> *Counselling*

- How do relationships get started successfully?
- How do relationships develop?
- What makes relationships decline and how can they be repaired?

As social psychologists become more aware of the ways in which relationships underpin almost everything in the social sciences, the need for an introductory book for students and scholars has further increased. This long-awaited second edition of a highly successful text summarizes the research on relationships, focusing not only on their growth and development but also on their negative aspects, breakdown and repair.

The author addresses the essential use of relationship issues within applied areas such as policing, health care, and the corporate world. He also emphasizes the importance of multidisciplinary studies and the integration of different frameworks and methods, by focusing less on static factors in relationships and more on the matter of process. Finally, he examines the need to contextualize relationship processes and take account of the daily issues of management by relational partners.

The second edition of *Relating to Others* is strongly grounded in a discussion of the contexts for relating, whether cultural, linguistic, or interpersonal. It focuses on a range of relationships, friendship, and types of marriage and is written in an engaging style for students of psychology and the wider social sciences by one of the top authorities in the scientific research on relationships.

## Contents
*The role of relationships in life – Contexts of relationships – Developing relationships and developing people – Developing a steady and exclusive partnership – Managing relationships – When relationships come apart – Putting relationships right – Overview – References – Index.*

176pp    0 335 20163 6 (paperback)    0 335 20164 4 (hardback)

**LEARNING TO USE STATISTICAL TESTS IN PSYCHOLOGY**
SECOND EDITION

**Judith Greene and Manuela d'Oliveira**

Praise for the first edition:

> An excellent textbook which is well planned, well written, and pitched at the correct level for psychology students. I would not hesitate to recommend Greene and d'Oliveira to all psychology students looking for an introductory text on statistical methodology.
>
> *Bulletin of the British Psychological Society*

The second edition of this widely acclaimed text is an accessible and comprehensible introduction to the use of statistical tests in psychology experiments: statistics without panic. Presented in a new textbook format, its key objective is to enable students to select appropriate statistical tests to evaluate the significance of data obtained from psychological experiments. Improvements in the organization of chapters emphasize even more clearly the principle of introducing complex experimental designs on a 'need to know' basis, leaving more space for an extended interpretation of analysis of variance. In an important development for the second edition, students are introduced to modern statistical packages as a useful tool for calculations, the emphasis being on understanding and interpretation.

This book shows psychology students:

* how psychologists plan experiments and statistical tests;
* why they must plan them within certain constraints;
* how they can analyse and make sense of their results.

The approach is that:

* theory is always presented together with practical examples;
* theoretical points are summarized and understanding of them tested;
* statistical principles are introduced as part and parcel of the principles of experimental design.

**Contents**
*Part I: Introduction – Introduction to experimental research – Introduction to experimental design – Introduction to statistical analysis – Selecting a statistical test – Part II: Non-parametric tests – General method for non-parametric tests – Non-parametric tests (two conditions) – Non parametric tests (three or more conditions) – Correlations – Chi-square test – Part III: Parametric tests – Requirements for parametric tests – General method for parametric tests – t test – One-way ANOVA – Multivariable experimental designs – Two-way ANOVA – Epilogue – References – Index.*

240pp    0 335 20377 9 (paperback)    0 335 20378 7 (hardback)